AWS for System Administrators

Build, automate, and manage your infrastructure
on the most popular cloud platform – AWS

Prashant Lakhera

BIRMINGHAM—MUMBAI

AWS for System Administrators

Group Product Manager: Wilson D'souza

Publishing Product Manager: Vijin Boricha

Acquisition Editor: Shrilekha Inani

Senior Editor: Arun Nadar

Content Development Editor: Romy Dias

Technical Editor: Yoginee Marathe

Copy Editor: Safis Editing

Project Coordinator: Neil Dmello

Proofreader: Safis Editing

Indexer: Priyanka Dhadke

Production Designer: Nilesh Mohite

First published: January 2021

Production reference: 1130121

Published by Packt Publishing Ltd.
Livery Place
35 Livery Street
Birmingham
B3 2PB, UK.

ISBN 978-1-80020-153-8

www.packt.com

`Packt.com`

Subscribe to our online digital library for full access to over 7,000 books and videos, as well as industry leading tools to help you plan your personal development and advance your career. For more information, please visit our website.

Why subscribe?

- Spend less time learning and more time coding with practical eBooks and Videos from over 4,000 industry professionals

- Improve your learning with Skill Plans built especially for you

- Get a free eBook or video every month

- Fully searchable for easy access to vital information

- Copy and paste, print, and bookmark content

Did you know that Packt offers eBook versions of every book published, with PDF and ePub files available? You can upgrade to the eBook version at `packt.com` and as a print book customer, you are entitled to a discount on the eBook copy. Get in touch with us at `customercare@packtpub.com` for more details.

At `www.packt.com`, you can also read a collection of free technical articles, sign up for a range of free newsletters, and receive exclusive discounts and offers on Packt books and eBooks.

Contributors

About the author

Prashant Lakhera (`lakhera2015` on Twitter) is an X-RHCA (Red Hat Certified Architect) and a seasoned Linux and open source specialist with over 15 years of enterprise open source experience.

Having a positive impact on the world is important to him, which is why he shares his knowledge with others through his website, blog posts, and YouTube channel, which also helps him to dig deep into topics and build on his expertise.

I would like to thank my wife, Pratima, for her support while writing this book, and my furry boy, Prince. Also, to my mother, who always supports and encourages me throughout my life.

About the reviewer

Saurabh Dhawan is an AWS- and Azure-certified cloud solution architect with over 16 years of IT experience. He has first-hand knowledge of building cloud-native solutions and a knack for Alexa programming. Saurabh has worked in India's largest IT company in the past and is currently part of the architecture team for the world's most iconic telecom company.

I would like to thank my wife for letting me get lost in my home office for hours on end!

Packt is searching for authors like you

If you're interested in becoming an author for Packt, please visit `authors.packtpub.com` and apply today. We have worked with thousands of developers and tech professionals, just like you, to help them share their insight with the global tech community. You can make a general application, apply for a specific hot topic that we are recruiting an author for, or submit your own idea.

Table of Contents

Section 2: Building the Infrastructure

3

Creating a Data Center in the Cloud Using VPC

4

Scalable Compute Capacity in the Cloud via EC2

Section 3: Adding Scalability and Elasticity to the Infrastructure

5

Increasing an Application's Fault Tolerance with Elastic Load Balancing

6

Increasing Application Performance Using AWS Auto Scaling

7

Creating a Relational Database in the Cloud using AWS Relational Database Service (RDS)

Section 4: The Monitoring, Metrics, and Backup Layers

8

Monitoring AWS Services Using CloudWatch and SNS

9

Centralizing Logs for Analysis

10

Centralizing Cloud Backup Solution

11
AWS Disaster Recovery Solutions

12
AWS Tips and Tricks

Other Books You May Enjoy

Index

Preface

AWS for System Administrators will teach you how to deploy, manage, and operate highly available systems on AWS. You'll start with the fundamentals of **Identity and Access Management (IAM)** to secure your environment before moving on to AWS networking and monitoring tools. As you make your way through the chapters, you'll get to grips with concepts such as **Virtual Private Cloud (VPC)**, **Elastic Compute Cloud (EC2)**, load balancers, auto-scaling, **Relational Database Service (RDS)** databases, CloudWatch, deployment, data management, and security. In the concluding chapters, you'll initiate AWS automated backups and learn how to keep track of and store log files. You will also acquire a knowledge of AWS APIs and how to use them, along with CloudFormation, Python Boto3 scripts, and Terraform to automate the infrastructure.

By the end of this book, you will be confident in building up your two-tier start-up with all the infrastructure, monitoring, and logging components in place. You will also acquire knowledge of AWS APIs and how to use them, along with Python Boto3 scripts and Terraform to automate the infrastructure.

Who this book is for

This book is aimed at the following people:

- System administrators and solution architects who want to build highly flexible and available AWS cloud platforms for their applications
- Software engineers and programmers who want to automate their AWS infrastructure using APIs
- IT project managers who want to understand technical aspects as well as billing requirements before adopting AWS in their organization
- IT architects who want to design their infrastructure using various solutions and then come up with an optimum solution

If you are planning to use AWS in your organization, this book is for you. It will show you how to build a highly available AWS environment from scratch.

What this book covers

Chapter 1, Setting Up the AWS Environment, provides a brief introduction to various AWS offerings. It's always a good idea to get a brief introduction to the various AWS services. We will start by exploring various services using the AWS console and then set up our environment to install tools such as the AWS CLI, Boto3, CloudFormation, and Terraform, which we can use in future chapters to automate the entire infrastructure.

Chapter 2, Protecting Your AWS Account Using IAM, provides a brief introduction to IAM and an in-depth overview of IAM policies and roles. Security is job zero for all of us, so it's important to understand IAM policies, such as how to make sure we assign only the minimum privileges to a user to do their job. We will also discuss two real-world scenarios where we will see how to restrict the user to launch only a particular instance and rotate their credentials on a regular basis to reduce the risk of leaking their access and secret keys.

Chapter 3, Creating a Data Center in the Cloud Using VPC, covers building two VPCs for high-availability and disaster recovery. We will use two subnets: public for setting up two EC2 instances and private to host databases. Once the VPCs are up, we will create a transit gateway so that services in these two VPCs communicate with each other. Finally, we will look at a real-world scenario to enable VPC flow logs.

Chapter 4, Scalable Compute Capacity in the Cloud via EC2, is the last chapter of the *Building Infrastructure* section, where the VPCs built in the previous chapter are used to create four instances in two availability zones. We need these four instances for high availability as well as for disaster recovery. We will also explore three real-world scenarios to save costs by shutting down instances in the development environment after XPM, clean up unused **Amazon Machine Images** (**AMIs**), and remove unattached volumes.

Chapter 5, Increasing an Application's Fault Tolerance with Elastic Load Balancing, explores how, to make our application robust, we add the layer of an application load balancer in front of instances. This helps to distribute the load to the backend EC2 instances, which make the application highly available as well as serve as the single point of contact for clients.

Chapter 6, Increasing Application Performance using AWS Auto Scaling, covers setting up the on-demand scaling of our application based on criteria such as load, I/O, and network. It provides a uniform user experience to our users by spinning up the instances in the backend when the load on the application increases and similarly tears down those instances when the load is back to normal.

Chapter 7, Creating a Relational Database in the Cloud Using AWS Relational Database Service (RDS), looks at adding a database layer to our application by using AWS RDS. As databases are a critical piece of our application, we will set them up in high-availability mode, both as primary and secondary as well as read-only replicas in different AWS regions to reduce the load on the main master server.

Chapter 8, Monitoring AWS Services Using CloudWatch and SNS, looks at monitoring critical pieces to maintain the uptime of the application, such as CPU, I/O, system uptime, as well as custom metrics such as memory and disk space. In the end, we will set up an automated alarm as well as notifications via email, SMS, and Slack.

Chapter 9, Centralizing Logs for Analysis, shows how to store logs in one centralized place (CloudWatch logs) and then forward them to Elasticsearch to perform anomaly detection.

Chapter 10, Centralizing Cloud Backup Solution, looks at how to back up our instances or databases using AWS solutions (DLM snapshots) and a custom solution, such as S3 scripts.

Chapter 11, AWS Disaster Recovery Solutions, shows how to use backups to perform data recovery in case of failure. Besides that, AWS offers various disaster recovery solutions, and we will see which solution to use in which scenario.

Chapter 12, AWS Tips and Tricks, teaches you 10 tips and tricks to get the most out of AWS. Some of these tricks are based on my experience, while others are derived from AWS blogs.

To get the most out of this book

Throughout this book, we will cover several AWS examples with a number of demonstrations. As a result, I suggest using an AWS account that is not used for a production workload. To follow along, you can use any Unix-based system as all these examples are already tested on Ubuntu:

Software/hardware covered in the book	OS requirements
AWS console	Any OS
AWS CLI, Terraform, and Boto3	Linux

To create a new AWS account, please follow this link:

```
https://aws.amazon.com/premiumsupport/knowledge-center/create-
and-activate-aws-account/
```

Installation of the AWS CLI, Boto3, and Terraform is covered in *Chapter 1, Setting Up the AWS Environment*.

Download the example code files

You can download the example code files for this book from GitHub at `https://github.com/PacktPublishing/AWS-for-System-Administrators/`.

If there's an update to the code, it will be updated on the existing GitHub repository.

Code in Action

Code in Action videos for this book can be viewed at `http://bit.ly/3ptc50K`.

Download the color images

We also provide a PDF file that has color images of the screenshots/diagrams used in this book. You can download it here: `https://static.packt-cdn.com/downloads/9781800201538_ColorImages.pdf`.

Conventions used

There are a number of text conventions used throughout this book.

`Code in text`: Indicates code words in text, database table names, folder names, filenames, file extensions, pathnames, dummy URLs, user input, and Twitter handles. Here is an example: "The `Principal` parameter (`*`) used within the resource-based policies is used to identify the user, account, or role."

A block of code is set as follows:

```
{
        "Sid": "Stmt1604259864802",
        "Action": "s3:*",
        "Effect": "Deny",
        "Resource": "arn:aws:s3:::myexamplebucket/*",
```

When we wish to draw your attention to a particular part of a code block, the relevant lines or items are set in bold:

```
    "Condition": {
        "NotIpAddress": {
            "aws:SourceIp": "192.168.1.10/24"
        }
    },
```

```
        "Principal": "*"
    }
```

Any command-line input or output is written as follows:

```
$ cd AWS-for-System-Administrators/Chapter4/html
```

Bold: Indicates a new term, an important word, or words that you see on screen. For example, words in menus or dialog boxes appear in the text like this. Here is an example: "If you are creating a new user, click on **Add user**."

> **Tips or important notes**
> Appear like this.

Get in touch

Feedback from our readers is always welcome.

General feedback: If you have questions about any aspect of this book, mention the book title in the subject of your message and email us at customercare@packtpub.com.

Errata: Although we have taken every care to ensure the accuracy of our content, mistakes do happen. If you have found a mistake in this book, we would be grateful if you would report this to us. Please visit www.packtpub.com/support/errata, selecting your book, clicking on the Errata Submission Form link, and entering the details.

Piracy: If you come across any illegal copies of our works in any form on the Internet, we would be grateful if you would provide us with the location address or website name. Please contact us at copyright@packt.com with a link to the material.

If you are interested in becoming an author: If there is a topic that you have expertise in and you are interested in either writing or contributing to a book, please visit authors.packtpub.com.

Reviews

Please leave a review. Once you have read and used this book, why not leave a review on the site that you purchased it from? Potential readers can then see and use your unbiased opinion to make purchase decisions, we at Packt can understand what you think about our products, and our authors can see your feedback on their book. Thank you!

For more information about Packt, please visit packt.com.

Section 1: AWS Services and Tools

This part will give you a brief introduction to various **Amazon Web Services** (**AWS**) services. After completion of *Section 1*, you will have skills in AWS services and understand the various ways to manage your AWS infrastructure. Then, we will look at **Identity and Access Management** (**IAM**) to fine-grain the user permissions and follow the principle of least privilege. We will then explore some real-world scenarios to solidify the concepts.

The following chapters are included in this section:

- *Chapter 1, Setting Up the AWS Environment*
- *Chapter 2, Protecting Your AWS Account Using IAM*

1

Setting Up the AWS Environment

Amazon Web Services (**AWS**) has changed the way we do system administration. Think of a pre-cloud era where if we planned to set up a new data center, it would go through a month of planning, which would involve choosing the location, ordering hardware, setting up the networking infrastructure (such as routers and switches); and the list goes on and on. With AWS, setting up a new data center can be performed with the help of few clicks or can be done with the help of **application programming interface** (**API**) calls.

This chapter will start by setting up the environment. We will begin by installing and configuring the AWS **command-line interface** (**CLI**), which we will use throughout the book. Next, we will install Boto3, a Python **software development kit** (**SDK**), and a feature-rich object-oriented API that provides low-level access to AWS services. Then, we will look at setting up CloudFormation and Terraform. Both these tools can be used to automate your AWS infrastructure, but there is a subtle difference between them. CloudFormation, on the one hand, is an AWS proprietary solution, whereas Terraform is an open source project. The other key difference between the two is that Terraform supports other cloud providers such as Google Cloud and Azure, whereas CloudFormation is native to AWS. The question of which one to use depends on your use case and requirement and your expertise.

Before we get our hands dirty with various AWS offerings, let's set up tools that we will use to interact with various AWS services and build the infrastructure.

In this chapter, we're going to cover the following main topics:

- Setting up the environment
- Introducing Python Boto3
- Introducing CloudFormation
- Introducing Terraform
- Installing tools in an automated way

Technical requirements

There are no special technical requirements to follow through and understand this chapter; however, familiarity with the Linux command line will help you better grasp the concepts that will be discussed.

Here is the GitHub link for solution scripts:

```
https://github.com/PacktPublishing/AWS-for-System-
Administrators/tree/master/Chapter1
```

Check out the following link to see the Code in Action video:

```
https://bit.ly/2WVTL4e
```

Setting up the environment

The AWS CLI is a significant way to automate the AWS infrastructure. Its features are as follows:

- Single unified tool for managing all AWS resources
- Supports Linux, macOS, and Windows
- Supports 200+ top-level commands

For the AWS CLI to interact with Amazon's API, it uses an AWS access key and a secret access key. These keys are used to authenticate and authorize any request sent to AWS. The steps to create an IAM user and retrieve the keys are as follows:

1. In order to generate these credentials, go to the **Identity and Access Management (IAM)** console (`https://aws.amazon.com/console/`) and log in with your credentials, and search for `IAM`, as illustrated in the following screenshot:

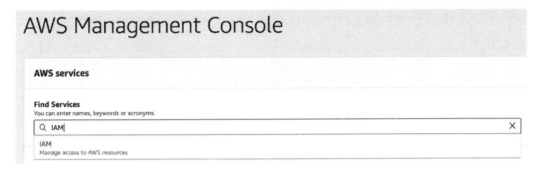

Figure 1.1 – AWS Management Console

2. Click on the **Users** tab: `https://console.aws.amazon.com/iam/home?#/users`.

3. Create a new user or use an existing user.

4. If you are creating a new user, click on **Add user**, which will take you to the following screen:

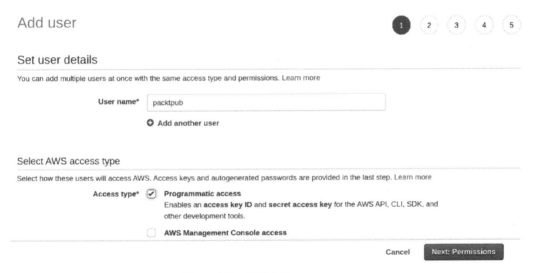

Figure 1.2 – IAM Add user screen

> **Important note**
> Please make sure you click on **Programmatic access** (as this will enable/create an access key and a secret access key).

5. Click **Next: Permissions**, and in the next screen, assign the **AdministratorAccess** policy to the user and click **Next: Tags**, as illustrated in the following screenshot:

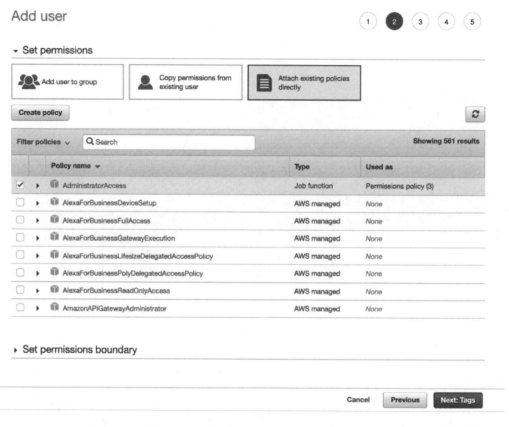

Figure 1.3 – IAM Set permissions screen

> **Important note**
>
> As an AWS security best practice, never give admin access to any user. Please follow the principle of least privilege. In the next chapter, we will tighten security and only assign the necessary privileges to the user.

6. The tag field is optional. I am leaving it blank, but please feel free to add tags to the newly created user depending upon your requirements. The field is shown in the following screenshot:

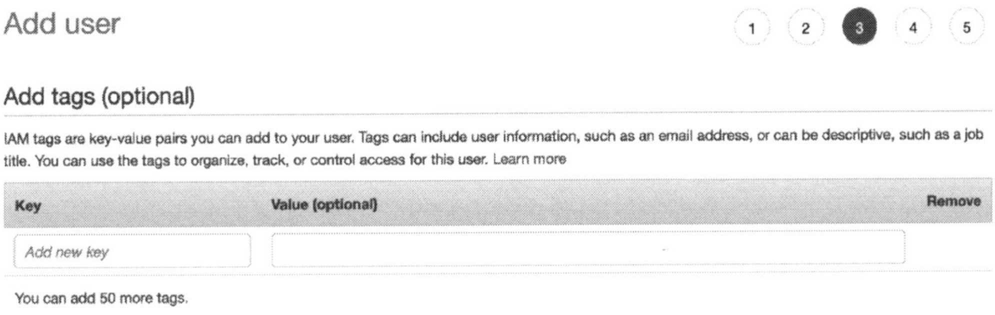

Add user

1 2 ③ 4 5

Add tags (optional)

IAM tags are key-value pairs you can add to your user. Tags can include user information, such as an email address, or can be descriptive, such as a job title. You can use the tags to organize, track, or control access for this user. Learn more

Key	Value (optional)	Remove
Add new key		

You can add 50 more tags.

Figure 1.4 – IAM tags (optional field)

7. Review all the settings such as **User name**, **AWS access type**, and **Permissions boundary**, and click **Create user**, as illustrated in the following screenshot:

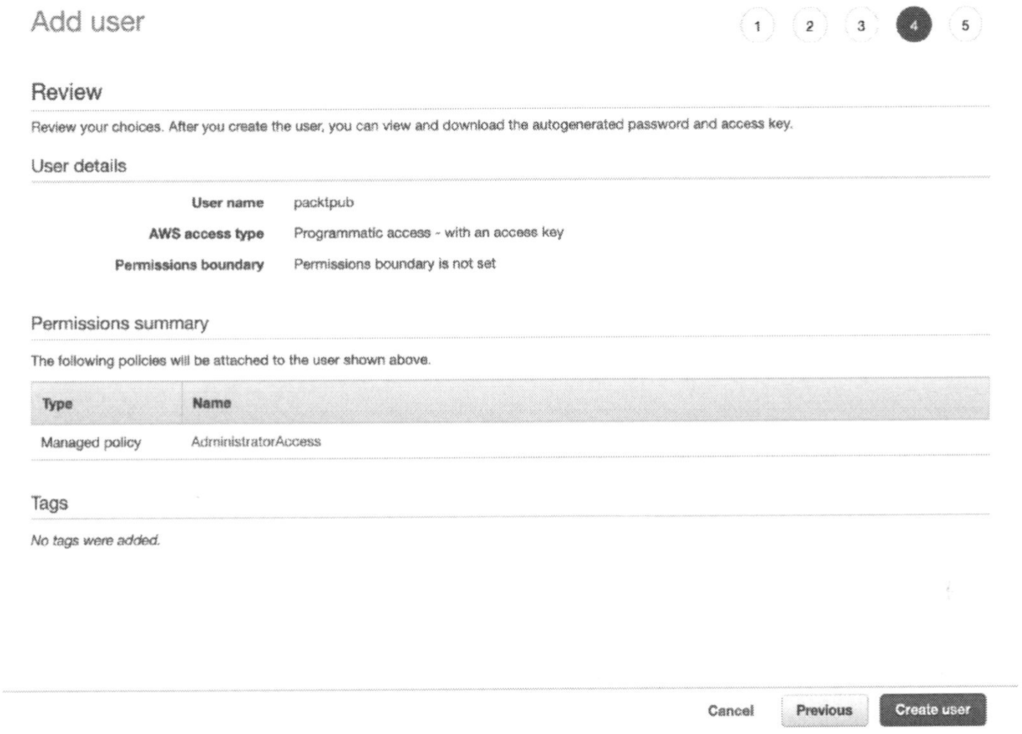

Add user

1 2 3 ④ 5

Review

Review your choices. After you create the user, you can view and download the autogenerated password and access key.

User details

User name	packtpub
AWS access type	Programmatic access - with an access key
Permissions boundary	Permissions boundary is not set

Permissions summary

The following policies will be attached to the user shown above.

Type	Name
Managed policy	AdministratorAccess

Tags

No tags were added.

Cancel   Previous   Create user

Figure 1.5 – Review user creation

8.   Please take a note of the **Access key ID** and **Secret access key** values, illustrated in the following screenshot:

	User	Access key ID	Secret access key
▶ ✓	packtpub	AKIAUCFHJCYTRRZFLARJ	********* Show

Figure 1.6 – The newly created IAM user

> **Important note**
> This is your only chance to see/retrieve the secret access key. There is no way to retrieve this key in the future. Keep this file confidential and *never* share this key, and never ever accidentally commit these keys to the GitHub/public code repository.

Installing the AWS CLI

The AWS CLI package works on Python and supports the following Python versions:

- 2.7.x and greater
- 3.4.x and greater

The AWS CLI installation is pretty straightforward. Run the following command to download, unzip, and install the AWS CLI:

```
curl "https://awscli.amazonaws.com/awscli-exe-linux-x86_64.zip"
-o "awscliv2.zip"
unzip awscliv2.zip
sudo ./aws/install -i /usr/local/aws-cli -b /usr/local/bin
```

> **Note**
> The AWS CLI v2 is still not available in the **Python Package Index** (**PyPI**) repository. Please check the bug at the following link for more info:
> `https://github.com/aws/aws-cli/issues/4947`.

Run the following command to verify the installation:

```
aws --version
aws-cli/2.0.24 Python/3.7.3 Linux/4.15.0-1065-aws
botocore/2.0.0dev28
```

> **Note**
>
> Throughout this book, we're going to discuss and use the AWS CLI version 2, which comes with its own set of features (for example: auto-prompt; wizard; **YAML Ain't Markup Language** (**YAML**) support). Please make sure to update or uninstall the AWS CLI v1 before continuing. See the following page for more information: https://docs.aws.amazon.com/cli/latest/userguide/install-cliv2-linux.html#cliv2-linux-upgrade.

Configuring command-line completion

To enable command-line completion, run the following command from the shell (for example: bash) that we are using:

```
$ complete -C '/usr/local/bin/aws_completer' aws
```

This command connects aws_completer to the aws command. As we execute these commands in the current shell, these changes will be lost as soon as we log out of this shell. To make this change permanent, add the preceding entry in ~/.bashrc.

Once the command-line completion is done, we can type any partial command and press the *Tab* key on the keyboard to see all the available commands, as illustrated in the following code snippet:

```
aws s<TAB>
s3                      sagemaker-runtime       securityhub
ses                     snowball                sso-oidc
```

We have configured the command-line completion, so let's go ahead and configure the AWS CLI.

Configuring the AWS command line

With command-line completion in place, our next step is to see how the AWS CLI will interact with the AWS API, and the fastest way to achieve this is via the aws configure command, as illustrated in the following code snippet:

```
aws configure
AWS Access Key ID [None]: XXXXXXXXXXX
AWS Secret Access Key [None]: XXXXXXXXXXX
Default region name [None]: us-west-2
Default output format [None]: json
```

As you can see, when we run this command, the AWS CLI asks for the following four sets of information:

- **Access key ID/secret access key ID**: Think of the access key and the secret key as a username/password. To access the AWS console, you need your username and password, but to access the AWS API, you need your access/secret keys. We already created an access key and a secret access key earlier in this chapter.

- **AWS region**: The location where we set up the AWS infrastructure (for example, us-west-2 if we set up our infrastructure in Oregon).

- **Output format**: Specifies how the result is formatted (supported formats: **JavaScript Object Notation (JSON)** (default), YAML, text, and table).

> **Note**
> Please make sure that the computer date and time is set correctly, because if it is not in sync or is way off, AWS will reject the request.

These credentials (access/secret key, region, and output) are stored in ~/.aws/ credentials, and the default region and output format are stored in ~/.aws/ config, as illustrated in the following code snippet:

```
cat ~/.aws/credentials
[default]
aws_access_key_id = XXXXXXXX
aws_secret_access_key = XXXXXXXXXXXX

cat ~/.aws/config
[default]
region = us-west-2
output = json
```

The AWS CLI stores this information (access/secret key, region, and output) in a default profile and the configuration file. In the next section, let's explore more about the location of the configuration file.

Understanding the AWS CLI command structure

The AWS CLI command is split into four parts and we need to specify these parts in order, as illustrated in the following code snippet:

```
aws <command> <subcommand> [options and parameters]
```

As you can see in the preceding command, the following apply:

- Everything starts with the `aws` program.
- The top-level command is the service supported by the AWS CLI (for example: `s3` in the following example).
- The sub command specifies the operation to perform (`ls` in the following example).
- Options or parameters required by the operation are provided (`s3://example-bucket`).

Examples of the preceding syntax commands are shown here:

```
$ aws s3 ls
2020-04-26 15:59:11 my-test-s3-bucket-XXXXXXX
$ aws s3 ls s3://example-bucket
2020-06-07 18:28:47          166 testfile
```

Other commands that can be used to verify the AWS CLI are listed here:

- `aws ec2 describe-instances`: This command describes the specified instances or all instances.
- `aws s3 mb s3://mytestbucket1235334`: This is used to create a **Simple Storage Service (S3)** bucket.
- `aws iam list-users`: This is used to list the IAM users.

We now have the AWS CLI configured and ready to use. In the next section, we will see how to install and configure Boto3.

Introducing Python Boto3

Python Boto3 is the AWS SDK for Python. It is useful for end users to manage their AWS services—for example, IAM or **Elastic Compute Cloud (EC2)**. Its features are as follows:

- Feature-rich object-oriented API
- Provides low-level access to various AWS services

Installing Python Boto3

Boto3 is written in Python. We can use the `pip` package installer for Python. This comes pre-installed with the OS in many OSes but is straightforward to install manually, with the following command:

```
sudo apt-get install python3-pip
```

Once we have `pip` installed in the system, the installation of AWS Boto3 is simple in Linux by running the following command:

```
pip3 install boto3
```

Before we begin using Boto3, we need to set up the authentication credentials, which Boto3 will use to connect to AWS. We already have these credentials configured as part of the AWS CLI setup, via the `aws configure` command.

Verifying the Boto3 setup

To verify the setup, please follow these steps:

1. First get the Python command, to get the python shell run the following command:

    ```
    python3
    Python 3.6.9 (default, Oct  8 2020, 12:12:24)
    [GCC 8.4.0] on linux
    Type "help", "copyright", "credits" or "license" for more
    information.
    ```

2. To use Boto3, we first need to import it, as follows:

    ```
    import boto3
    ```

3. We need to tell Boto3 which service to use (for example: S3 in this case), as follows:

    ```
    s3 = boto3.resource("s3")
    ```

4. Print all the bucket names, like this:

    ```
    for bucket in s3.buckets.all():
    ...         print(bucket.name)
    ...
    my-test-s3-bucket-XXXXXX
    ```

Here, I have given you a brief introduction to Boto3. Boto3 is powerful, and in a future chapter, we will see how it will be helpful in automating recurring tasks.

Introducing CloudFormation

If you are looking for a tool that will automate your entire AWS infrastructure deployment, then CloudFormation is the right solution. It gives you the ability to create resource templates to define the AWS resource you need to create. You can version-control these templates, and using these templates replicate your infrastructure quickly and in a repeatable manner, as illustrated in the following screenshot:

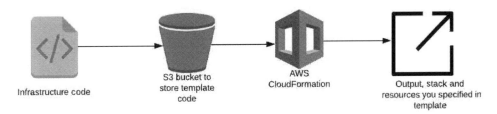

Figure 1.7 – How CloudFormation works

For example, we can instruct the CloudFormation template to do the following:

- Create a security group.
- Create an EC2 machine using this security group.

CloudFormation creates this for us, in exactly the right order and with the exact configuration that we provide.

Here are some advantages of using CloudFormation:

- We can version-control the CloudFormation code using Git (GitHub, GitLab, Bitbucket...).
- You can code your infrastructure using JSON or YAML.
- Before pushing the change, someone in the team can review the code.
- CloudFormation works as **Infrastructure as Code (IaC)**; that is, no resources are created manually.
- CloudFormation is free of charge.
- It automatically creates a diagram for your template.
- It involves declarative programming, which means we define the end goal, and CloudFormation will figure out how to achieve that goal.

> **Important note**
>
> For CloudFormation, we don't need to install any separate tool. The AWS CLI is sufficient in order to create the stack from the command line, and we can also create it with the help of the AWS console.

Writing your first CloudFormation template

Let's start with a basic CloudFormation stack template that simply launches an EC2 instance. A CloudFormation stack is a group of AWS resources. To create an AWS resource, we can create, update, or delete the stack.

To create a stack, we need the following:

- **AWSTemplateFormatVersion section (optional)**: AWS only allows you to use 2010-09-09 as a template version (only valid value). The version of the template defines what this template is capable of.

- **Description (optional)**: If you want to define your template or add a comment, you can add that in a description section.

- **Resources (required)**: This is the mandatory section of the CloudFormation template, where you define the resource you want to create—for example, for an Amazon EC2 instance (AWS::EC2::Instance) or an Amazon S3 bucket (AWS::S3::Bucket).

- **Amazon Machine Image (AMI)**: This is an operating system image used to run EC2 instances. For this example, I am using the ami-0bc06212a56393ee1 CentOS 7 image.

  To find out the AMI ID for the CentOS 7 image, run the following command (the last column of the query returns the AMI ID—for example: ami-0bc06212a56393ee1):

```
aws ec2 describe-images --owners aws-marketplace
--filters Name=product-code,Values=aw0evgkw8e5c1q413zg
y5pjce --query 'Images[*].[CreationDate,Name,ImageId]'
--filters "Name=name,Values=CentOS Linux 7*" --region
us-west-2 --output table | sort -r
|   2020-03-09T21:54:48.000Z|   CentOS Linux 7 x86_64 HVM
EBS ENA 2002_01-b7ee8a69-ee97-4a49-9e68-afaee216db2e-ami-
0042af67f8e4dcc20.4   |   ami-0bc06212a56393ee1   |
|   2019-01-30T23:43:37.000Z|   CentOS Linux 7 x86_64 HVM
EBS ENA 1901_01-b7ee8a69-ee97-4a49-9e68-afaee216db2e-ami-
05713873c6794f575.4   |   ami-01ed306a12b7d1c96   |
```

```
|    2018-06-13T15:58:14.000Z|    CentOS Linux 7 x86_64 HVM
EBS ENA 1805_01-b7ee8a69-ee97-4a49-9e68-afaee216db2e-ami-
77ec9308.4            |    ami-3ecc8f46                |
|    2018-05-17T09:30:44.000Z|    CentOS Linux 7 x86_64 HVM
EBS ENA 1804_2-b7ee8a69-ee97-4a49-9e68-afaee216db2e-ami-
55a2322a.4 |    ami-5490ed2c             |
|    2018-04-04T00:11:39.000Z|    CentOS Linux 7 x86_64 HVM
EBS ENA 1803_01-b7ee8a69-ee97-4a49-9e68-afaee216db2e-ami-
8274d6ff.4            |    ami-0ebdd976                |
|    2017-12-05T14:49:18.000Z|    CentOS Linux 7 x86_64 HVM
EBS 1708_11.01-b7ee8a69-ee97-4a49-9e68-afaee216db2e-ami-
95096eef.4 |    ami-b63ae0ce             |
|
DescribeImages                                              |
    --------------------------------------------------------
    --------------------------------------------------------
    -------------------------------------------------------
    +-----------------------------+--------------------------
    --------------------------------------------------------
    ---------------------------+------------------------+
    +-----------------------------+--------------------------
    --------------------------------------------------------
    ---------------------------+------------------------+
```

- **Instance type**: The type of EC2 instance to run, as every instance type provides different capabilities (CPU, memory, **input/output (I/O)**). For this example, I am using t2.micro (one virtual CPU; 1 GB memory).

The CloudFormation template will look like this. Save the following code as ec2-instance. yml or download the file from https://github.com/PacktPublishing/ AWS-for-System-Administrators/blob/master/Chapter1/ cloudformation/ec2-instance.yml:

```
{
  "AWSTemplateFormatVersion" : "2010-09-09",
  "Description" : "Simple Stack to launch an EC2 instance.",
  "Resources" : {
    "Ec2Instance" : {
      "Type" : "AWS::EC2::Instance",
      "Properties" : {
        "InstanceType": "t2.micro",
```

```
        "ImageId" : "ami-0bc06212a56393ee1"
    }
  }
}
}
```

Now, we have created our first CloudFormation template. In the next section, we will create our first stack using this template.

Creating a CloudFormation stack using the AWS console

To create a stack on the AWS CloudFormation console, follow these steps:

1. Go to the AWS console and search for CloudFormation (`https://us-west-2.console.aws.amazon.com/cloudformation/home?region=us-west-2#/`).

2. In the CloudFormation screen, click on **Create stack**, as illustrated in the following screenshot:

Figure 1.8 – CloudFormation stack creation wizard

3. Click on **Upload a template file** and upload the earlier-mentioned CloudFormation template, then click **Next**.

4. Provide a **Stack name** and click **Next**, as illustrated in the following screenshot:

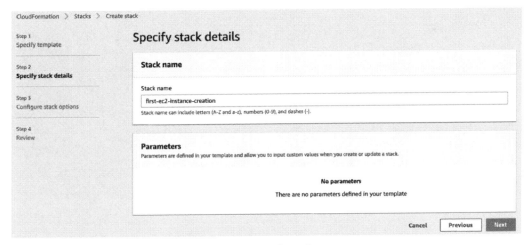

Figure 1.9 – Specify stack name

5. Keep the rest of the parameters as default and click the **Create stack** button at the bottom of the page, as illustrated in the following screenshot:

Figure 1.10 – Create stack

6. Monitor the progress of stack creation by clicking on the **Events** tab, as illustrated in the following screenshot:

Figure 1.11 – CloudFormation Events

Once the stack creation is completed, the **CREATE_COMPLETE** event is displayed, as shown in the following screenshot:

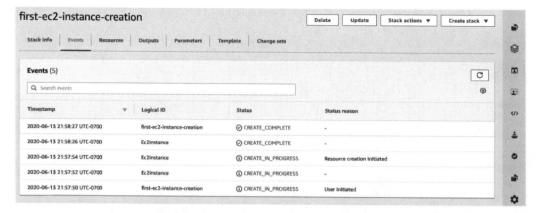

Figure 1.12 – CloudFormation Events completion

7. Verify the instance ID (**Physical ID**) under the **Resources** section, as illustrated in the following screenshot:

Figure 1.13 – CloudFormation resource

8. The instance ID can also be verified via the EC2 console (`https://console.aws.amazon.com/ec2/v2/home?region=us-west-2`), as illustrated in the following screenshot:

Figure 1.14 – EC2 console

Up to this point, you now understand how to create a CloudFormation stack using the AWS console. In the next part, you will see how to create it using the AWS CLI.

Creating a CloudFormation stack using the AWS CLI

In the previous example, you created the CloudFormation stack using the AWS console. We can perform the same steps with the help of the AWS CLI, to assist in automating the entire process, as follows:

1. Validate the template to make sure there is no syntax error, as follows:

    ```
    aws cloudformation validate-template --template-body
    file://ec2-instance.yml
    {
        "Parameters": [],
        "Description": "Simple Stack to launch an EC2
    instance."
    }
    ```

2. Create the stack by specifying the template file and the necessary IAM capabilities, as follows:

    ```
    aws cloudformation create-stack --stack-name first-ec2-
    instance-creation --template-body file://ec2-instance.yml
    --capabilities "CAPABILITY_IAM" "CAPABILITY_NAMED_IAM"
    {
        "StackId": "arn:aws:cloudformation:us-west-
    2:XXXXXXXX:stack/first-ec2-instance-creation/cf6e6100-
    b3ed-11ea-b69a-0a233d312e0a"
    }
    ```

3. The command will wait, and the user will not get Command Prompt back until the stack creation is complete, as illustrated in the following code snippet:

    ```
    aws cloudformation wait stack-create-complete --stack-
    name first-ec2-instance-creation
    aws cloudformation describe-stacks --stack-name first-
    ec2-instance-creation
    ```

4. Execute the `describe-stacks` command, which will return the description of the created stack, as follows:

    ```
    aws cloudformation describe-stacks --stack-name
    first-ec2-instance-creation --query 'Stacks[].
    [StackName,StackStatus]' --output text
    first-ec2-instance-creation     CREATE_COMPLETE
    ```

5. To verify all the resources have been created successfully, we are going to use `describe-stack-resources` with `aws cloudformation`. From the output, we can verify the newly created instance ID (`PhysicalResourceId"` : `"i-0dfaad58d59b59717`), as follows:

```
aws cloudformation describe-stack-resources --stack-name
first-ec2-instance-creation
{
    "StackResources": [
        {
            "StackName": "first-ec2-instance-creation",
            "StackId": "arn:aws:cloudformation:us-west-
2:XXXXXX:stack/first-ec2-instance-creation/cf6e6100-b3ed-
11ea-b69a-0a233d312e0a",
            "LogicalResourceId": "Ec2Instance",
            "PhysicalResourceId": "i-0dfaad58d59b59717",
            "ResourceType": "AWS::EC2::Instance",
            "Timestamp": "2020-06-
21T18:34:51.773000+00:00",
            "ResourceStatus": "CREATE_COMPLETE",
            "DriftInformation": {
                "StackResourceDriftStatus": "NOT_CHECKED"
            }
        }
    ]
}
```

6. Once you are done with your testing (as this will cost you), to clean up the CloudFormation stack, please pass `delete-stack` to the `cloudformation` command, as follows:

```
aws cloudformation delete-stack --stack-name first-ec2-
instance-creation
```

In this section, you have understood different CloudFormation components and how to create a stack using the CloudFormation template. In the next section, we will learn about another popular infrastructure automation tool Terraform.

Introducing Terraform

To provision your AWS infrastructure, there are a variety of tools available, and Terraform is one of them. Terraform is an open source **Infrastructure as Code (IAC)** tool created by HashiCorp that enables users to provision an infrastructure or manage IAC. Terraform also supports multiple cloud providers such as AWS, **Google Cloud Platform (GCP)**, Azure, and more, as illustrated in the following diagram:

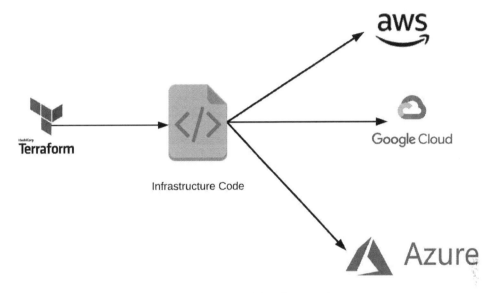

Figure 1.15 – How Terraform works

The way Terraform works is by reading the code and translating it to API calls to providers (AWS, in our case).

Here are some of the Terraform features:

- We can write Terraform code in **HashiCorp Configuration Language (HCL)** or, optionally, in JSON.

- All code files end with the extension of .tf.

- It is a declarative language (we need to define what infrastructure we want and Terraform will figure out how to create it).

In this section, you have learned what Terraform is and about its advantages. In the next section, we will explore how to install it and create your AWS resources using it.

Installing Terraform

To install Terraform, find the appropriate package for your system (`https://www.terraform.io/downloads.html`) and download the ZIP archive by following these steps:

1. Download the package, like this:

```
wget https://releases.hashicorp.com/terraform/0.12.26/
terraform_0.12.26_linux_amd64.zip
```

2. Unzip it, like this:

```
unzip terraform_0.12.26_linux_amd64.zip
```

3. Add the binary to the `PATH` environment variable and change the permission, as follows:

```
sudo cp terraform /usr/local/bin/
```
```
sudo chmod +x /usr/local/bin/terraform
```

4. Log out and log back in.

5. Verify the installation by running the following command:

```
terraform version
```
```
Terraform v0.12.26
```

Creating resources using Terraform

As with the AWS CLI and Boto3, for Terraform to interact with the AWS environment, it needs to know the credentials to authenticate with AWS, which we already set up as a part of the `aws configure` command. To create resources via Terraform, we need to define the following prerequisites:

- **Resource**: This defines one or more infrastructure objects such as an `ec2` instance or an `s3` bucket.

- **Logical name**: Then, we need to define the logical name, such as `test_instance`. The name is used to refer to this resource from elsewhere in the same Terraform code/module, but has no significance outside of the scope of a module.

- **Instance type**: The type of EC2 instance to run, as every instance type provides different capabilities (CPU, memory, I/O). For this example, I am using `t2.micro` (one virtual CPU; 1 GB memory).

You can verify the instance type supported in each region, as follows:

```
aws ec2 describe-instance-type-offerings --query
InstanceTypeOfferings --output table
-----------------------------------------------------
|              DescribeInstanceTypeOfferings         |
+---------------+-------------+----------------+
|  InstanceType  |  Location   |  LocationType   |
+---------------+-------------+----------------+
|  m5dn.8xlarge  |  us-west-2  |    region      |
|  m5ad.8xlarge  |  us-west-2  |    region      |
|   z1d.metal    |  us-west-2  |    region      |
|  g3s.xlarge    |  us-west-2  |    region      |
|  r5dn.16xlarge |  us-west-2  |    region      |
|   m5n.large    |  us-west-2  |    region      |
|  m5.16xlarge   |  us-west-2  |    region      |
|   t2.medium    |  us-west-2  |    region      |
|   t2.micro     |  us-west-2  |    region      |
|  i3en.xlarge   |  us-west-2  |    region      |
|  c5d.12xlarge  |  us-west-2  |    region      |
|  c5.12xlarge   |  us-west-2  |    region      |
```

- **AMI**: This is an operating system image used to run EC2 instances. For this example, I am using the `ami-0bc06212a56393ee1` CentOS 7 image.

Creating an AWS instance using Terraform

Now that we have all the prerequisites in place, let's follow these steps to create a Terraform resource:

1. First, let's create our first Terraform code with a filename ending with `.tf` (for example: `ec2-instance.tf`), as follows:

```
resource "aws_instance" "test_instance" {
    ami = "ami-0bc06212a56393ee1"
    instance_type = "t2.micro"
}
```

2. The next step is to clone the GitHub repository, like this:

    ```
    git clone https://github.com/PacktPublishing/AWS-for-
    System-Administrators
    ```
    ```
    cd AWS-for-System-Administrators/tree/master/Chapter1/
    terraform
    ```

3. The first command we are going to run to set up our instance is `terraform init`. This downloads code for a provider (AWS) that we are going to use. The command is shown here:

    ```
    terraform init
    ```

    > **Important note**
    > It is safe to run the `terraform init` command multiple times as it is idempotent.

4. The next command we are going to run is `terraform plan`, which tells us what Terraform will execute (+, -, and ~ sign, where + means the addition of resources, - is the deletion of resources, and the ~ sign is a modification of resources) before making any changes, as follows:

    ```
    terraform plan
    ```

    This is an effective way of making any sanity check before making actual changes to the environment.

    The output of the `terraform plan` command looks like the Linux `diff` command, and is described here:

    - (+ sign): Resource going to be created

    - (- sign): Resource going to be deleted

    - (~ sign): Resource going to be modified

    We need to manually specify the region where we want to set up the infrastructure (for example: `us-west-2`). We will discuss more about how to automate this process in future chapters.

    If this is the first time you are using the CentOS AMI, you might see this error:

    ```
    Error launching source instance: OptInRequired
    ```

In order to use this AWS Marketplace product, you need to accept the terms and subscribe. To do so, please visit `https://aws.amazon.com/marketplace/pp?sku=aw0evgkw8e5c1q413zgy5pjce`. The CentOS AMI console is shown in the following screenshot:

Figure 1.16 – Centos AMI console

5. To apply these changes, run the `terraform apply` command, as follows:

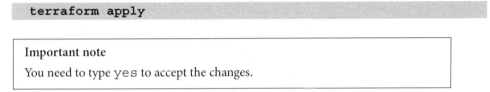

```
terraform apply
```

> **Important note**
> You need to type `yes` to accept the changes.

6. Go to the EC2 console and verify that it is creating an instance, as illustrated in the following screenshot:

	Name	▽	Instance ID	Instance state ▽	Instance type ▽
☐	PacktPub		i-0a0ea0cdbf242c5be	⊘ Running ⊕⊖	t2.micro

Figure 1.17 – EC2 console

7. To perform a cleanup of resources we have created so far, run the `terraform destroy` command, as follows:

```
terraform destroy
```

> **Important note**
> As with `plan` and `apply`, you need to specify the region, and you need to type `yes` to accept changes.

Terraform makes the life of a system administrator or DevOps engineer easy by creating an infrastructure using a few code lines. In this chapter, you have learned how to install it. In future chapters, we will create our AWS infrastructure using this tool.

Installing tools in an automated way

So far, we have installed all these tools manually, but wouldn't it be great if we had an automated way to install these tools?

Here is the script that automates the installation process of all these tools:

```
git clone https://github.com/PacktPublishing/AWS-for-System-
Administrators
cd AWS-for-System-Administrators/tree/master/Chapter1
chmod +x env_setup.sh
sudo bash env_setup.sh
```

In this section, you have learned how rather than installing tools manually with the help of a simple shell script, we can automate the installation of tools such as the AWS CLI, Boto3, and Terraform.

Summary

In this chapter, we learned about the installation of tools such as the AWS CLI, Boto3, CloudFormation (verification), and Terraform. We also wrote simple code to verify these applications. Now that we have installed all the tools and set up the environment, we will use these tools in future chapters to build the AWS infrastructure.

In the next chapter, we will see how to tighten security using AWS IAM, by applying IAM policies and roles. We will also look at some real-world examples on how to restrict users to specific instance types using IAM policy, and rotate access and secret keys using a Python Boto3 script.

2
Protecting Your AWS Account Using IAM

In the previous chapter, while setting up AWS tools, we assigned administration access to the user. However, there is a significant risk involved in doing this as that particular user can perform any action, such as deleting the instance, wiping out S3 buckets, and so on. To address that, in this chapter, we will see how IAM is a set of features that allows us to create and manage users and groups and, at the same time, give them allow or deny permissions via IAM policies to access AWS resources.

In this chapter, we're going to cover the following main topics:

- Creating IAM users and groups
- Understanding IAM policies
- Creating IAM roles
- Introducing AWS Security Token Service (STS)
- Real-time use case of launching a specific instance using CloudFormation
- Rotating IAM credentials using Boto3

Let's get started!

Technical requirements

To gain the most from this chapter, you should have basic knowledge and awareness of the IAM service. You should also have basic knowledge of CloudFormation and Terraform, which we covered in *Chapter 1, Setting Up the AWS Environment*.

The solution scripts for this chapter can be found in this book's GitHub repository at:

```
https://github.com/PacktPublishing/AWS-for-System-
Administrators/tree/master/Chapter2
```

Check out the following link to see the Code in Action:

```
https://bit.ly/3ptQTHY
```

Creating IAM users and groups

Before we dig deeper into IAM users and groups, let's try to understand where IAM fits into the security realm with the help of logging in, which requires authentication and authorization.

To log into any system, two critical pieces of information are required:

- **Authentication**: This will define who that person is. IAM users and groups handle this.

- **Authorization**: What action a user is allowed to perform. IAM policies handle this.

Introducing IAM users

A user can be a person who logs into the AWS console using their username and password or a service account with the help of access and secret access keys. We can assign one or more IAM policies to the user, which specify the action this user can perform.

> **Note**
>
> IAM is a global service and is not tied to any specific region. No region needs to be specified when you define user permissions. IAM users can use an AWS service in any geographic region if it's allowed by a specific IAM policy.

Creating a new IAM user using the AWS CLI

The `create-user` command creates an IAM user with username, `prashant1` (or any username that is provided), in the current AWS account:

```
aws iam create-user --user-name prashant1
{
    "User": {
        "Path": "/",
        "UserName": "prashant1",
        "UserId": "AIDAUCFHJCYT3IYYKKCRU",
        "Arn": "arn:aws:iam::XXXXXXXXX:user/prashant1",
        "CreateDate": "2020-06-22T00:38:26+00:00"
    }
}
```

Once you run the `aws iam create-user --user-name <provided username>` command, you will get the following output between curly braces { }:

- `Path`: This is the path to the username, and it defaults to slash (/).
- `UserName`: The username you provided during IAM user creation.
- `UserId`: This is the string that identifies the user.
- `Arn`: This is used to identify AWS resources uniquely (we'll look at this in more detail in the *Introducing ARN* section).
- `CreateDate`: The date when the user was created.

Listing all the IAM users in this account

The `list-users` command lists all the IAM users in the current AWS account:

```
aws iam list-users --query Users[].[UserName,Arn] --output
table
---------------------------------------------------------------
                            ListUsers

+------------------+------------------------------------------+
|    packtpub      |   arn:aws:iam::XXXXXXXXX:user/packtpub   |

|    plakhera      |   arn:aws:iam::XXXXXXXXX:user/plakhera   |
```

```
|   plakhera.dev   |   arn:aws:iam::XXXXXXXXX:user/plakhera.dev
|
+----------------+-----------------------------------------------------+
```

With that, we know how to create an IAM user using the command line. Now, let's focus on IAM groups.

Introducing IAM groups

An IAM group is a collection of IAM users. Groups can let you specify multiple users, making it easier for you to manage the permissions for those users. One of the group's typical use cases is to create an admin group and assign the necessary policy to it. Then, you can add all the users who need that permission, or if any new user joins the organization and needs admin privilege, we can add that person as a member of this group. Similarly, if that person moves to a different team, rather than editing their permission manually, we can remove them from this group.

> **Note**
> The IAM group is not a real identity because we cannot mention it in
> a permission policy. It's merely a way to attach policies to multiple users at
> one time.

Creating a new group

The following create-group command creates an IAM group named Admins in the current account:

```
aws iam create-group --group-name Admins
{
    "Group": {
        "Path": "/",
        "GroupName": "Admins",
        "GroupId": "AGPAUCFHJCYTXQTOW6OQU",
        "Arn": "arn:aws:iam::XXXXXXXXX::group/Admins",
        "CreateDate": "2020-06-22T00:42:35+00:00"
    }
}
```

Listing all the IAM groups

The `list-groups` command lists all the IAM groups on the current account:

```
aws iam list-groups --query Groups[].GroupName --output table
---------------------
|      ListGroups    |
+-------------------+
|  Admins            |
|  EC2LimitedAccess  |
|  mytestgrp         |
+-------------------+
```

Adding a user to a group

The `add-user-to-group` command adds an IAM user named `prashant1` to the IAM group named `Admins`:

```
aws iam add-user-to-group --user-name prashant1 --group-name
Admins
```

Now that we know how to create, list, and add a user to an IAM group using the command line, let's move on to the next topic: understanding IAM policies.

Understanding IAM policies

An IAM policy is a JSON-formatted document that defines which action a user, group, or role can perform on AWS resources. When users or roles make a request, the AWS policy engine evaluates these policies and, depending on the permission defined in the policy request, is either allowed or denied. Once again, I want to re-emphasize the point that IAM policies are used for authorization. For authentication purposes, we are going to use IAM users.

> **Note**
> By default, all requests are implicitly denied, and IAM identities (user, group, or role) have no permissions or policies attached by default.

AWS supports four types of policies:

- **Identity-based policies**: To grant permission to any identity, which can be users, groups, or roles, we can use identity-based policies.

- **Resource-based policies**: This policy is mostly used with resources, such as an S3 bucket or KMS keys to grant permissions to a principal.

- **Permissions boundaries**: Permissions boundaries don't grant any permission, but they define the maximum permission any identity-based policy can grant to any resource.

- **Organizations SCPs**: The **service control policy (SCP)** is used by an account member of an organization or **organizational unit (OU)**, and it defines the maximum number of permissions that can be made for account members of an organization.

IAM policy structure

As we mentioned earlier, the IAM policy is a JSON-formatted document that consists of one or more statements. To build the JSON document, we need to adhere to a certain structure. The policy's structure is divided into four main parts:

- **Effect**: This is either `Allow` or `Deny`, which indicates whether the following actions are allowed or denied.

- **Action**: This is a list of service-level actions that are allowed or denied access; for example, `s3:GetObject` (where `s3` is the service name and `GetObject` is the action that's performed by service).

- **Resource**: This specifies the list of specific resources within services; for example, `arn:aws:ec2:::instance`.

- **Condition**: This specifies the condition under which the access that's been defined is valid. For example, in this case, we specify the condition that allows access from a specific IP:

```
"Condition": {
    "NotIpAddress": {
        "aws:SourceIp": [
            "192.0.2.0/24",
            "203.0.113.0/24"
        ]
    }
}
```

Combining all these parts will make the IAM policy structure look like this:

```
{
    "Statement":[{
        "Effect":"effect",
        "Action":"action",
        "Resource":"arn",
        "Condition":{
            "condition":{
            "key":"value"
            }
        }
    }]
}
```

One real-world example is blocking traffic to an S3 bucket unless the traffic is from a specific IP. In this case, we are using Condition, along with the aws:SourceIp key, which allows requests from a specific IP:

```
{
    "Id": "Policy1604259866496",
    "Version": "2012-10-17",
    "Statement": [
        {
            "Sid": "Stmt1604259864802",
            "Action": "s3:*",
            "Effect": "Deny",
            "Resource": "arn:aws:s3:::myexamplebucket/*",
            "Condition": {
                "NotIpAddress": {
                    "aws:SourceIp": "192.168.1.10/24"
                }
            },
            "Principal": "*"
        }
    ]
}
```

Now that we understand the different components of an IAM policy and how to build one, let's dig deeper into how to use an **Amazon Resource Name** (**ARN**) alongside the IAM policy.

Introducing ARN

An ARN is used to identify any AWS resource uniquely. One of the primary reasons we need an ARN is to specify a resource precisely across all of AWS; for example, IAM policies or API calls. The following is the general format of an ARN, but it usually depends on the type of resource being used. For example, in the case of S3, you don't need to specify the region or account number, but specifying an IAM, EC2 region, or account ID may not be optional:

```
arn:partition:service:region:account-id:resource-id
```

Let's break down the different components of an ARN one by one:

- `partition`: A partition is a group of AWS regions in which the resource is located. The supported partitions are as follows:

  - `aws`: AWS Regions

  - `aws-cn`: AWS China Regions

  - `aws-us-gov`: AWS GovCloud (US) Regions

- `service`: This identifies the AWS product; for example, `iam` or `s3`.

- `region`: This specifies the AWS region; for example, `us-west-2`.

- `account-id`: This is the account ID of the AWS account that owns the resources; for example, `123456789012`.

- `resource-id`: This can be the name or ID of the resource; for example, `my_test_bucket`.

Let's take a look at some ARN examples, where in the case of `iam` and `ec2`, an account ID (`123456789012`) is required, whereas in the case of `s3`, which is a global resource, an account ID is not needed:

```
arn:aws:iam::123456789012:user/Prod/test1234/*
arn:aws:s3:::my_test_bucket/*
arn:aws:ec2:us-west-2:123456789012:instance/instance-id
```

The ARN is an important concept to understand and is especially helpful while defining which resource to allow or deny.

IAM policy evaluation

In this section, we are going to learn how the AWS policy engine evaluates requests. It performs a series of checks to determine which request to allow or deny. Here is the sequence of steps it performs:

1. By default, all requests are implicitly denied (except the root user, who has full access).

2. The AWS policy engine, after policy evaluation, decides whether the request is allowed or denied.

3. For the given resources, AWS gathers all the policies.

4. If there is an explicit *allow* in resource-based policy, it will override the explicit *deny*.

5. If other AWS policies such as **Service Control Policy** (**SCP**) or permissions boundaries is present, it will override the *allow* with an implicit *deny*.

6. If an explicit *deny* is found in any policy, this always overrides any *allow*.

The following is a flowchart of the IAM policy evaluation process:

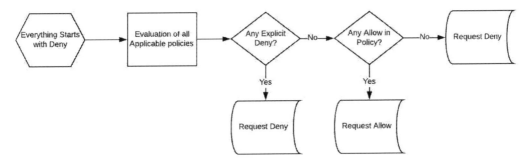

Figure 2.1 – IAM policy evaluation

> **Note**
> In this case, we are going to assume that both the resource and request are from the same account.

Creating the IAM policy using the AWS CLI

To create an IAM policy using the AWS CLI, follow these steps:

1. Here, we are assuming, you have saved the policy to a file called `ec2-instance.json`. In this example, we are going to create a policy that allows a user to perform stop/start, describe, and delete key pair for a specific instance (`arn:aws:ec2:us-west-2:XXXXXX:instance/i-02ba5c9e4250bf322`):

> **Important note**
> Please replace XXXXXX with your AWS account ID. To find out what your AWS account ID is, please run the `aws sts get-caller-identity --query Account` command.

```
{
    "Version": "2012-10-17",
    "Statement": [
        {
            "Sid": "VisualEditor0",
            "Effect": "Allow",
            "Action": [
                "ec2:StartInstances",
                "ec2:StopInstances"
            ],
            "Resource": "arn:aws:ec2:us-west-
2:XXXXXX:instance/i-02ba5c9e4250bf322"
        },
        {
            "Sid": "VisualEditor1",
            "Effect": "Allow",
            "Action": [
                "ec2:DescribeInstances",
                "ec2:DeleteKeyPair"
            ],
            "Resource": "*"
        }
    ]
}
```

2. To create the policy, use the `put-user-policy` command, which attaches a policy to the IAM user `plakhera`:

```
aws iam put-user-policy --user-name plakhera --policy-
name ec2_restrict --policy-document file://ec2-instance.
json
```

`--policy-name` is the name of the policy, while `--policy-document` is the policy (`ec2-instance.json`) we defined earlier.

3. To list the policy we created earlier, use the `get-user-policy` command:

```
aws iam get-user-policy --user-name  plakhera --policy-
name ec2_restrict
{
    "UserName": "plakhera",
    "PolicyName": "ec2_restrict",
    "PolicyDocument": {
        "Version": "2012-10-17",
        "Statement": [
            {
                "Sid": "VisualEditor0",
                "Effect": "Allow",
                "Action": [
                    "ec2:StartInstances",
                    "ec2:StopInstances"
                ],
                "Resource": "arn:aws:ec2:us-west-
2:XXXXXX:instance/XXXXXXXX"
            },
            {
                "Sid": "VisualEditor1",
                "Effect": "Allow",
                "Action": [
                    "ec2:DescribeInstances",
                    "ec2:DeleteKeyPair"
                ],
                "Resource": "*"
            }
```

```
            ]
        }
    }
```

The AWS CLI is just one of the ways we can create an IAM policy. We can also create a policy using the AWS console.

Creating IAM roles

Think of an IAM role as being similar to an IAM user. It's an AWS identity that defines a group of permissions for making AWS service requests. The IAM role is assumed by the following:

- Applications
- External users

Advantages of using an IAM role

The advantages of using an IAM role are as follows:

- It provides temporary security credentials for your role session.
- We no longer need to embed permanent credentials inside applications.
- You can grant users in one AWS account access to resources in another account.
- It easily federates external users.

Creating an IAM role using Terraform

Let's try to understand an IAM role with the help of an example. We can attach an IAM role to an EC2 instance in order to use other AWS services, such as an S3 bucket. To demonstrate this example, I will be using Terraform.

Create a file called iam_role.tf and copy the code provided at https://github. com/PacktPublishing/AWS-for-System-Administrators/blob/master/ Chapter2/terraform/iam_role.tf into it.

Let's break down the code and understand what's going on:

1. In this example, we are using `sts:AssumeRole` as `Action` and `ec2.amazonaws.com` as `Service`, which grants an EC2 service permission to assume a role:

```
resource "aws_iam_role" "my-test-iam-role" {
  name = "my-test-iam-role"

    assume_role_policy = <<EOF
{
"Version": "2012-10-17",
"Statement": [
{
"Action": "sts:AssumeRole",
"Principal": {
  "Service": "ec2.amazonaws.com"
},
"Effect": "Allow"
}
]
}
EOF

  tags = {
      tag-key = "my-test-iam-role"
  }
}
```

2. The preceding Terraform code creates an IAM role, but it is not linked to an EC2 instance. To do this, we need to create an EC2 instance profile.

3. Now, let's create an EC2 instance profile:

```
resource "aws_iam_instance_profile" "my-test-iam-
instance-profile" {
  name = "my-test-iam-instance-profile"
  role = "${aws_iam_role.my-test-iam-role.name}"
}
```

Even though we have an IAM role and instance profile, there is no permission attached to it.

4. Next, we will add the IAM policy, which restricts EC2 users to only running specific commands, to an S3 bucket:

```
resource "aws_iam_role_policy" "my-test-policy" {
  name = "my-test-iam-policy"
  role = "${aws_iam_role.my-test-iam-role.id}"

  policy = <<EOF
{
    "Version": "2012-10-17",
    "Statement": [
        {
            "Sid": "VisualEditor0",
            "Effect": "Allow",
            "Action": [
                "s3:ListBucket",
                "s3:PutObject",
                "s3:GetObject"
            ],
            "Resource": "*"
        }
    ]
}
EOF
}
```

5. Finally, we will attach the created role to an EC2 instance using `iam_instance_ profile`. During the launch instance, it will use a specific role:

```
resource "aws_instance" "test_ec2_role" {
    ami                 = "ami-0d5fad86866a3a449"
    instance_type       = "t2.micro"
    iam_instance_profile = "${aws_iam_instance_profile.
my-test-iam-instance-profile.name}"
    key_name            = "packtpub"
}
```

> **Note**
>
> All these `aws_instance` parameters were discussed in the *Setting up the AWS environment* section of *Chapter 1, Setting Up the AWS Environment*.

6. Now, it's time to execute the code and create an IAM role using Terraform. Run the following commands to clone the repository and navigate to the `terraform` folder:

```
git clone https://github.com/PacktPublishing/AWS-for-
System-Administrators.git
AWS-for-System-Administrators/tree/master/Chapter2/
terraform
```

7. The following command will initialize the Terraform working directory or download any plugins for a provider (for example, `aws`):

```
terraform init
```

8. The `terraform plan` command will generate and show the execution plan before making the actual changes:

```
terraform plan
```

9. To create the instance, we need to run the `terraform apply` command:

```
terraform apply
```

10. To verify whether an IAM role is now attached to an EC2 instance, log into the `ec2` instance using your public key and the public IP of that instance:

```
ssh -i <public key> ec2-user@<public ip of the instance>
```

11. You can now use the instance metadata service (`http://169.254.169.254/latest/meta-data/`) from your running instance to get the IAM role from the instance profile ID:

```
curl http://169.254.169.254/latest/meta-data/iam/info
{
  "Code" : "Success",
  "LastUpdated" : "2020-06-28T05:18:17Z",
    "InstanceProfileArn" : "arn:aws:iam::XXXXXXX:instance-profile/test-iam-profile1",
    "InstanceProfileId" : "XXXXXXX"
}
```

12. Similarly, to get credentials, you can query the instance metadata service, which is available in each running instance:

```
curl http://169.254.169.254/latest/meta-data/iam/security-credentials/test_iam_role1
{
  "Code" : "Success",
  "LastUpdated" : "2020-06-28T05:19:15Z",
  "Type" : "AWS-HMAC",
  "AccessKeyId" : "XXXXXXXXXX",
  "SecretAccessKey" : "XXXXXXXX",
  "Token" : "XXXXXXXXXXXXXXXXXXXXX",
  "Expiration" : "2020-06-28T11:53:17Z"
}
```

Now that we understand how to create IAM roles using Terraform, let's shift gear and look at the Security Token Service.

Introducing AWS Security Token Service (AWS STS)

AWS STS is a web service that allows you to request temporary, limited privilege credentials (lasting from 15 minutes to 36 hours) for AWS IAM users or federated users:

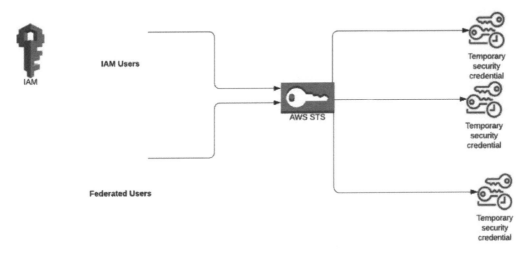

Figure 2.2 – AWS STS

The application makes an API request to AWS STS for credentials; STS generates these credentials dynamically. Once the credentials expire, new ones may be requested (as long as the user has permission to do so).

Advantages of AWS STS

The advantages of AWS STS are as follows:

- Provides temporary security credentials.
- Short-term credentials lasting from 15 minutes to 36 hours.
- Credentials are dynamically assigned as requested.
- No need to rotate/revoke password or access keys.

Use cases

Here are some of the use cases of AWS STS:

- Identity federation (grants users from outside AWS access to the service)
- Cross-account access (users or services from other accounts are granted access to your account)
- Applications on Amazon EC2 instances that need access to services

With that, you understand what STS is, how it works, and some of its use cases. Now, let's solidify this concept with the help of a use case example where you will see how STS can be helpful in the case of cross accounts.

IAM cross-account access

To illustrate this example, we are going to do the following:

1. Use two AWS accounts (Account A and Account B).

2. Create an IAM role in Account B and attach the Administration Policy to it.

3. Log into Account A and attach the assume role policy.

4. Log into the AWS Management Console for Account A and switch roles to Account B.

Let's perform each of these steps one by one:

1. Create an IAM role in Account B and attach the Administration Policy to it.

2. Go to `https://console.aws.amazon.com/iam/home#/roles` and click on **Create role | Another AWS account**.

3. To get the account ID of Account A, run the following command on the Terminal:

```
aws sts get-caller-identity --query Account
```

4. Paste Account A's `Account ID` into the **Account ID*** field, as shown in the following screenshot:

Figure 2.3 – IAM Create role screen (Another AWS account)

5. Now, click **Next: Permissions** and under **Attach permission policies**, select **AdministratorAccess** under **Policy name**. Then, click **Next: Tags**:

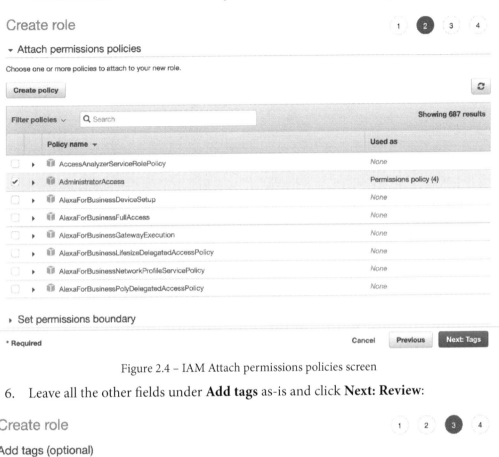

Figure 2.4 – IAM Attach permissions policies screen

6. Leave all the other fields under **Add tags** as-is and click **Next: Review**:

Create role   1   2   ③   4

Add tags (optional)

IAM tags are key-value pairs you can add to your role. Tags can include user information, such as an email address, or can be descriptive, such as a job title. You can use the tags to organize, track, or control access for this role. Learn more

Key	Value (optional)	Remove
Add new key		

You can add 50 more tags.

Cancel   Previous   Next: Review

Figure 2.5 – IAM Add tags (optional) screen

7.   Under the **Review** section, provide a **Role name***, as shown in the following screenshot. Once you've done this, scroll down to the bottom of the page and click **Create role**:

Figure 2.6 – IAM Review screen

8.   Please take a note of our **Role ARN**:

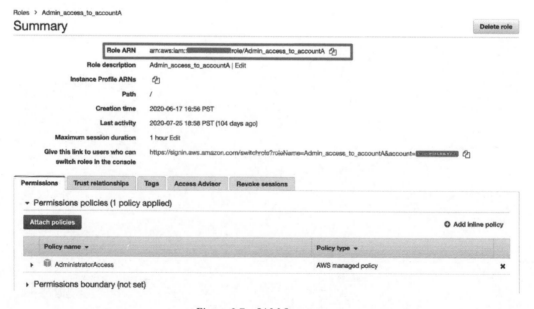

Figure 2.7 – IAM Summary

9. Now, click on the **Trust relationships** tab. You will see that the trust relationship has been established between Account A and Account B (Account A's ID is shown under **Trusted entities**):

Figure 2.8 – IAM Trust relationships screen

So far, we have established the trust relationship between Account A and Account B. Next, we are going to log into Account A and attach the assume role policy (by assuming a role on Account A will obtain temporary credentials) by following these steps:

1. Log into Account A.

2. Go to the IAM console (`https://console.aws.amazon.com/iam/home?region=us-west-2#/home`) and create a new user or use an existing user. We learned how to do this in the previous chapter.

3. Click on **Add inline policy**:

Figure 2.9 – IAM Add inline policy

4. Under **Create policy**, go to **Service** and search for STS. Then, go to **Action** and, under **Write**, search for AssumeRole. After that, go to **Resources** and choose **Specific** and then specify the role ARN we created in the previous step (arn:aws:iam::XXXXXX:role/Admin_access_to_accountA). Finally, click on the **Review policy** button:

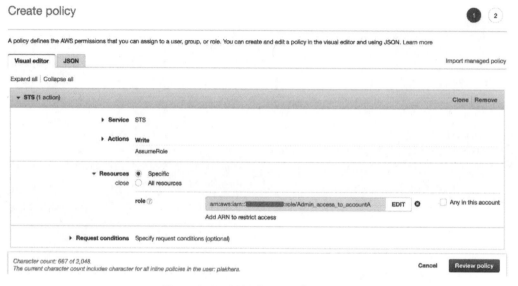

Figure 2.10 – IAM Create policy screen

5. On the **Review policy** page, give the policy a meaningful name. For example, I chose **AccountA_to_AccountB_Trust**, but feel free to choose whatever name suits your requirements. Then, click on **Create policy**:

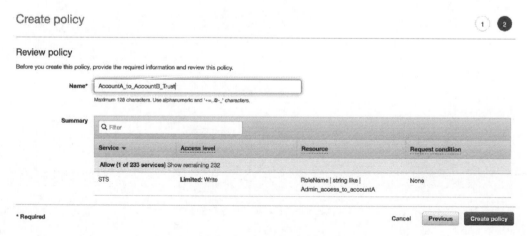

Figure 2.11 – IAM Review policy screen

So far, we have created the IAM policy and established a trust relationship between Account A and Account B. Now, let's switch roles to Account B from Account A. To do that, go back to the AWS Management Console:

1. Go back to the **AWS Management Console** page of Account A and click on **Switch Role**:

Figure 2.12 – Switch Role

2. Enter the **Account** number of Account B, the name of our **Role** name, which we had created earlier (`Admin_access_to_accountA`), and provide a **Display Name**. Then, click on **Switch Role**:

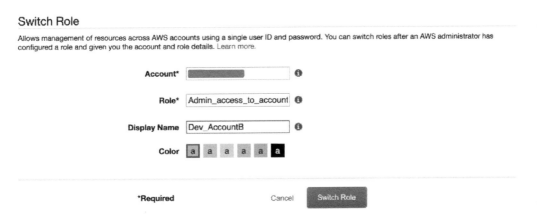

Figure 2.13 – Switch Role – adding details

3. We have now switched to Account B:

Figure 2.14 – Switching role to Account B

4.   To log back to Account A, click **Back to <user id>**:

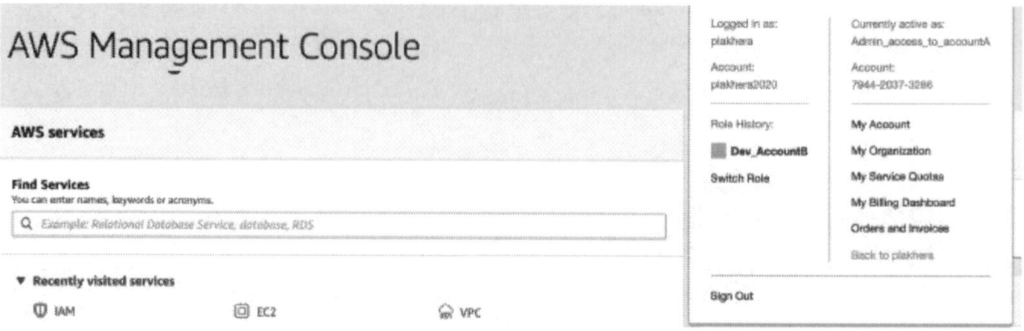

Figure 2.15 – Switching back to the previous user

With that, you know how to give a user in one account access to the resources in another account. This is one of the common tasks we encounter as part of our daily job, where a user in one account asks for access to a specific resource in another account.

Real-time use case of launching a specific instance using CloudFormation

This is one of the requirements that most of us face in a non-production or development environment, where we want to restrict users to launching specific instance types to save costs. Let's learn how to achieve this with the help of an IAM policy. We are going to look at a real-time use case for an IAM policy where we must do the following:

1.   First, we need to create two IAM users, `plakheraprod` and `plakheradev`.

2.   Next, we must create an IAM group called `EC2LimitedAccess`.

3.   Now, we must create an IAM policy that restricts a user to performing only specific actions (`RunInstances`, `StopInstances`, and `StartInstances`), as well as launching only specific instance types (`t2.small` and `t2.medium`).

With that in mind, let's start creating the stack template:

1.   Create a file named `iam-resource-creation.yml`. You can find it here: `https://github.com/PacktPublishing/AWS-for-System-Administrators/blob/master/Chapter2/cloudformation/iam-resource-creation.yml`.

2. Add some boilerplate syntax that is common to all templates; for example, `AWSTemplateFormatVersion` and `Description`. We covered this in *Chapter 1, Setting Up the AWS Environment*.

3. Now, create a resource. The first resource we are going to create is an IAM group named `EC2LimitedAccess` with `AWS::IAM::Group` as its type.

4. Next, we will create an IAM policy that provides limited access to EC2 to run, stop, and start an instance on a specific instance family (`t2.medium` or `t2.small`). Attach this policy to the IAM group (`EC2LimitedAccess`) we created in the previous step.

5. Finally, we will create two users (`plakheraprod` and `plakheradev`) and attach them to `EC2LimitedAccess`.

6. Validate the template to make sure there are no syntax errors. To do that, we are going to use the `validate-template` command, which will validate the `iam-resource-creation.yml` file:

```
aws cloudformation validate-template --template-body
file://iam-resource-creation.yml
{.
    "Parameters": [],
    "Description": "CloudFormation Script to Create
User, Groups and IAM Policy to restrict user to specific
instance family",
    "Capabilities": [
        "CAPABILITY_NAMED_IAM"
    ],
    "CapabilitiesReason": "The following resource(s)
require capabilities: [AWS::IAM::User]"
}
```

7. Create the IAM stack and add the necessary IAM capabilities. To create a stack, we will use the `create-stack` command, which creates a stack called `iam-resource-creation`:

```
aws cloudformation create-stack --stack-name
iam-resource-creation --template-body file://
iam-resource-creation.yml --capabilities "CAPABILITY_
IAM" "CAPABILITY_NAMED_IAM"
{
    "StackId": "arn:aws:cloudformation:us-west-
```

```
2:XXXXXXX:stack/iam-resource-creation/e37509d0-b972-11ea-
9117-064fbe1c973c"
}
```

> **Note**
>
> In some cases, we need to specify capabilities for AWS CloudFormation to create the stack. In the case of IAM, a new user might contain resources that will impact the permission of your AWS account. This is why we explicitly specify capabilities such as CAPABILITY_IAM and CAPABILITY_NAMED_IAM.

8. To verify that the stack has been created successfully, we will use the `describe-stack` command, which provides a summary of the stack. If the stack has been created, it will show `StackStatus": "CREATE_COMPLETE` as its status:

```
aws cloudformation describe-stacks --stack-name
iam-resource-creation
{
    "Stacks": [
        {
            "StackId": "arn:aws:cloudformation:us-west-
2:XXXXXXXXXX:stack/iam-resource-creation/e37509d0-b972-
11ea-9117-064fbe1c973c",
            "StackName": "iam-resource-creation",
            "Description": "CloudFormation Script to
Create User, Groups and IAM Policy to restrict user to
specific instance family",
            "CreationTime": "2020-06-
28T19:09:28.247000+00:00",
            "RollbackConfiguration": {},
            "StackStatus": "CREATE_COMPLETE",
        }
    ]
}
```

9. To get the details of the resources in the specified stack, we can run `describe-stack-resources`:

```
aws cloudformation describe-stack-resources --stack-name
iam-resource-creation
{
    "StackResources": [
        {
            "StackName": "iam-resource-creation",
            "StackId": "arn:aws:cloudformation:us-west-
2:XXXXXXXX:stack/iam-resource-creation/e37509d0-b972-
11ea-9117-064fbe1c973c",
            "LogicalResourceId": "EC2LimitedAccess",
            "PhysicalResourceId": "EC2LimitedAccess",
            "ResourceType": "AWS::IAM::Group",
            "Timestamp": "2020-06-
28T19:10:07.903000+00:00",
            "ResourceStatus": "CREATE_COMPLETE",
            "DriftInformation": {
                "StackResourceDriftStatus": "NOT_CHECKED"
            }
        }
    ]
}
```

In this section, we learned how to restrict a user to performing a particular action and limited them to launching a specific instance type using CloudFormation.

Rotating IAM credentials using Boto3

Rotating an access key (including access key IDs and secret access keys) regularly is a security best practice. It reduces the blast radius of damage if the security key is compromised.

> **Note**
> AWS strongly recommends the use of IAM roles as it uses temporary security credentials. STS will automatically take care of rotating and expiring those credentials, so we don't need to worry about this. However, in cases where our application runs somewhere other than EC2, we need to add key rotation as part of the application life cycle.

Prerequisites

Before executing the Boto3 script, please create a new key for the user, in addition to the one that is in use. IAM only allows two access keys. Before generating a new key for the user, we need to list the existing keys; if the user already has two keys, our Boto3 script will fail if we try to generate a new key (third key). Listing a key is an important step as it will provide us with a safety check before we proceed with our Boto3 script:

1. To list the existing key, we will use the `list-access-keys` command, which lists the access keys IDs for the user `plakhera.dev`:

```
aws iam list-access-keys --user-name plakhera.dev
{
    "AccessKeyMetadata": [
        {
            "UserName": "plakhera.dev",
            "AccessKeyId": "AKIAUCFHJCYTRHD7C2UN",
            "Status": "Active",
            "CreateDate": "2020-07-08T00:29:50Z"
        }
    ]
}
```

Next, let's create a new key for the user.

2. To create a new key, we will use the `create-access-key` command, which will create an access key ID and secret access key for the user `plakhera.dev`:

```
aws iam create-access-key --user-name plakhera.dev
{
    "AccessKey": {
        "UserName": "plakhera.dev",
        "AccessKeyId": "AKIAUCFHJCYT55F2RTE4",
        "Status": "Active",
```

```
        "SecretAccessKey":
"Jau+Bq3YmP4bEYitPjqwTcWvuMYvtPcyGZ79BCQQ",
        "CreateDate": "2020-07-08T00:32:33Z"
    }
}
```

Now, update your applications so that they can use the new access key and make sure it's working as expected. Updating the new key is required as we are disabling the existing key, which is in use, so make sure to update your application so that it can use the new key and check that all the functionalities work as expected. This usually requires some automation or canary deployment, where you update a portion of your application; for example, if your application is running using 10 nodes, then update one node and check if you are getting the desired behavior.

Creating a Boto3 script to rotate credentials

To rotate credentials, we are going to import Boto3, as well as the `datetime` Python module. A Python module is merely Python code, and by importing a module, we are gaining access to code from another module. In this case, we are importing Boto3, which is an AWS SDK for Python. We are going to use the `datetime` module to make the key inactive based on the current date.

> **Important note**
> For this script, I used 60 days as the maximum key age, but this depends on your company/security requirements.

Follow these steps to rotate the credentials using a Boto3 script:

1. First, we must import all the standard libraries; that is, `boto3` and `datetime`. Next, we must define the `KEY_MAXIMUM_AGE` variable in order to define the maximum key age:

    ```
    import boto3
    from datetime import datetime, timezone
    KEY_MAXIMUM_AGE = 60
    ```

2. Next, we must set up a variable for the IAM client. This will give us low-level access to the IAM service:

    ```
    iam = boto3.client("iam")
    ```

3. Now, we can define a variable that will hold the list specifying all the IAM users that
    are present in this account:

    ```
    iam_all_users = iam.list_users()
    ```

4. Next, we can calculate the difference between the current date and the date when
    the key for the particular user was created:

    ```
    def key_age(access_key_creation_date):
        current_date = datetime.now(timezone.utc)
        age = current_date - user_creation_date
        return age.days
    ```

5. By using the `iam_all_users` variable that we created earlier, we can get a list of
    all the individual users.

6. Next, we will create a new variable name response to get the list of access keys for
    each user:

    ```
    for user in iam_all_users['Users']:
        iam_user = user['UserName']
        response = iam.list_access_keys(UserName=iam_user)
    ```

7. Now, iterate over the response object we created in the previous step (response)
    to get the `access_key` ID and key creation date for each user.

8. Print the username, access key ID, and key creation date. This is for verbosity and
    to verify that everything is working as expected:

    ```
    for access_key in response['AccessKeyMetadata']:
        access_keyid = access_key['AccessKeyId']
        access_key_creation_date = access_key['CreateDate']
        print(f'IAM UserName: {iam_user} {access_keyid}
    {access_key_creation_date}')
    ```

9. Next, we will call the `key_age` function that we created earlier to calculate the
    difference between the current date and when the key is created for a particular user:

    ```
    age = key_age(access_key_creation_date)
    ```

10. Next, we need to perform a condition check to see if our key is older than 60 days. If so, we will deactivate the key by using `iam.update_access_key` and setting its status to `Inactive`:

```
if age < KEY_MAXIMUM_AGE:
continue
        print(f'Deactivating the key for a particular
user {iam_user} as it exceed the maximum key age')
                        iam.update_
access_key(UserName=iam_user,AccessKeyId=access_
keyid,Status='Inactive')
```

11. Finally, the user who is executing this script must have the following IAM permissions. They must be able to list IAM users and list and update access keys:

```
"iam:ListAccessKeys",
"iam:ListUsers",
"iam:UpdateAccessKey"
```

12. Now, if you execute the preceding script, you will see the following output:

```
python3 iam_rotate_key.py
IAM UserName: plakhera XXXXXXXXX 2020-04-18
04:50:38+00:00
Deactivating the key for a particular user plakhera as it
exceeds the maximum key age
IAM UserName: prashant XXXXXXXXXX 2020-06-17
17:20:37+00:00
Deactivating the key for a particular user prashant as it
exceeds the maximum key age
IAM UserName: testuser XXXXXXXXX 2020-05-24
15:08:53+00:00
Deactivating the key for a particular user testuser as it
exceeds the maximum key age
```

In this section, we learned how to rotate IAM keys for a user on regular cadence using the Boto3 script.

Summary

In this chapter, we learned how to create IAM users and groups and the significance of using them. We explored different IAM policies, how to create them, and how to always use the fundamental of least privilege so that we only assign the minimum access rights to the user so that they can do their job. We also looked at the importance of IAM roles, how AWS STS works, and how temporary credentials reduce the chance of IAM keys being leaked to the internet.

Finally, we wrapped things up with two real-world examples. First, we restricted the user to a specific instance using CloudFormation. By doing this, we can save costs so that users can only launch specific instance types. Then, we looked at how to deactivate the user's access/secret key once a specific day's threshold has been met. We used Boto3 to reduce the security blast radius.

In the next chapter, we will focus on networking components, VPC, and how to create it. We will also learn what a transit gateway is and its benefits.

Section 2:
Building the
Infrastructure

It's time to get our hands dirty and start building our infrastructure as per the architectural diagram. We will start building a **virtual private cloud** (**VPC**) that will provide us with the networking component and will later use this VPC—which is going to host our application—to build our instances. We will explore some real-world scenarios to solidify the concepts.

The following chapters are included in this section:

- *Chapter 3, Creating a Data Center in the Cloud Using VPC*
- *Chapter 4, Scalable Compute Capacity in the Cloud via EC2*

3
Creating a Data Center in the Cloud Using VPC

In the previous chapter, you learned how to tighten security with the help of IAM policies and how to use IAM roles to assign temporary credentials to role sessions so that you no longer need to embed them inside your application. IAM provides security at the authentication level, that is, who is allowed or denied, and the authorization level is what that authenticated user or role is allowed to do. In the next level of defense, we need to secure our network so that only the users from the trusted network can access our service, and that is where VPC comes into the picture.

AWS **Virtual Private Cloud** (**VPC**) is your data center in the cloud. In VPC, you can define your own private network, which resembles a network in a traditional data center but with the advantage of using AWS's scalable infrastructure. Some of the benefits of using AWS VPC are as follows:

- **Simple**: Creating VPC is pretty quick and straightforward using the AWS Management Console.

- **Secure**: VPC provides security features such as security groups and **network access control lists** (**NACLs**) to filter incoming and outgoing traffic.

- **Customizable**: You can select your own IP address range, configure the route table and network gateways, and create your subnet.

With a security focus in mind, in this chapter, we are going to cover the following networking topics:

- Setting up two VPCs

- Introducing AWS Transit Gateway

- Setting up a transit gateway

- Real-time use case to enable a VPC flow log

Technical requirements

To gain the most from this chapter, you should have basic knowledge and awareness of the network service. You should be familiar with terms such as routing, IP address, and **Classless Inter-Domain Routing** (**CIDR**).

The GitHub link for solution scripts is `https://github.com/PacktPublishing/AWS-for-System-Administrators/tree/master/Chapter3`.

Check out the following link to see the Code in Action video:

`https://bit.ly/3o2nJ2e`

Setting up two VPCs

Think of VPC as your data center in the cloud, but instead of spending months or years setting up that data center, it's now a matter of a few clicks (API calls).

VPC provides you with a logically isolated section in the cloud where you can launch your AWS resources inside the virtual network you provide. Network isolation offers you other advantages, such as choosing your IP address range, defining your subnets, and configuring the route table and gateways, which we will discuss in detail later in this chapter.

The architecture we will build in this chapter is as follows:

- A VPC in two availability zones (us-west-2 Oregon) and (us-east-2 Ohio).

- Each availability zone will have two subnets (Oregon: 10.0.1.0/24, 10.0.4.0/24 in us-west-2a, 10.0.2.0/24, 10.0.5.0/24 in us-west-2b, and 10.0.3.0/24, 10.0.6.0/24 in us-west-2c; Ohio: 172.16.1.0/24, 172.16.4.0/24 in us-east-2a, 172.16.2.0/24, 172.16.5.0/24 in us-east-2b, and 172.16.3.0/24, 172.16.6.0/24 in us-east-2c). In each availability zone, the following subnet will act as a public subnet ([Oregon: 10.0.1.0/24, 10.0.3.0/24, 10.0.5.0/24], [Ohio: 172.16.1.0/24, 172.16.3.0/24, 172.16.5.0/24]) and the following subnet will act as a private subnet ([Oregon: 10.0.2.0/24, 10.0.4.0/24, 10.0.6.0/24], [Ohio: 172.16.2.0/24, 172.16.4.0/24, 172.16.6.0/24]).

- A transit gateway in each region to connect to each VPC:

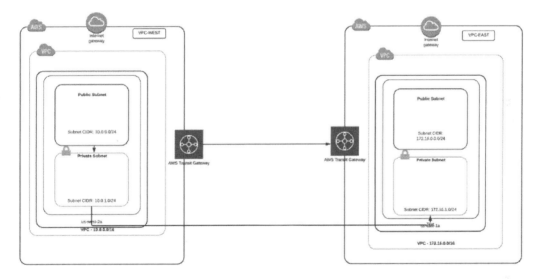

Figure 3.1 – Multi-region VPC architecture

Let's get started with creating a VPC using the AWS console and later using CloudFormation. Creating a VPC will also cover the creation of the subnet (public and private). In the last part of this chapter, we will see how to create a transit gateway.

Creating your first VPC using the AWS console

You need to perform the following steps to create your first VPC:

1. Choose a CIDR/IP address range.

2. Divide a network into subnetworks to provide high availability (different availability zones). We will discuss more about availability zones later in the chapter.

3. Create an internet gateway – set up an internet gateway, to connect your VPC to the internet.

4. Create a custom route table to set up routing. This will allow a subnet to access the internet through the internet gateway (via a route table).

Choosing a CIDR/IP address range

You need to specify the CIDR block (/16 or smaller) as suggested by RFC1918 for an IPv4 private address range:

- 10.0.0.0 – 10.255.255.255 (10/8 prefix)

- 172.16.0.0 – 172.31.255.255 (172.16/12 prefix)

- 192.168.0.0 – 192.168.255.255 (192.168/16 prefix)

Follow these steps to choose the CIDR/IP address range for VPC creation:

1. In the AWS console, **VPC** can be found under **Networking & Content Delivery** or you can use the direct link, https://console.aws.amazon.com/vpc/, and click on **VPC**:

Figure 3.2 – VPC link under Networking and Content Delivery

2. Next, click on **Your VPCs** and **Create VPC** as shown in the following screenshot:

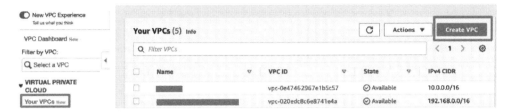

Figure 3.3 – Create a VPC console

3. Under **Create VPC**, fill in all the details:

    Name tag: Enter the name of the VPC; for example, `prod-vpc`.

    IPv4 CIDR block: Provide the CIDR block under **IPv4 CIDR block**. For this example, I am using `10.0.0.0/16` (which will provide me with the `65536` IP address), but you can choose any subnet block as discussed earlier: `172.16.0.0/12` or `192.168.0.0/16`.

    IPv6 CIDR block: Choose **No IPv6 CIDR Block** as we are not using IPv6.

    Tenancy: **Tenancy** can be **Default** or **Dedicated**. The difference between **Default** and **Dedicated** is, in the case of **Default**, your VPC is sharing hardware with other customers, but in the case of dedicated tenancy, your VPC runs on dedicated hardware, but it will incur an extra cost. Here, we will choose **Default** and then click on **Create**:

VPCs > Create VPC

Create VPC

A VPC is an isolated portion of the AWS cloud populated by AWS objects, such as Amazon EC2 instances. You must specify an IPv4 address range for your VPC. Specify the IPv4 address range as a Classless Inter-Domain Routing (CIDR block; for example, 10.0.0.0/16. You cannot specify an IPv4 CIDR block larger than /16. You can optionally associate an IPv6 CIDR block with this VPC.

Name tag	prod-vpc
IPv4 CIDR block*	10.0.0.0/16
IPv6 CIDR block	● No IPv6 CIDR Block
	○ Amazon provided IPv6 CIDR block
	○ IPv6 CIDR owned by me
Tenancy	Default

* Required   Cancel   Create

Figure 3.4 – Create VPC details

> **Note**
> You can use websites such as `https://cidr.xyz/` to calculate CIDR blocks. Also, please check with your network team to determine the CIDR block you can use so that there will be no overlapping CIDR range between your data center and AWS VPC. Overlapping CIDR will create conflict in cases where you want to connect your on-premises data center with AWS VPC via VPN or Direct Connect, or maybe you want to set up VPC peering.

An important point to note is, the moment you create a VPC, AWS will create a few resources such as *route tables*, *security groups*, and a *NACL* for you. Let's explore each of these one by one.

4. Go back to the VPC console page (`https://console.aws.amazon.com/vpc/`) and in the top-right corner, under **Filter by VPC**, select the VPC you have just created (you may need to refresh the page or press the *F5* key if your newly created VPC is not showing under **Filter by VPC**):

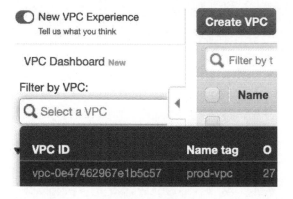

Figure 3.5 – Search for a particular VPC

> **Note**
> You will see one more VPC under the search bar and that VPC is called a default VPC. It's created for you by AWS at the time of AWS account provisioning. A default VPC is helpful for a newbie who wants to explore AWS, and when they launch their first instance, by default, it's launched under a default VPC.

5. Next, click on **Route Tables**. As the name suggests, it takes care of routing decisions. It's used to determine where network traffic needs to be directed:

Figure 3.6 – Route Tables

6. Next, click on **Network ACLs. NACLs** provide an additional security layer by controlling traffic going in and out of one or more subnets. The default NACL allows all the traffic to flow in and out of the subnets with which it is associated:

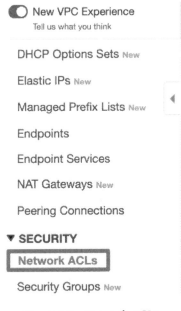

Figure 3.7 – Network ACLs

7. Next, click on **Security Groups**. A security group works as a virtual firewall, and it's used to control the traffic associated with the instance. All VPCs come with a default security group. Any instance not associated with a security group during launch is by default associated with the default security group:

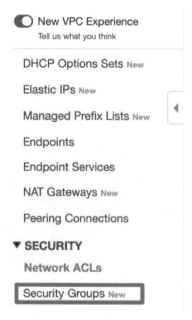

Figure 3.8 – Security Groups

So far, we have chosen the CIDR range for our VPC. In the next step, we are going to divide our network into subnetworks.

Dividing into subnetworks to provide high availability

One of the primary reasons to divide a network into subnetworks is to provide high availability. If one of the availability zones goes down, your service can always fall back to other availability zones provided you have configured your service/application in multiple **availability zones**.

Let's create subnets to provide high availability to our application:

1. Go back to the VPC console page (`https://console.aws.amazon.com/vpc/`) and click on **Subnets**:

Figure 3.9 – Subnets

2. Click on **Create subnet** as shown in the following screenshot:

Figure 3.10 – Create subnet

3. Under **Create subnet**, fill in all the details:

    Name tag: Enter the name of the subnet, for example, `vpc-prod-us-west-2a`.

    VPC: From the dropdown, select the VPC you have just created.

    Availability Zone: The availability zone where you want to create the subnet, for example, `us-west-2a` if you are setting your environment in this region.

    IPv4 CIDR block: The IPv4 address you use for the subnet. In this example, I am using `10.0.1.0/24`, which will give you 256 (actually, 251; for more details check the following note) usable IP addresses. It entirely depends upon your architectural requirement which subnet mask you choose. We already discussed this in the *Choosing a CIDR/IP address range* section.

Now, click on **Create**:

Figure 3.11 – Create subnet details page

4. You need to repeat the same steps for the us-west-2b (IP address: 10.0.2.0/24) and us-west-2c (IP address: 10.0.3.0/24) availability zones, and then again for the us-west-2a (IP address: 10.0.4.0/24), us-west-2b (IP address: 10.0.5.0/24), and us-west-2c (IP address: 10.0.6.0/24) availability zones. Here, I am showing it for the first three subnets, but it's going to be the same for the remaining three subnets (10.0.4.0/24, 10.0.5.0/24, and 10.0.6.0/24). The reason we choose six subnets and one subnet from each availability zone is to provide high availability. If one of the availability zones goes down, we can fail over to another availability zone.

5. In this case, we are creating a subnet in us-west-2b using CIDR 10.0.2.0/24:

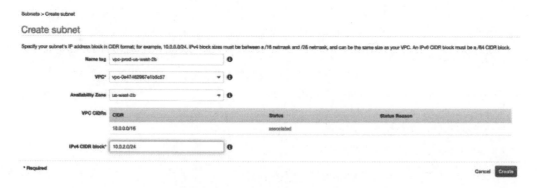

Figure 3.12 – Create subnet details page

6. In this case, we are creating a subnet in `us-west-2c` using CIDR `10.0.3.0/24`:

Figure 3.13 – Create subnet details page

7. In the end, you should see the three created subnets as shown in the following screenshot:

	Name	Subnet ID	State	VPC	IPv4 CIDR	Available IPv4	IPv6 CIDR
■	vpc-prod-us...	subnet-05092c71e8f07167a	available	vpc-0e47462967e1b5c57 ...	10.0.3.0/24	250	-
	vpc-prod-us...	subnet-05c1d5e1541ffbe71	available	vpc-0e47462967e1b5c57 ...	10.0.6.0/24	251	-
	vpc-prod-us...	subnet-07714eb09171b1f7e	available	vpc-0e47462967e1b5c57 ...	10.0.4.0/24	251	-
	vpc-prod-us...	subnet-0b0a071bce16f9347	available	vpc-0e47462967e1b5c57 ...	10.0.1.0/24	249	-
	vpc-prod-us...	subnet-0cca9fdeb1b95003c	available	vpc-0e47462967e1b5c57 ...	10.0.5.0/24	251	-
	vpc-prod-us...	subnet-0e87d62c04db49b80	available	vpc-0e47462967e1b5c57 ...	10.0.2.0/24	250	-

Figure 3.14 – Subnets

> **Note**
> Whatever CIDR block you choose, you cannot use its first four and the last IP addresses.

For example, say you choose `10.0.0.0/24`:

- `10.0.0.0`: Network address
- `10.0.0.1`: Reserved for AWS VPC router
- `10.0.0.2`: Reserved for AWS DNS server
- `10.0.0.3`: Reserved for AWS future use
- `10.0.0.255`: Network broadcast address

At this stage, we have chosen the CIDR range for our VPC and divided the network into subnetworks. The next step is to create an internet gateway that allows communication between your VPC and the internet.

Creating an internet gateway

As the name suggests, an internet gateway acts as a gateway to connect your VPC to the internet. To create an internet gateway, follow these steps:

1. Go back to the VPC console page (`https://console.aws.amazon.com/vpc/`) and click on **Internet Gateways**:

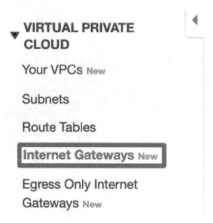

Figure 3.15 – Internet Gateways

2. Next, click on **Create internet gateway**:

Figure 3.16 – Create internet gateway

3. Give your internet gateway a name under **Name tag** (for example, `prod-vpc-igw`) and click on **Create internet gateway**:

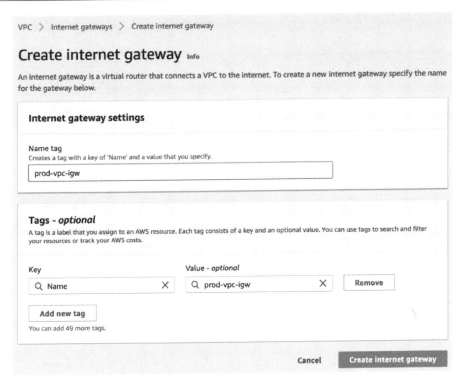

Figure 3.17 – Create internet gateway details page

4. Once the internet gateway is created, you will see a screen like this and, by default, its state is **Detached**:

Figure 3.18 – Create internet gateway final screen

5.   To attach it to the VPC, click on **Actions | Attach to VPC**:

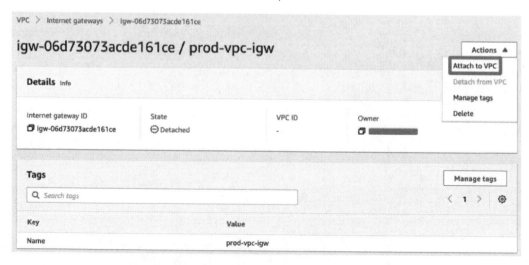

Figure 3.19 – Attaching the internet gateway to VPC

6.   Search for the VPC (you created in the earlier step) and then click on
     Attach internet gateway:

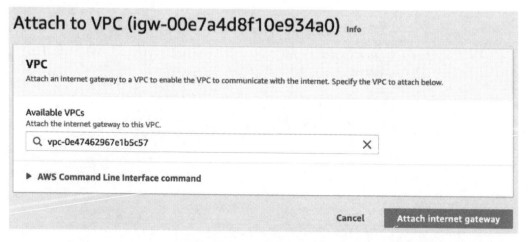

Figure 3.20 – Final attachment screen while attaching the internet gateway to VPC

Now your VPC has a gateway, which connects your VPC to the internet. In the last step,
we will create the route table.

Creating a custom route table

The route table contains a collection of rules that determine where traffic needs to be directed.

To create a custom route table, follow these steps:

1. Go back to the VPC console page (`https://console.aws.amazon.com/vpc/`) and click on **Route Tables** and click **Create route table** as shown in the following screenshot:

Figure 3.21 – Create route table

2. Give your route table a name under **Name tag** (for example, `vpc-prod-rt`), and from the **VPC** dropdown, select the VPC. Then, click on **Create**:

Figure 3.22 – Fill in the details for the route table

3. Select the newly created route table and then click on **Routes** as shown in the following screenshot:

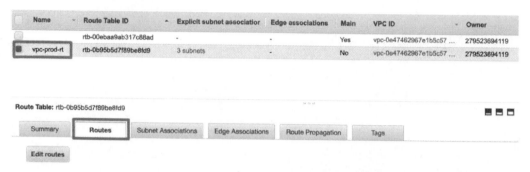

Figure 3.23 – Select the route table and routes

4. Under the **Routes** tab, you will see the entry, which is the default route. The default route defines the traffic from the VPC to stay within the VPC. In order for us to send traffic to the internet, we need to connect it to an internet gateway. Click on **Edit routes**:

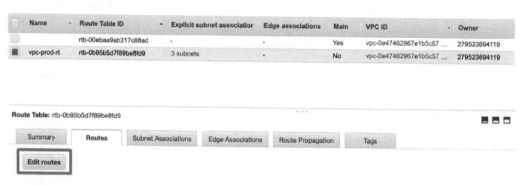

Figure 3.24 – Route table local route

5. Click on **Add route** and add the 0.0.0.0 route to the internet gateway that we created in the earlier steps. It sends any traffic destined for outside the VPC to the internet gateway. Next, click on **Save routes**:

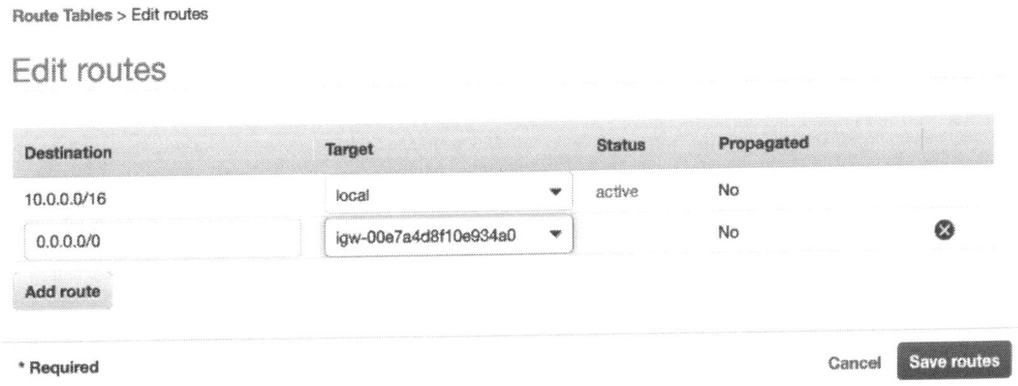

Route Tables > Edit routes

Edit routes

Destination	Target		Status	Propagated	
10.0.0.0/16	local	▾	active	No	
0.0.0.0/0	igw-00e7a4d8f10e934a0	▾		No	✖

Add route

* Required   Cancel   **Save routes**

Figure 3.25 – Adding a route to the internet gateway

6. Now, click on **Subnet Associations** and then click on **Edit subnet associations**:

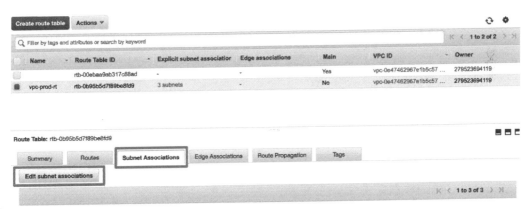

Figure 3.26 – Edit subnet route associations

7. Select the subnets (`10.0.1.0/24`, `10.0.2.0/24`, and `10.0.3.0/24`), which means that now `10.0.1.0/24`, `10.0.2.0/24`, and `10.0.3.0/24` are our public subnets as they're associated with a route table that has a route to an internet gateway. `10.0.4.0/24`, `10.0.5.0/24`, and `10.0.6.0/24` are by default associated with a default route table with no route to the internet, and, logically, it is called the **private subnet**. Click **Save**:

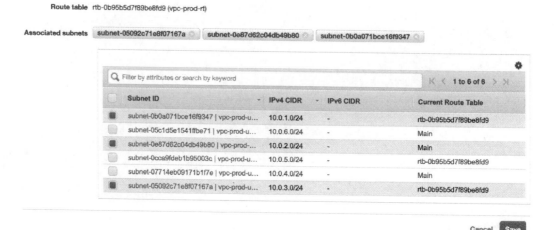

Figure 3.27 – Associating a subnet with routes

8. As the last step, click on **Subnets**, select the subnet (`10.0.1.0/24`, which you have associated with the public route table), and click on **Actions**. What this will do is, when we launch an instance under the public subnet, it will assign a public IP to it:

Figure 3.28 – Associating a subnet to a public IP

9. Under **Actions**, select **Modify auto-assign IP settings**:

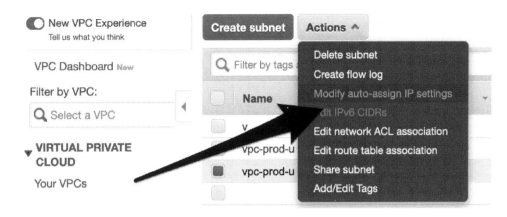

Figure 3.29 – Modify auto-assign IP settings

10. Select **Auto-assign IPv4** and click **Save**:

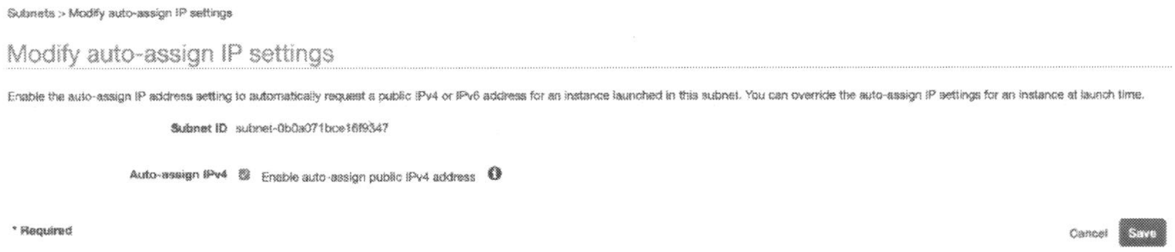

Subnets > Modify auto-assign IP settings

Modify auto-assign IP settings

Enable the auto-assign IP address setting to automatically request a public IPv4 or IPv6 address for an instance launched in this subnet. You can override the auto-assign IP settings for an instance at launch time.

Subnet ID   subnet-0b0a071bce16f9347

Auto-assign IPv4 ☑ Enable auto-assign public IPv4 address ⓘ

* Required   Cancel   Save

Figure 3.30 – Auto-assign IPv4

11. Please repeat the same step (**Modify auto-assign IP settings**) for the `10.0.2.0/24` and `10.0.3.0/24` subnets.

With this, we have launched our first VPC using the AWS console. Some key takeaways are as follows.

When creating a VPC using the AWS console, these resources are created for us by default:

- **NACLs**
- Security groups
- Route tables

The resources we need to create are as follows:

- Internet gateways
- Subnets
- Custom route tables

In the next section, you will see how to automate this entire process using CloudFormation.

Creating a second VPC using CloudFormation

In the last section, we saw how to create a VPC using the AWS console. Let's automate the entire process using CloudFormation.

In this section, you will create a VPC in the Ohio region (us-east-2), which acts as **Disaster Recovery (DR)** for our application. The Ohio region (us-east-2) acts as our DR region if our primary, Oregon (us-west-2), goes down. We can fail over our application to the Ohio (us-east-2) region.

Creating VPCs and subnets using CloudFormation

With that in mind, let's begin by creating the CloudFormation stack template:

1. Create a file named vpc-dr.yml.

2. Add boilerplate syntax, which is common to all templates (for example, AWSTemplateFormatVersion and Description):

   ```
   AWSTemplateFormatVersion: "2010-09-09"
   Description: "Second VPC for DR"
   ```

3. Then, we specify the parameters (VpcCidrPrefix) with the help of a regular expression where you can specify the first two octets of your subnet block. For example, if you are using 172.16.0.0, then using the AllowedPattern regex, you can specify 172.16 during stack creation. In the next section, you will see how we use it along with VPC resources:

   ```
   Parameters: We can specify multiple parameters here, but
   in our use case, we only have one parameter. As per the
   CloudFormation template, we can only use Parameters (the
   parameter is an invalid keyword). That's why I am using
   the Parameters vs. parameter.
     VpcCidrPrefix:
       Type: "String"
       AllowedPattern: "(\\d{1,3})\\.(\\d{1,3})"
   ```

4. You are creating the actual VPC using the intrinsic function (`Join`) where you need to combine `VpcCidrPrefix`, discussed in the previous step, with the hardcoded value (`0.0/16`). At the end of the resource block, you are also specifying `Tags`, which will get the value from whatever `StackName` you have passed during CloudFormation stack creation (you will see how to pass `StackName` during the actual CloudFormation stack creation command using the `-stack-name` parameter):

```
Resources:
  Vpc:
    Type: "AWS::EC2::VPC"
    Properties:
      CidrBlock: !Join [ "", [!Ref VpcCidrPrefix,
".0.0/16"]]
      EnableDnsSupport: True
      EnableDnsHostnames: True
      Tags:
      - Key: Name
        Value: !Ref "AWS::StackName"
```

5. The next step is to create three subnets, one public subnet (to host a web server), and two private subnets (one for the database and the second one for backup purposes). The new thing introduced here is the use of a `Select` function that gives the list of availability zones for a given region. In this case, we are picking the first, second, and third availability zones for each subnet. The main idea behind that is that you don't need to hardcode the value of the subnet per availability zone. For the first subnet, `MapPublicIpOnLaunch` is set to `true`, which we are treating as a public subnet, and `false` (the default value) for the remaining two subnets, which sets these subnets as private subnets:

```
PublicsubnetA:
  Type: "AWS::EC2::Subnet"
  Properties:
    AvailabilityZone: !Select [0, !GetAZs ""]
    CidrBlock: !Join [ "", [!Ref VpcCidrPrefix,
".1.0/24"]]
    MapPublicIpOnLaunch: true
    Tags:
```

```
        - Key: Name
          Value: vpc-dr-us-east-2a
      VpcId: !Ref Vpc


  PrivatesubnetB:
    Type: "AWS::EC2::Subnet"
    Properties:
      AvailabilityZone: !Select [1, !GetAZs ""]
      CidrBlock: !Join [ "", [!Ref VpcCidrPrefix,
".2.0/24"]]
      MapPublicIpOnLaunch: false
      Tags:
        - Key: Name
          Value: vpc-dr-us-east-2b
      VpcId: !Ref Vpc


  PrivatesubnetC:
    Type: "AWS::EC2::Subnet"
    Properties:
      AvailabilityZone: !Select [2, !GetAZs ""]
      CidrBlock: !Join [ "", [!Ref VpcCidrPrefix,
".3.0/24"]]
      MapPublicIpOnLaunch: false
      Tags:
        - Key: Name
          Value: vpc-dr-us-east-2c
      VpcId: !Ref Vpc
```

6. In the output section, we are exporting several values, which later on will be
    used with other templates; for example, referencing the VPC ID (!Ref Vpc)
    once it's created, which later on is exported to a particular name (!Sub
    ${AWS::StackName}-VpcId). You will see how to use this in a later section:

```
  Outputs:
    VpcId:
      Description : "VPC ID"
      Value:  !Ref Vpc
```

```
        Export:
          Name: (!Sub ${AWS::StackName}-VpcId)


    VpcCidr:
      Description : "VPC CIDR"
      Value:   !GetAtt Vpc.CidrBlock
      Export:
        Name: !Sub ${AWS::StackName}-VpcCidr


    PublicsubnetA:
      Description : "Public A Subnet ID"
      Value:   !Ref PublicsubnetA
      Export:
        Name: !Sub ${AWS::StackName}-PublicsubnetA


    PrivatesubnetB:
      Description : "Private B Subnet ID"
      Value:   !Ref PrivatesubnetB
      Export:
        Name: !Sub ${AWS::StackName}-PrivatesubnetB


    PrivatesubnetC:
      Description : "Private C Subnet ID"
      Value:   !Ref PrivatesubnetB
      Export:
        Name: !Sub ${AWS::StackName}-PrivatesubnetC
```

Now you understand the CloudFormation code. The next step is to create the stack.

7. As you are creating these resources in the Ohio region (us-east-2), the first step is to export the region:

```
export AWS_DEFAULT_REGION=us-east-2
```

8. Validate the template to make sure there is no syntax error. To do that, we are going to choose the `validate-template` command, which will validate the `vpc-dr.yml` file:

```
aws cloudformation validate-template --template-body
file://vpc-dr.yml
{
    "Parameters": [
        {
            "ParameterKey": "VpcCidrPrefix",
            "NoEcho": false
        }
    ],
    "Description": "Second VPC for DR"
}
```

9. To create a stack, we will use a `create-stack` command that creates a stack with the name `vpc-dr` and passes the `VpcCidrPrefix` parameter as `172.16`:

```
aws cloudformation create-stack --stack-name vpc-dr
--template-body file://vpc-dr.yml --parameters
ParameterKey=VpcCidrPrefix,ParameterValue=172.16
{
    "StackId": "arn:aws:cloudformation:us-east-
2:XXXXXXX:stack/vpc-dr/e576b370-c95b-11ea-9d80-
0af17cbfa87c"
}
```

10. To get the list of exports, which are `VPCId`, `CidrBlock`, and the created subnets, run the following command:

```
aws cloudformation list-exports --query 'Exports[].
[Name,Value]' --output table
-------------------------------------------------------------
|                         ListExports                       |
+-------------------------------+---------------------------+
|  vpc-dr-PrivatesubnetB        |  subnet-0d9cdde1411af6ba3 |
|  vpc-dr-PrivatesubnetC        |  subnet-0d9cdde1411af6ba3 |
|  vpc-dr-PublicsubnetA         |  subnet-05ddb3dd0fc1c3aaf |
```

```
|   vpc-dr-VpcCidr          |   172.16.0.0/16             |
|   vpc-dr-VpcId            |   vpc-08e8817913600dff0     |
+---------------------------+-----------------------------+
```

In the first part of the CloudFormation code, you have seen how we created a VPC and a subnet. Next, we will create an internet gateway and route table.

To follow along with the code, please use the following GitHub link: `https://github.com/PacktPublishing/AWS-for-System-Administrators`.

Creating an internet gateway and route table using CloudFormation

In this section, we will be creating an internet gateway and route table and will then associate the internet gateway with the route table to make one of the subnets public as we did via the AWS console:

1. In the first step, we will create the internet gateway and attach it with the VPC that we created in an earlier step via CloudFormation:

```
Resources:

  InternetGateway:
    Type: AWS::EC2::InternetGateway
    Properties:
      Tags:
      - Key: Name
        Value: !Ref AWS::StackName

  InternetGatewayAttachment:
    Type: AWS::EC2::VPCGatewayAttachment
    Properties:
      InternetGatewayId: !Ref InternetGateway
      VpcId:
        Fn::ImportValue:
          !Sub ${NetworkStack}-VpcId
```

2. Once the internet gateway is created, the next step is to create the route table and attach it to the internet gateway and one of the subnets (similarly to how we created it via the AWS console):

```
publicRouteTable:
   Type: AWS::EC2::RouteTable
   Properties:
     VpcId:
       Fn::ImportValue:
         !Sub ${NetworkStack}-VpcId
     Tags:
     - Key: Name
       Value: vpc-dr-public-route-table


publicRouteToInternet:
   DependsOn: InternetGatewayAttachment
   Type: AWS::EC2::Route
   Properties:
     DestinationCidrBlock: 0.0.0.0/0
     GatewayId: !Ref InternetGateway
     RouteTableId: !Ref publicRouteTable


publicRouteTableAssociationA:
   Type: "AWS::EC2::SubnetRouteTableAssociation"
   Properties:
     RouteTableId: !Ref publicRouteTable
     SubnetId:
       Fn::ImportValue:
         !Sub ${NetworkStack}-PublicsubnetA
```

Once we have the CloudFormation code ready, we will follow the standard practice.

3. Validate the template to make sure there is no syntax error. To do that, we are going to choose the `validate-template` command, which will validate the `gateway-route.yml` file:

```
aws cloudformation validate-template --template-body
file://gateway-route.yml
{
    "Parameters": [
        {
            "ParameterKey": "NetworkStack",
            "NoEcho": false,
            "Description": "Creating Networking Stack for
Resources"
        }
    ],
    "Description": "Creating Internet Gateway and Route
Table"
}
```

4. To create a stack, we will use a `create-stack` command that creates a stack with the name `gateway-route` and passes the `NetworkStack` parameter with the value `vpc-dr` as we did while creating the VPC and subnets:

```
aws cloudformation create-stack --stack-name gateway-route
--template-body file://gateway-route.yml --parameters
ParameterKey=NetworkStack,ParameterValue=vpc-dr
{
    "StackId": "arn:aws:cloudformation:us-east-
2:XXXXXX:stack/gateway-route/90fd0360-c962-11ea-96a7-
0aa2bf13b672"
}
```

So far, we have learned how to create a VPC using the AWS console and CloudFormation. A VPC is a critical component in AWS and, usually, VPC creation is the first step after you figure out which AWS account to use. In the next step, you will see how to set up a transit gateway and attach the existing VPC to it.

Introducing AWS Transit Gateway

AWS Transit Gateway is a network service using which customers can connect their on-premises VPC using a single gateway. A transit gateway works like a virtual router, and you can connect the following resources to your transit gateway:

- One or more VPCs
- One or more VPN connections
- One or more direct connections
- One or more transit gateway peering connections

The following diagram shows the workflow of AWS Transit Gateway:

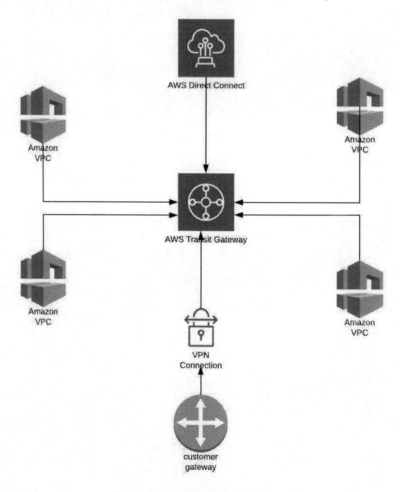

Figure 3.31 – AWS Transit Gateway

The features of AWS Transit Gateway are as follows:

- It can scale horizontally (for example, three VPN connections every 1.25 Gbps combined will give 3.75 Gbps).

- It can scale up to 5,000 VPCs.

- It uses hub-and-spoke network topology.

- 50 Gbps of max throughput tested by AWS so far.

- Support for direct connections.

- Supports 10,000 routes in each route table (for VPC, the limit is 100).

Creating your first transit gateway using the AWS console

A transit gateway is available under the VPC console. You need to follow this series of steps to create one:

1. Go to the VPC console (`https://us-west-2.console.aws.amazon.com/vpc`) and click on **Transit Gateways**:

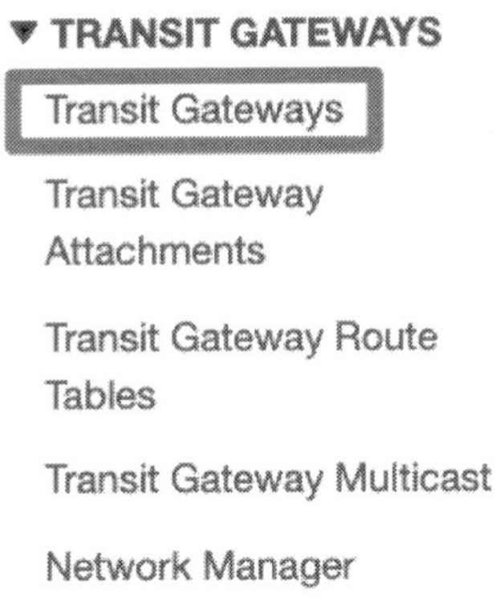

▼ TRANSIT GATEWAYS

Transit Gateways

Transit Gateway
Attachments

Transit Gateway Route
Tables

Transit Gateway Multicast

Network Manager

Figure 3.32 – Selecting Transit Gateways

2. Click on **Create Transit Gateway**:

You do not have any Transit Gateways in this region

Click the Create Transit Gateway button to create your first Transit Gateway

Create Transit Gateway

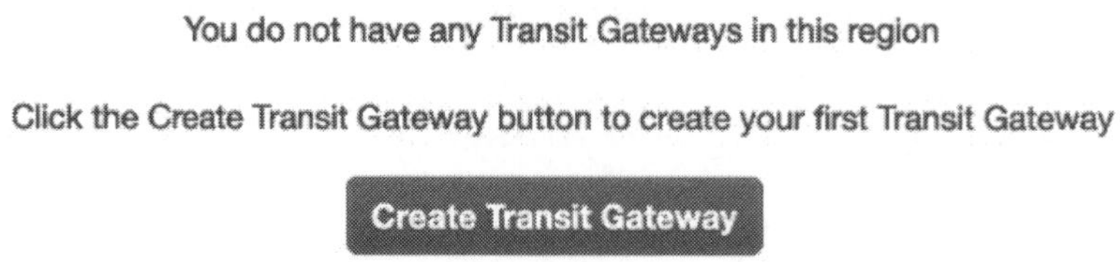

Figure 3.33 – Create Transit Gateway

3. On the next screen, fill in all the details:

Name tag: Give a meaningful name to your transit gateway; for example, `vpc-prod-tgw`.

Description: Add a description; for example, `Transit Gateway for Production VPC`.

Amazon side ASN: This is the **Autonomous System Number** (**ASN**) of your transit gateway. You can use a private ASN, which spans from `64512` to `65534` or in the `4200000000` to `4294967294` range. You can use an existing ASN allocated to your network.

DNS support: To enable domain name resolution for a VPC attached to a transit gateway (for example, if you have two VPCs connected to a transit gateway, this will enable name resolution between the two VPCs).

VPN ECMP support: **Equal cost multipath** (**ECMP**) supports routing between VPN connections. If the connection advertises the same CIDRs, the traffic will be distributed equally between them.

Default route table association: It automatically associates a transit gateway attachment with the transit gateway default route table.

Default route table propagation: It automatically propagates a transit gateway attachment with the transit gateway default route table.

Auto accept shared attachments: This is useful if you are planning to spread your transit gateway attachment to multiple accounts. In those cases, it automatically accepts the cross-account attachment.

4. Once you've filled everything in, click on **Create Transit Gateway**:

Transit Gateways > Create Transit Gateway

Create Transit Gateway

A Transit Gateway (TGW) is a network transit hub that interconnects attachments (VPCs and VPNs) within the same account or across accounts.

Name tag   vpc-prod-tgw   ❶

Description   Transit Gateway for Production VPC   ❶

Configure the Transit Gateway

Amazon side ASN   64512   ❶

DNS support   ☑ enable   ❶

VPN ECMP support   ☑ enable   ❶

Default route table association   ☑ enable   ❶

Default route table propagation   ☑ enable   ❶

Configure sharing options for cross account

Auto accept shared attachments   ☐ enable   ❶

* Required   Cancel   Create Transit Gateway

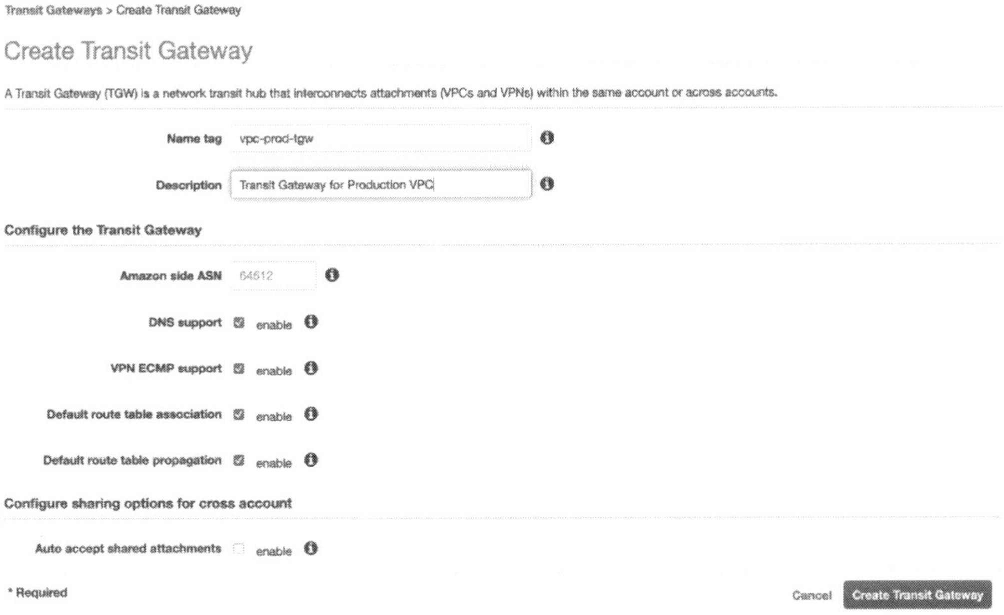

Figure 3.34 – Create Transit Gateway details

Once the transit gateway is created, the next step is to attach the existing VPC to the transit gateway.

Attaching your existing VPC to the transit gateway

To attach an existing VPC to the transit gateway, we need to follow these steps:

1. Click on **Transit Gateway Attachments**:

▼ **TRANSIT GATEWAYS**

Transit Gateways

Transit Gateway
Attachments

Transit Gateway Route
Tables

Transit Gateway Multicast

Network Manager

Figure 3.35 – Transit Gateway Attachments

2.   Next, click on **Create Transit Gateway Attachment**:

| Create Transit Gateway Attachment | Actions ∨ |

Q Filter by tags and attributes or search by keyword

You do not have any Transit Gateway Attachments in this region

Click the Create Transit Gateway Attachment button to create your first Transit Gateway Attachment

Create Transit Gateway Attachment

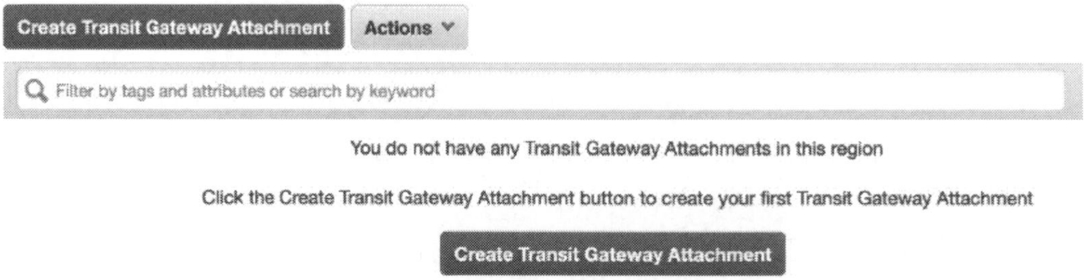

Figure 3.36 – Create Transit Gateway Attachment

3.   Select the Transit Gateway ID you created while setting up the transit gateway and fill in all the details:

Attachment type: Should be **VPC** (or depends upon your requirement, whether you are trying to connect a VPN or another transit gateway).

Attachment name tag: Give a meaningful name to the attachment tag; for example, `prod-vpc-tgw-attachment`.

DNS support: This will enable DNS support between VPC attachments.

IPv6 support: Leave it blank.

VPC ID: From the dropdown, select the VPC you want to attach to the transit gateway.

Subnet IDs: Select at least one subnet per availability zone. This will create a transit gateway VPC attachment in that particular subnet.

4.   Once you've filled everything in, click on **Create attachment**:

Figure 3.37 – Attaching a VPC to a transit gateway

So far, we have created a transit gateway and attached the existing VPC to it. This will enable a path from the transit gateway to the VPC, but there is no return path, that is, from the VPC back to the transit gateway. In the next step, we will update the route table to have a path between the VPC and the transit gateway.

Updating the route table

As you can see in the following transit gateway route table, there is a route between the transit gateway and the VPC:

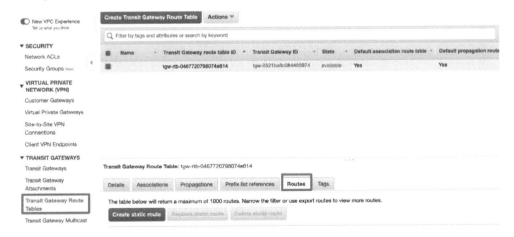

Figure 3.38 – Transit Gateway route table

To create the route between the VPC and the transit gateway, follow these steps:

1. Go back to the VPC console: `https://us-west-2.console.aws.amazon.com/vpc`.

2. Click on **Route Tables**, select the route table for the particular VPC, click on the **Routes** tab, and then **Edit routes**:

Figure 3.39 – VPC route table

3. Next, click on **Add route** and under **Destination**, add the `10.0.0.0/8` subnet, which will cover all routes, and for **Target**, select the transit gateway created earlier from the dropdown. Once done, click on **Save routes**:

Figure 3.40 – Add route to transit gateway

Up to this point, you have learned how to create a transit gateway using the AWS console. In the next step, we will automate the entire transit gateway creation using Terraform.

Creating a second transit gateway using Terraform

You have just created a transit gateway using the AWS console. In this section, we will see how to automate the entire process using Terraform.

The entire code is divided into three sections. In the first section, we will pull some read-only resources from vpc-dr (the VPC ID, subnet CIDR, and route table). In the second section, we will create the transit gateway, and in the third and final section, we will create a transit gateway route table.

As you created the second VPC (vpc-dr) using CloudFormation, in this section, we are going to use the Terraform data resource, which acts as a read-only resource to pull data such as VPC ID, subnet CIDR, and route table for vpc-dr:

1. To get the VPC ID for vpc-dr, we are going to filter it based on the tag that we gave during the VPC creation; that is, vpc-dr:

    ```
    data "aws_vpc" "vpc-dr" {
      filter {
        name   = "tag:Name"
        values = ["vpc-dr"]
      }
    }
    ```

    Similarly, we will get the subnet CIDR based on the VPC ID (which we pulled in the previous step):

    ```
    data "aws_subnet_ids" "vpc-dr-subnet" {
      vpc_id = data.aws_vpc.vpc-dr.id
    }
    ```

    Similarly, based on the tag, we can get the route table of vpc-dr:

    ```
    data "aws_route_table" "vpc-dr-rt" {
      filter {
        name   = "tag:Name"
        values = ["vpc-dr-public-route-table"]
      }
    }
    ```

2.   In the next step, create a transit gateway and then attach `dr-vpc`:

```
resource "aws_ec2_transit_gateway" "tgw-dr" {
   description                          = "transit gateway for
DR environment"
   amazon_side_asn                      = 64512
   auto_accept_shared_attachments   = "disable"
   default_route_table_association = "enable"
   default_route_table_propagation = "enable"
   dns_support                          = "enable"
   vpn_ecmp_support                     = "enable"


   tags = {
     Name = "tgw-dr"
   }
}


resource "aws_ec2_transit_gateway_vpc_attachment"
"tgw-dr-attachment" {
   transit_gateway_id = aws_ec2_transit_gateway.tgw-dr.id
   vpc_id              = data.aws_vpc.vpc-dr.id
   dns_support         = "enable"
   subnet_ids          = data.aws_subnet_ids.vpc-dr-subnet.
ids



   tags = {
     Name = "tgw-dr-subnet"

   }
}
```

3.   As we know, there is a path from the transit gateway to the VPC but there is no
     return path, that is, from the VPC back to the transit gateway. To create the return
     path, we are going to use the `aws_route` Terraform resource:

```
resource "aws_route" "my-tgw-route" {
   route_table_id            = data.aws_route_table.
vpc-dr-rt.id
```

```
    destination_cidr_block = "172.0.0.0/16"
    transit_gateway_id      = aws_ec2_transit_gateway.
  tgw-dr.id
  }
```

If you want to follow along, here is the Terraform GitHub link for creating a transit gateway: `https://github.com/PacktPublishing/AWS-for-System-Administrators/tree/master/Chapter3/terraform`.

At this stage, we have all our code ready to create a new transit gateway using Terraform. Now, it's time to execute the code:

1. Clone the Git repo:

    ```
    git clone https://github.com/PacktPublishing/AWS-for-
    System-Administrators.git
    ```

2. Go to the directory where the Terraform code is located:

    ```
    Administrators/tree/master/Chapter3/terraform
    ```

3. The following command will initialize the Terraform working directory or it will download plugins for a provider (for example, `aws`):

    ```
    terraform init
    ```

4. The `terraform plan` command will generate and show the execution plan before making the actual changes:

    ```
    terraform plan
    ```

5. To create the transit gateway, we need to run the following command:

    ```
    terraform apply
    ```

Transit Gateway is a newly released feature by AWS, and it dramatically simplifies networking architecture. At this point, you have a firm knowledge of different components of Transit Gateway and how to create it via both the AWS console and Terraform.

Real-time use case to enable a VPC flow log

A real-time use case to enable VPC flow logs is useful in troubleshooting any network-related issues as it captures information about the IP traffic flowing in and out of your network interfaces in VPC.

> **Note**
> VPC flow logs are not enabled by default.

The real-time use case we are discussing here is enabling VPC flow logs. VPC flow logs are useful in debugging network-related issues, and this might be a requirement of your security team where they want every newly created VPC. In your account, VPC flow logs must be enabled by default. To achieve that, we will write an AWS Lambda function using the Python Boto3 library, which continually monitors the `CreateVpc` event using CloudWatch events. If any new VPC is created, it will enable the flow logs for it. To achieve that, we need to perform the following steps:

1. You need to allow the VPC Flow Logs service to assume the IAM role. Create a file named `trustpolicy.json`:

```
{
    "Version": "2012-10-17",
    "Statement": [{
      "Effect": "Allow",
      "Principal": {
        "Service": [
          "vpc-flow-logs.amazonaws.com"
        ]
      },
      "Action": "sts:AssumeRole"
    }]
}
```

2. We then execute the following command to create the role:

```
aws iam create-role --role-name VPCFlowLogsRole --assume-
role-policy-document file://trustpolicy.json
{
    "Role": {
        "Path": "/",
        "RoleName": "VPCFlowLogsRole",
        "RoleId": "AROAUCFHJCYTWW62S6XEQ",
        "Arn": "arn:aws:iam::XXXXXXXXX:role/
VPCFlowLogsRole",
        "CreateDate": "2020-07-20T00:56:02+00:00",
```

```json
        "AssumeRolePolicyDocument": {
            "Version": "2012-10-17",
            "Statement": [
                {
                    "Effect": "Allow",
                    "Principal": {
                        "Service": [
                            "vpc-flow-logs.amazonaws.com"
                        ]
                    },
                    "Action": "sts:AssumeRole"
                }
            ]
        }
    }
}
```

Please make a note of Arn as you are going to use it in the Lambda function.

3.   As a next step, grant this role permission to create a CloudWatch log group. Create a file named vpcflowlog.json:

```json
{
    "Version": "2012-10-17",
    "Statement": [{
        "Action": [
            "logs:CreateLogGroup",
            "logs:CreateLogStream",
            "logs:PutLogEvents",
            "logs:DescribeLogGroups",
            "logs:DescribeLogStreams"
        ],
        "Resource": "*",
        "Effect": "Allow"
    }]
}
```

We then execute the following command to give the necessary permission:

```
aws iam put-role-policy --role-name VPCFlowLogsRole
--policy-name VPCFlowLogsPolicy --policy-document file://
vpcflowlog.json
```

4. Create the IAM role for the Lambda function. In this case, create a trust policy document (lambdatrustpolicy.json) and policy document (vpcflowlogsenable.json).

    Here, we are defining a policy (lambdatrustpolicy.json) that will give Lambda the permission to assume the IAM role:

    ```
    cat lambdatrustpolicy.json
    {
        "Version": "2012-10-17",
        "Statement": [{
          "Effect": "Allow",
          "Principal": {
            "Service": [
              "lambda.amazonaws.com"
            ]
          },
          "Action": "sts:AssumeRole"
        }]
    }
    ```

5. Execute the following command to create the IAM role (VPCFlowLogsEnableRole):

    ```
    aws iam create-role --role-name VPCFlowLogsEnableRole
    --assume-role-policy-document file://lambdatrustpolicy.
    json
    ```

6. In this step, we use the policy (vpcflowlogsenable.json) and attach it to the IAM role (VPCFlowLogsEnableRole) we created in the previous step. This policy will give the Lambda function the permission to create a log group and put events to the log group:

    ```
    cat vpcflowlogsenable.json
    {
        "Version": "2012-10-17",
    ```

```
    "Statement": [{
        "Effect": "Allow",
        "Action": [
            "logs:CreateLogGroup",
            "logs:CreateLogStream",
            "logs:PutLogEvents"
        ],
        "Resource": "arn:aws:logs:*:*:*"
    },
    {
        "Effect": "Allow",
        "Action": [
            "ec2:CreateFlowLogs",
            "ec2:DescribeFlowLogs",
            "iam:PassRole"
        ],
        "Resource": "*"
    }
    ]
}
aws iam put-role-policy --role-name VPCFlowLogsEnableRole
--policy-name vpcflowlogenablepolicy --policy-document
file://vpcflowlogsenable.json
```

You can create all these resource IAM policies and roles manually, as mentioned, or you can use the following script:

```
git clone https://github.com/PacktPublishing/AWS-for-System-
Administrators
AWS-for-System-Administrators/blob/master/Chapter3/python/role_
creation.sh
```

We have the IAM role (VPCFlowLogsEnableRole) created, which we will use in the next step while creating the Lambda function.

Creating the Lambda function

Now we have all the IAM roles in place. The next step is to create a Lambda function:

1. Go to the Lambda console (`https://us-west-2.console.aws.amazon.com/lambda/home`) and click on **Create function**:

Figure 3.41 – AWS Lambda console

2. Provide the following details:

    Function name: Give your Lambda function a name; for example, `enablingvpcflowlogs`.

    Runtime: Choose **Python 3.7**.

    Choose or create an execution role: Select **Use an existing role** and from the dropdown, select **VPCFlowLogsEnableRole**.

3. Once everything is filled in, click on **Create function**:

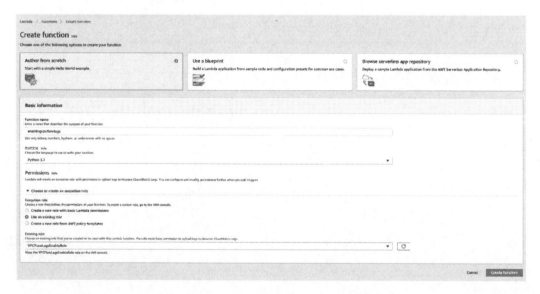

Figure 3.42 – AWS Lambda Create function

Next, we are going to use the following Python code. Let's try to understand the code step by step:

1. In the first step, we are importing all the modules (`boto3`, `botocore.exception`, and `os`), setting up the ROLE_ARN variable (as it's required later when enabling flow logs), and setting up the client for EC2 and CloudWatch logs:

```
import boto3
from botocore.exceptions import ClientError
import os

ROLE_ARN = os.environ['ROLE_ARN']

ec2 = boto3.client('ec2')
logs = boto3.client('logs')
```

2. In the next part of the code, we need to create a CloudWatch log group. To do that, we need to use the AWS API call via CloudTrail (refer to *Figure 3.47* for a more detailed explanation). We are using an AWS API call via CloudTrail because there are certain AWS services that don't emit events (in this example, we need to get the VPC ID and CloudWatch log group name). In those cases, we can use API calls recorded by AWS CloudTrail. In the following code, we are trying to get the VPC ID based on the CloudTrail events and then create a CloudWatch log group. The CloudWatch log group is the `vpcflowcloudwatch` suffix prepended with vpcid). Furthermore, we do some sanity checks to see whether the CloudWatch log group already exists. If it already exists, then under the exception block, print `This Log group '{cloudwatchloggrp}' already exists`:

```
def lambda_handler(event, context):

    try:

        vpcid = event['detail']['responseElements']
['vpc']['vpcId']

        cloudwatchloggrp = 'vpcflowcloudwatch' + vpcid

        print('VPC Id: ' + vpcid)
```

```
        try:
            response = logs.create_log_group(
                logGroupName=cloudwatchloggrp)
        except ClientError:
            print(f"This Log group '{cloudwatchloggrp}'
already exists.")
```

3. In this step, we are capturing the response; if the length is greater than 0, then flow logs are enabled, else they're disabled. Then we are simply enabling it using create_flow_logs:

```
        response = ec2.describe_flow_logs(
            Filter=[
                {
                    'Name': 'resource-id',
                    'Values': [
                        vpcid,
                    ]
                },
            ],
        )

        if len(response['FlowLogs']) > 0:
            print('VPC Flow Logs already ENABLED for this
VPC')
        else:
            print('VPC Flow Logs are DISABLED for this
VPC')

        response = ec2.create_flow_logs(
            ResourceIds=[vpcid],
            ResourceType='VPC',
            TrafficType='ALL',
            LogGroupName=cloudwatchloggrp,
            DeliverLogsPermissionArn=ROLE_ARN,
        )
```

```
      print('Created Flow Logs:' +
response['FlowLogIds'][0])


      except Exception as e:
          print('Error - reason "%s"' % str(e))
```

4. The final code in the lambda console will look as follows:

Figure 3.43 – AWS Lambda function code

5. On the same page, scroll down and click on **Manage environment variables**:

Environment variables (0)   Edit

Key   Value

No environment variables

No environment variables associated with this function.

Manage environment variables

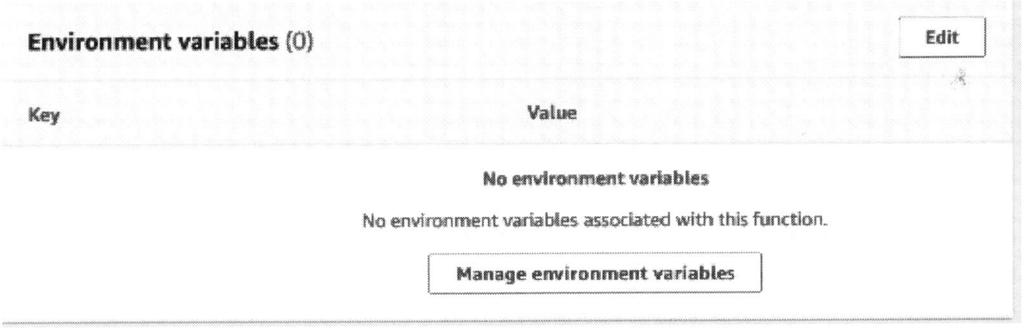

Figure 3.44 – AWS Lambda Manage environment variables

6. Next, click on **Add environment variable**:

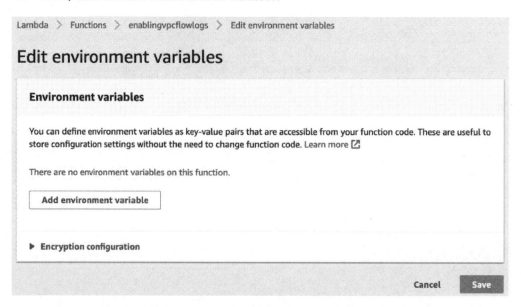

Figure 3.45 – AWS Lambda Add environment variable

7. Remember, I had asked you to make a note of `Arn` – please add it here. Click on the **Save** button:

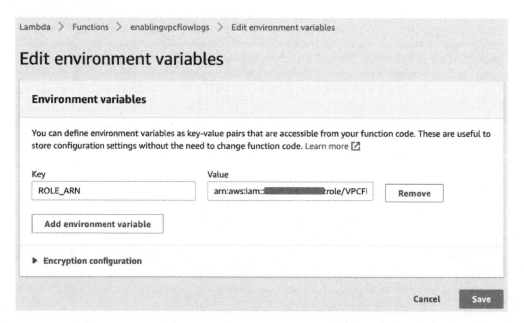

Figure 3.46 – AWS Lambda – add ROLE_ARN as an environment variable

8. Don't forget to click on the **Save** button in the top-right corner:

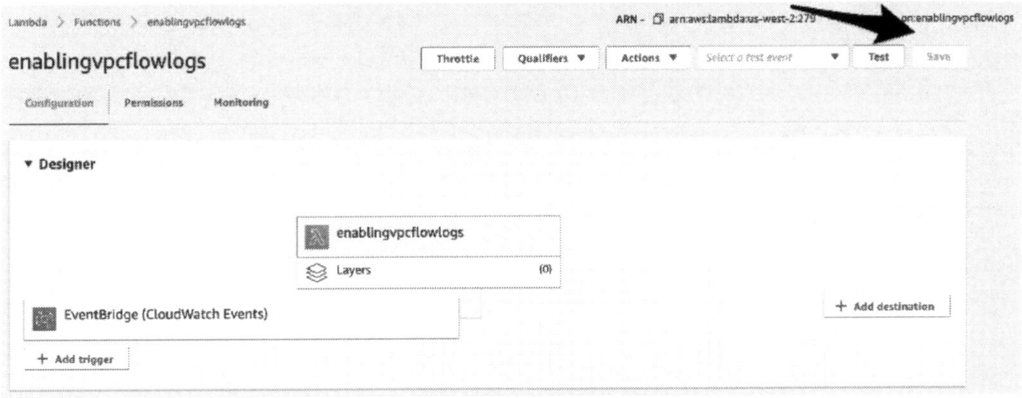

Figure 3.47 – Click on Save to save your Lambda code

Now our lambda function is ready. To trigger this function, we need to use the CloudWatch event.

Invoking the Lambda function using the CloudWatch event

CloudWatch events help us to respond to any state changes in our AWS resources. When any AWS resource changes, the state changes send events into the event stream. We can create a rule that matches the selected events in the stream and routes them to the Lambda function to take any appropriate action:

1. Go to the **CloudWatch** console (`https://us-west-2.console.aws.amazon.com/cloudwatch/home`) and click on **Rules** and **Create rule**:

Figure 3.48 – CloudWatch rules

2. Fill in the following details:

    Event Source: Select **Event Pattern**.

    Service Name: Choose **EC2** from the dropdown.

Event Type: Select **AWS API call via CloudTrail** from the dropdown.

Then, select **Specific operation(s)** and add `CreateVpc`.

On the right-hand side under **Targets**, select **Lambda function** and choose the Lambda function created earlier from the dropdown (**enablingvpcflowlogs**).

Once done, click on **Configure details** as shown in the following screenshot:

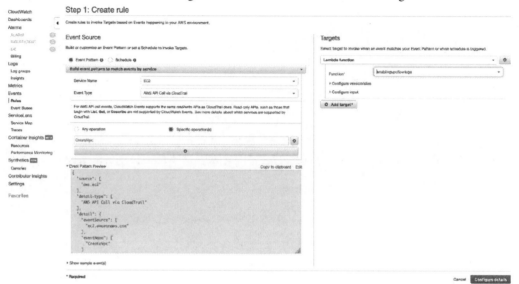

Figure 3.49 – CloudWatch rules – configure rule details

3. Give the CloudWatch rule a name – for example, `enablevpcflowlogs` – and click on **Create rule**:

Figure 3.50 – CloudWatch rules – configure rule details to name your rule

4. Now, let's test the Lambda function. To test your newly create lambda function, try to create a VPC using the following command:

```
aws ec2 create-vpc --cidr-block 172.17.0.0/16 --region
us-west-2
```

5. Go back to the **Lambda** console (`https://us-west-2.console.aws.amazon.com/lambda/home`), and click on **Monitoring** and then **View logs in CloudWatch**:

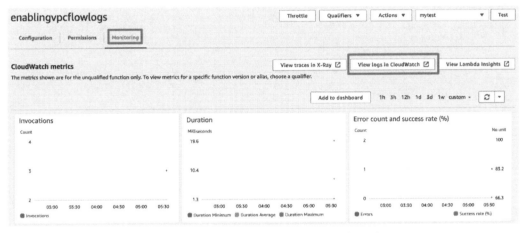

Figure 3.51 – View Lambda logs in CloudWatch

6. Click on one of the log streams and you will see the log created by the lambda function:

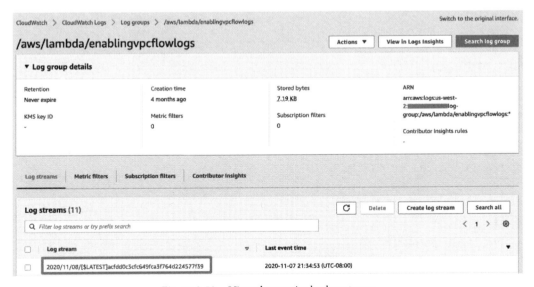

Figure 3.52 – View the particular log stream

7. You will see something like this, where the CloudWatch log indicates that the Lambda function is enabling VPC flow logs for the new VPC:

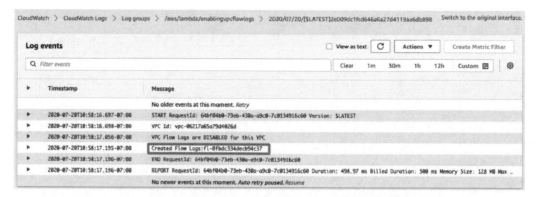

Figure 3.53 – CloudWatch logs to verify the lambda function is working as expected

8. You can also verify this using the **VPC** console (`https://us-west-2.console.aws.amazon.com/vpc/home`) by clicking on the particular VPC and then clicking on **Flow logs**. You will see a flow log is enabled for a specific VPC as it's shown under **Flow log ID**:

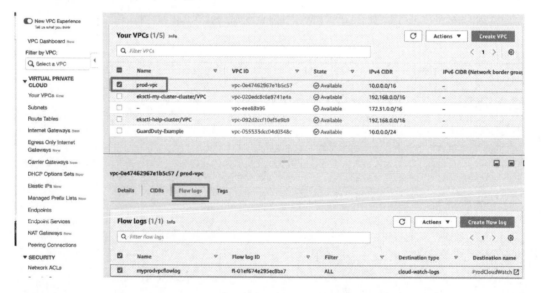

Figure 3.54 – Verify VPC logs via the VPC console

VPC flow logs are a great way to troubleshoot any network issue as they contain information such as the source and destination server address, protocol, and port number. It's good if flow logs are enabled by default, or you can use the solution we discussed earlier.

Summary

In this chapter, we learned about one of the critical networking components of AWS offering VPC and Transit Gateway. You learned how to create a VPC using the AWS console and CloudFormation and how it resembles a traditional data center. You learned about the recently launched feature by AWS called Transit Gateway and how it simplifies networking architecture. We wrapped up the chapter with a real-world example, where we saw how to enable VPC Flow Logs, which is helpful in network debugging.

In the next chapter, we will focus on one of the most popular AWS services, EC2. It allows us to create a virtual machine in the cloud where we can deploy our applications.

4
Scalable Compute Capacity in the Cloud via EC2

In the previous chapter, you learned how to set up your networking using VPC, which acts as your own data center in the cloud. Once you have a networking component ready, the next step is to create virtual machines, also known as instances in AWS terminology, where you will host your code.

AWS EC2 is one of the most well-known components of the AWS cloud and provides scalable compute capacity in the cloud. It eliminates the need to invest upfront in hardware so that you can develop and deploy your application faster in the cloud. It enables you to scale up or down to handle changes in demand/spikes based on your requirements.

This chapter will start by setting up an EC2 instance using the AWS console. Setting up an EC2 instance requires a lot of manual effort. We will look at how to automate the entire process using CloudFormation. We'll also look at one of the critical tasks of managing our AWS bill by setting up an AWS billing alarm. We will further extend the concept of saving our AWS bill by looking at three real-world examples: how to shut down instances not in use, how to clean up an unused **Amazon Machine Image** (**AMI**), and how to detach an unused EBS volume.

In this chapter, we are going to cover the following main topics:

- Setting up EC2 instances
- Creating an AWS billing alarms
- Real-time use case to clean up an unused AMI
- Real-time use case to detach unused EBS volumes
- Real-time use case to shutdown instances on a daily basis

Technical requirements

To gain the most from this chapter, you should have basic knowledge and awareness of the AWS service. You should be familiar with terms such as a hypervisor, virtual machine, elastic block storage, and **Amazon Machine Image** (**AMI**). Besides that, you should have basic knowledge of CloudFormation and Terraform, which was already covered in *Chapter 1*, *Setting Up the AWS Environment*.

The solution scripts for this chapter can be found at the following link:

```
https://github.com/PacktPublishing/AWS-for-System-
Administrators/tree/master/Chapter4
```

Check out the following video to see the Code in Action:

```
https://bit.ly/2L1TMAW
```

Setting up EC2 instances

Elastic Compute Cloud (**EC2**) is your virtual machine in a cloud, but instead of paying thousands of dollars to own that machine, you can choose a pay-as-you-go model. With the pay-as-you-go model, you only pay for the amount of time you use that resource.

The other advantage of using the cloud is that you can easily switch to a higher or lower family of resources based on your requirement. For example, if you start your application instance with 1 CPU and 1 GB of memory, later on, if your application demand increases, you can easily switch to 2 CPUs and 2 GB of memory (sometimes without any downtime). In the traditional environment, you're stuck with 1 CPU and a 1 GB machine forever, but you can easily switch to a bigger instance (2 CPUs and 2 GB) in the cloud.

Creating your first EC2 instance using the AWS console

To set up your application, the first step is to launch the EC2 instance, which will host your application, and for a newbie, the easiest way to do it is via the AWS console.

To launch an instance via the AWS console, you need to follow a series of steps:

1. The first step is to go to the EC2 console at `https://us-west-2.console.aws.amazon.com/ec2/v2/home`.

2. Click on **Instances** and **Launch Instances**:

Figure 4.1 – Launching your first EC2 instance using the AWS console

3. An AMI is an ISO image that holds an operating system and application. In the **Choose an Amazon Machine Image (AMI)** step (Figure 4.2), for this demo, let's use the Amazon Linux AMI, but please feel free to use any AMI based on your requirement (for example, CentOS, Red Hat, or Windows):

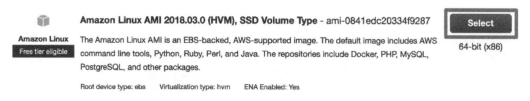

Figure 4.2 – Selecting the Amazon Linux AMI

4. The next step is to choose the instance type. AWS provides a wide range of instance types depending upon your requirement and use cases. For this demo, let's use **t2.micro**, which provides 1 **virtual CPU (vCPU)** and 1 GiB of memory:

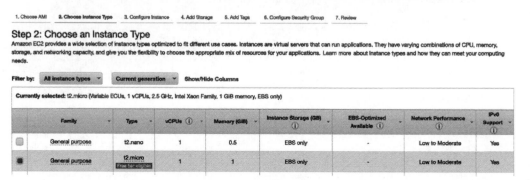

Figure 4.3 – Selecting an instance type

5. In the next section (**Configure Instance Details**), you will only select a handful of parameters and keep the rest of the settings as the default. Some of the parameters you will choose are, from the **Network** dropdown, the VPC that you created in *Chapter 3*, *Creating a Data Center in the Cloud Using VPC*, (prod-vpc); **Subnet**, in a us-west-2a availability zone; and the **User data** script (under **Advanced Details**). The script can be found at https://github.com/ PacktPublishing/AWS-for-System-Administrators/blob/master/ Chapter4/html/install_apache.sh. This script will install Apache, start it, clone the GitHub repo, and copy the directory images to the Apache document root. Now, click on **Next: Add Storage**:

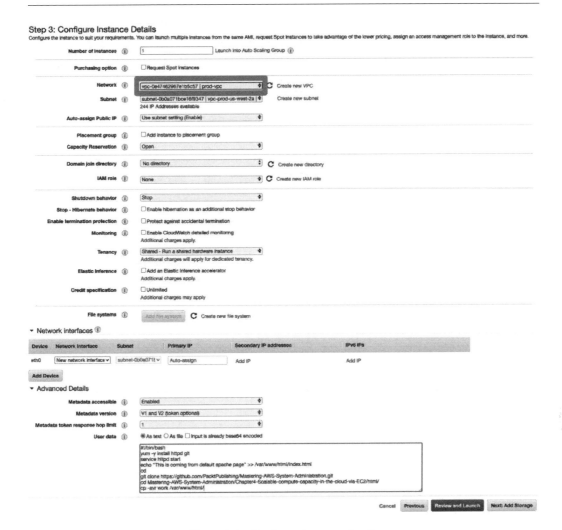

Figure 4.4 – Configure instance details

6. Under **Add Storage**, keep all the settings as the default, that is, keep the size of the root volume as 8 GB. The root volume is the location where your operating system/AMI is going to be installed. Next, click on **Next: Add Tags**:

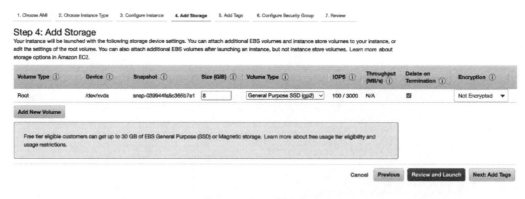

Figure 4.5 – Add Storage

7. Under **Add Tags**, add a tag to your instance. Tags are metadata (key-value pairs) and are useful to track your resources. For example, you can use Name for **Key** and prod-server for **Value**. Click on **Next: Configure Security Group**:

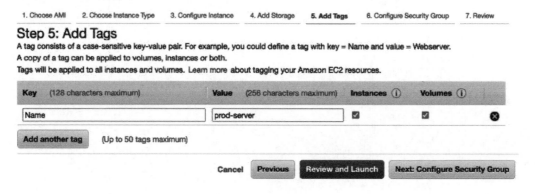

Figure 4.6 – Adding tags

8. Under **Configure Security Group**, keep the default rule, which allows traffic on **SSH** (port 22) and add a rule for **HTTP** (port 80) by clicking on **Add Rule**. For **Type**, from the dropdown, choose **HTTP**; have **Protocol** as **TCP**; **Port Range** as 80; **Source** as **Custom**, and the IP as 0.0.0.0/0 (which allows traffic from anywhere). Allowing traffic from everywhere is bad security practice, and you must always allow traffic from a specific subnet/IP, but for this exercise, you are allowing it from everywhere. A security group acts as a virtual firewall and allows traffic based on the security group rule. Click on **Review and Launch**:

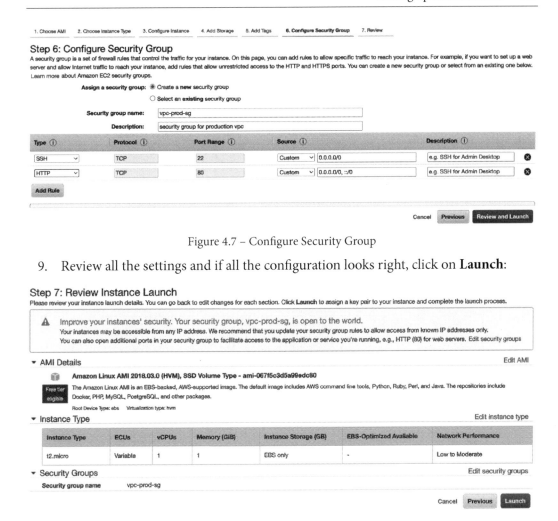

Figure 4.7 – Configure Security Group

9.   Review all the settings and if all the configuration looks right, click on **Launch**:

Figure 4.8 – Review launch configuration

10. As a final step, before launching the instance, you need a key pair to log in to the newly created instance. You can create a new key pair by giving it a meaningful name, such as vpc-prod, and then click on **Download Key Pair**. Once you download the key pair, click on **Launch Instances**:

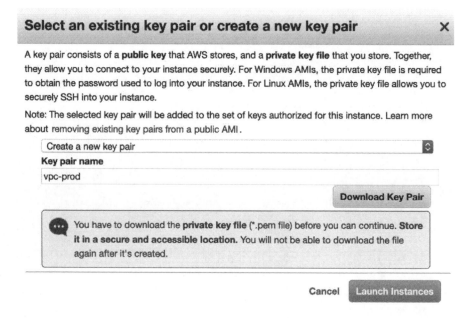

Figure 4.9 – Create a key pair

11. You will see a screen like the following. Click on the instance (for example, **i-0ea882bccd75ad1de** in this case; it will be different as per your AWS account):

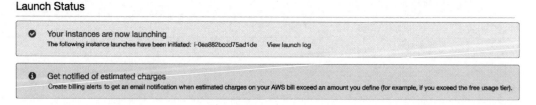

Figure 4.10 – Launch Status

12. To log in to this instance, you need a public key (created in the previous step) and the public IP of the instance (this you will get after clicking on the instance, as mentioned in the last step):

Figure 4.11 – Getting a public IP of an instance

13. Before logging in to the instance, you need to change the permission of the key to 400 (which means only the user has the read permission to it) to make it more secure. This is the same key you downloaded in step 10, and it's generally stored in your downloaded location:

```
chmod 400 vpc-prod.pem
```

14. To log in to the instance, you need a key (created in *Figure 4.10*) and username, which is AMI specific. ec2-user is the username for the AWS AMI you are using in this example. It is different for different operating system vendors. For example, in the case of CentOS and Ubuntu, the usernames are centos and ubuntu, respectively. To log in to the instance, pass the key, username, and public IP of the instance:

```
ssh -i <key name> <username>@<public ip>
ssh -i vpc-prod.pem ec2-user@54.185.177.217
```

At this stage, you know how to create instances using the AWS console. Launching instances via the AWS console is convenient if you need to launch only a few instances, but in cases where you need to launch many instances, you need an automated way to perform these steps – this is where AWS CloudFormation comes in handy. In the next section, you will see how to perform the same task of launching an instance using AWS CloudFormation.

Creating an EC2 instance using AWS CloudFormation

In this section, you will see how to automate the entire EC2 instance creation process using CloudFormation. Let's break down the CloudFormation VPC code and understand it step by step:

1. In the first step, you need to create a security group that acts as a virtual firewall to allow traffic on port 22 (SSH port) from anywhere. In this example, you will use the resource `AWS::EC2::SecurityGroup` and then specify the port as 22 and the protocol as `tcp`. `CidrIp (0.0.0.0)` signifies that it allows traffic from anywhere, which is useful in a demo situation, but please make sure that you are only allowing traffic from specific subnet ranges in the production environment. In the last section, to ensure security, a group will be created in the existing VPC. You need to import the value of the current VPC ID using the `ImportValue` function:

```
Description: EC2 Instance creation using CloudFormation
Parameters:
  NetworkStack:
    Type: "String"
    Description: "Creating Networking Stack for
Resources"
Resources:
  SecurityGrouptoallowsshtraffic:
    Type: AWS::EC2::SecurityGroup
    Properties:
      GroupName: prod-sg
      SecurityGroupIngress:
      - IpProtocol: tcp
        FromPort: 22
        ToPort: 22
        CidrIp: 0.0.0.0/0
        Description: To allow ssh traffic from anywhere
      GroupDescription: Security Group for prod
environment
      VpcId:
        Fn::ImportValue:
          !Sub ${NetworkStack}-VpcId
```

2. With the security group creation in place, the next step is to create an instance using the `AWS::EC2::Instance` type and specify all the necessary parameters, such as availability zone, root volume, AMI type, key name (we discussed all these parameters in the previous section). Just as in previous steps, you need to import the value of the subnet from the existing VPC, and to reference the security group you created in the last step:

```
EC2InstanceProdEnv:
    Type: AWS::EC2::Instance
    Properties:
      AvailabilityZone: "us-east-2a"
      BlockDeviceMappings:
      - DeviceName: "/dev/sda1"
        Ebs:
          DeleteOnTermination: 'true'
          VolumeSize: '8'
          VolumeType: gp2
      ImageId: "ami-07c8bc5c1ce9598c3"
      InstanceType: "t2.micro"

      NetworkInterfaces:
      - Description: "Primary network interface"
        DeviceIndex: "0"
        SubnetId:
          Fn::ImportValue:
            !Sub ${NetworkStack}-PublicsubnetA
        GroupSet:
        - Ref: SecurityGrouptoallowsshtraffic
```

Now that you understand the CloudFormation code, the next step is to create the stack where we are going to create an actual AWS resource:

1. In the first step, create a file named `ec2-instance.yml`, and copy-paste the preceding CloudFormation code. The entire code can be found at `https://github.com/PacktPublishing/AWS-for-System-Administrators/tree/master/Chapter4/cloudformation/ec2-instance.yml`. As you create these resources in the Ohio region (`us-east-2`), the next step is to export the region in your Linux command line:

```
export AWS_DEFAULT_REGION=us-east-2
```

2. Validate the template to make sure there is no syntax error. To do that, you are going to run the `validate-template` command, which will validate the `ec2-instance.yml` file:

```
aws cloudformation validate-template --template-body
file://ec2-instance.yml
{
    "Parameters": [
        {
            "ParameterKey": "NetworkStack",
            "NoEcho": false,
            "Description": "Creating Networking Stack for
Resources"
        }
    ],
    "Description": "EC2 Instance creation using
CloudFormation"
}
```

3. To create a stack, you will use the `create-stack` command, which creates a stack with the name `ec2-dr`:

```
aws cloudformation create-stack --stack-name ec2-dr
--template-body file://ec2-instance.yml --parameters
ParameterKey=NetworkStack,ParameterValue=vpc-dr
{

    "StackId": "arn:aws:cloudformation:us-east-
2:XXXXXXXXXXXX:stack/ec2-dr/263d0d50-d393-11ea-ada1-
```

```
06eba8d6f1ae"
}
```

4. To verify that the instance is created correctly, go to the EC2 console (https://
    us-east-2.console.aws.amazon.com/ec2/v2/home?region=us-
    east-2#Instances:sort=instanceId) and check the instance status under
    the **Status Checks** tab (in the next few minutes, its status should change from
    Initializing to **Running**):

Figure 4.12 – AWS EC2 instance console

At this stage, you know how to create an EC2 instance using the AWS console, as well as
how to automate it using CloudFormation.

Creating an AWS billing alarms

One of the critical tasks you will need to perform as a sysadmin or DevOps engineer is
to create a billing alarm so that a team will be notified when a certain billing threshold is
reached. This is also useful if you forget to shutdown AWS resources that are not in use.
In those cases, a billing alarm will be triggered once the threshold is reached, and it will
work like a sanity check so that you can go back to the particular account and see which
AWS resource you can shut down/clean up to save costs. Now let's see how you can create
a billing alarm, but before that, some pre-requisites need to be met before creating it:

- You must be logged in as a root user or an IAM user who has the permission to view
  billing information.

- You need to select the us-east (N Virginia) region in the AWS console, as billing
  metric data is stored in this region.

- You need to enable **Receive Billing Alerts**, which will mean you receive an email
  notification when charges reach a specific threshold.

The following are the steps you need to follow to enable a billing alarm:

1. Once you've logged in to the AWS console using the root account (the account you created while first setting up the AWS account) at `https://aws.amazon.com/console/`, go to the billing and cost management console at `https://console.aws.amazon.com/billing/`, click on **Billing preferences**, and then check **Receive Billing Alerts**. Click on **Save preferences**:

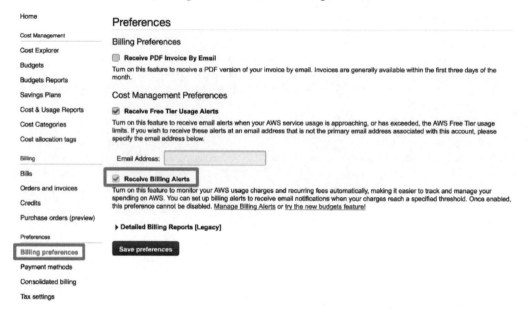

Figure 4.13 – AWS billing console

2. Go to the CloudWatch console at `https://console.aws.amazon.com/cloudwatch/home?region=us-east-1` and make sure you are in the N. Virginia region (**us-east-1**):

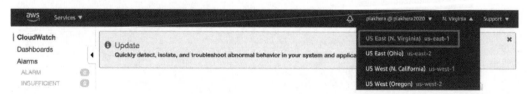

Figure 4.14 – Selecting the N. Virginia region for billing

3. Click on **Alarms** and then **Create alarm**:

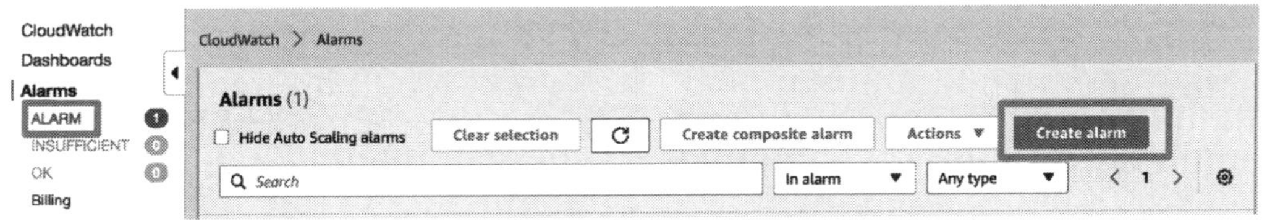

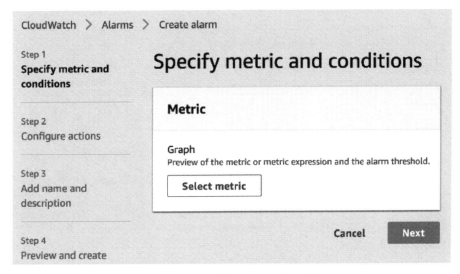

Figure 4.15 – Creating a CloudWatch Alarm

4. Then click on **Select metric** as shown in the following screenshot:

CloudWatch > Alarms > Create alarm

Step 1
Specify metric and conditions

Specify metric and conditions

Metric

Graph
Preview of the metric or metric expression and the alarm threshold.

Step 2
Configure actions

Select metric

Step 3
Add name and description

Step 4
Preview and create

Cancel   Next

Figure 4.16 – Specify metric and condition

5. Now, on the following screen, select **Billing**:

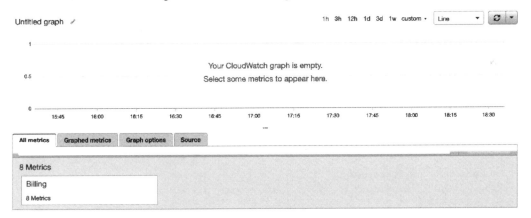

Figure 4.17 – Select Billing as a metric

6.   From the next screen, select **Total Estimated Charge**:

Figure 4.18 – Select Total Estimated Charge

7.   Select **USD** and then click on **Select metric**:

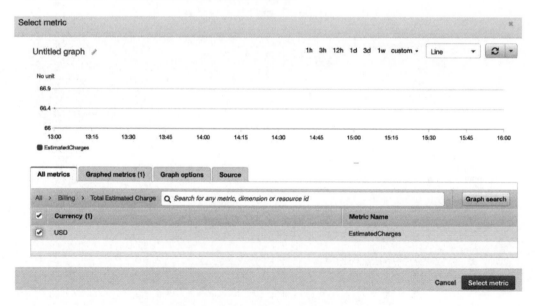

Figure 4.19 – Select USD as the currency

Keep all the settings as the default and select the threshold based on your requirement (for example, in this case, you can choose **5** (USD), which means once your AWS bill exceeds $5, you will receive an alert). Change this threshold value based on your requirement and click on **Next**:

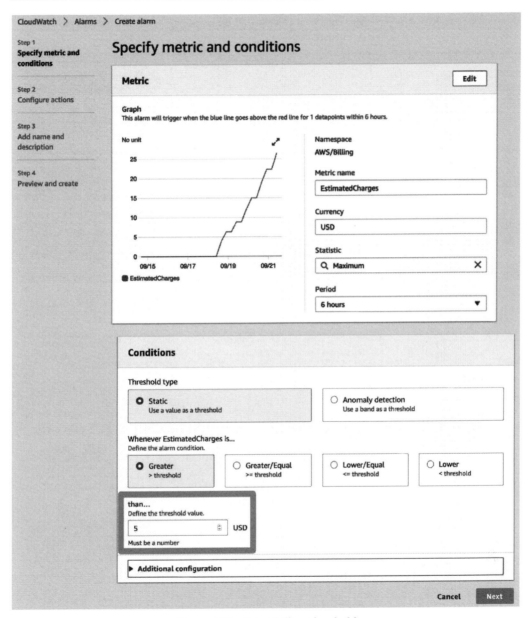

Figure 4.20 – Select billing threshold

8. On the next screen, click on **Create new topic** or choose an existing **Simple Notification Service** (**SNS**) topic (AWS SNS is a fully managed message delivery service by AWS, which will deliver a notification via email when a certain threshold is reached). Click on **Create topic**. At the bottom of the screen, click on **Next**:

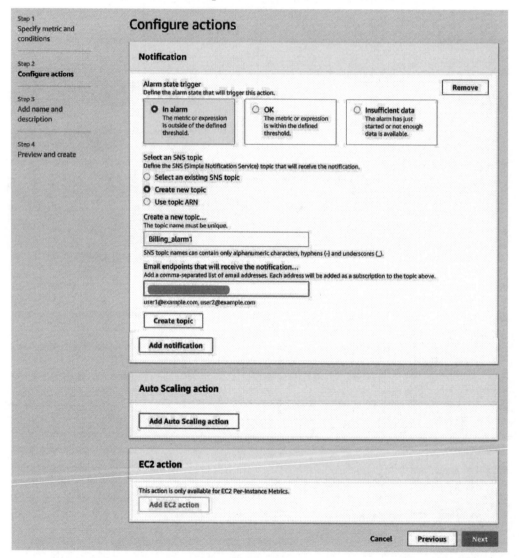

Figure 4.21 – SNS topic

9. You will receive an email, as shown in the following screenshot. Please make sure to click on **Confirm subscription**. Only after that will you receive an email when the threshold is exceeded:

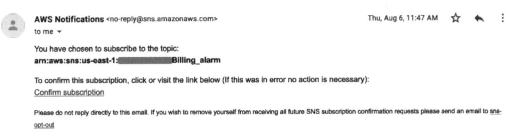

You have chosen to subscribe to the topic:
arn:aws:sns:us-east-1:▓▓▓▓▓▓Billing_alarm

To confirm this subscription, click or visit the link below (If this was in error no action is necessary):
Confirm subscription

Please do not reply directly to this email. If you wish to remove yourself from receiving all future SNS subscription confirmation requests please send an email to sns-opt-out

Figure 4.22 – SNS Subscription confirmation

10. On the next screen, fill in **Alarm name**—give your alarm a meaningful name (for example, `Billing_Alarm`)—and **Alarm Description**—give a meaningful description (for example, `Billing Alarm when threshold reached 5 dollars`). Once done, click on **Next**:

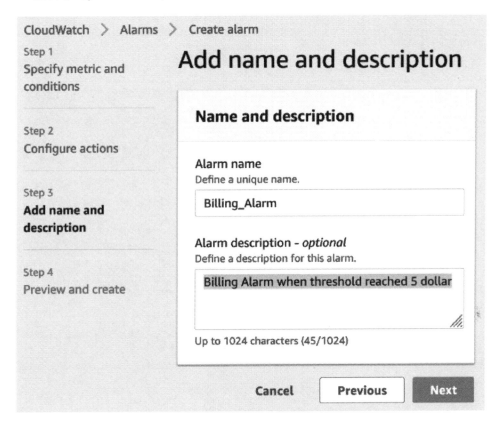

Figure 4.23 – SNS alarm name and description

11. In the preview stage, review all the settings and click on **Create alarm**:

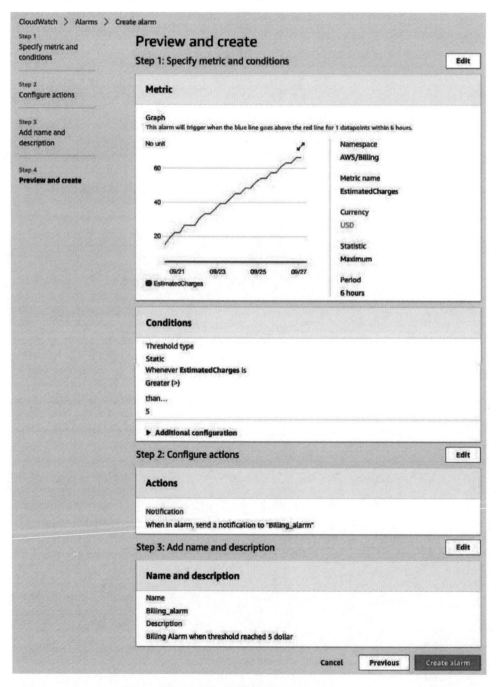

Figure 4.24 – Billing alarm preview

Now you have an automated process, and when your budget threshold exceeds $5, you will receive an alarm. This is an excellent way to perform a sanity check and make sure you do not exceed the existing budget. In the next few sections, you will see how to reduce your AWS bill by cleaning up unused resources.

Real-time use case to clean up an unused AMI

One way you can save costs in AWS is by cleaning up or removing old AMIs that are not in use. The process is called deregistering an AMI, and it will not impact the existing running instance, but you will not be able to launch a new instance from the AMI.

There are multiple ways to achieve the end goal (cleaning up an AMI), but the way we will do it is with a combination of Lambda and CloudWatch rules. The following are the steps you need to follow:

1. The first step is to create a Lambda function. Go to the Lambda console at `https://us-west-2.console.aws.amazon.com/lambda/home` and click on **Create Function**:

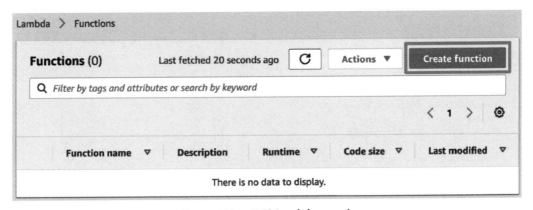

Figure 4.25 – AWS Lambda console

2. Fill in the following details:

    - **Function name**: Give your Lambda function a name, for example, `cleanupunusedami`.

    - **Runtime: Python3.7**

    - **Choose or create an execution role**: Choose a **Create a new role with basic Lambda permissions**

Click on **Create function**:

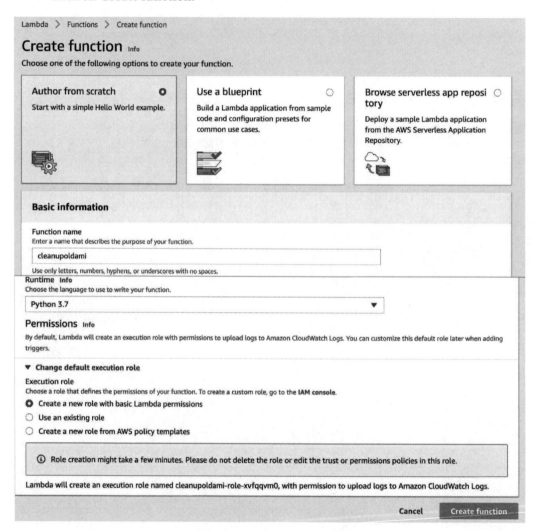

Figure 4.26 – Create Lambda function

3.   On the next screen, click on **Permissions**:

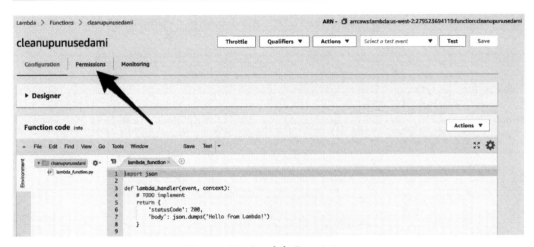

Figure 4.27 – Lambda Permissions

4. On the next screen, click on **Edit**:

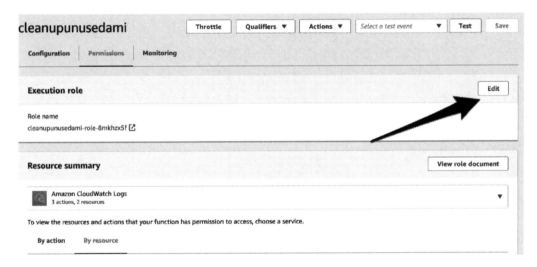

Figure 4.28 – Lambda Edit IAM permissions

5. Click on the role (for example, `cleanupunusedami-role-8mkhzx5f` – this is going to be different in your case):

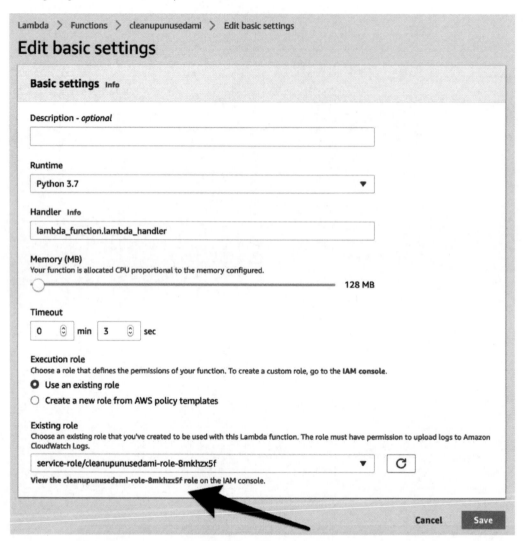

Figure 4.29 – Lambda IAM role

6. Click on the policy (for example, `AWSLambdaBasicExecutionRole-2e608e42-2653-4c1c-a7ea-9` in this case – it is going to be different in your case) and then **Edit policy**. After **Edit policy**, click on **JSON**:

Figure 4.30 – Lambda JSON policy

7. Replace the code under **JSON** with the following code. The reason you are
    replacing the default IAM policy is our Python script needs some extra IAM
    permissions; for example, `DescribeImages`, which is used to list all the
    images, `ec2:DescribeRegions`, to get the list of all AWS regions, and
    `ec2:DeregisterImage`, the actual permission to deregister/clean up the AMI.
    The IAM permissions, which are needed along with default permission, is to create
    a CloudWatch log group (`logs:CreateLogGroup`), CloudWatch log stream
    where Lambda logs get stored (`logs:CreateLogStream`), and finally, the
    permission to put logs into the CloudWatch logs (`logs:PutLogEvents`):

```
"Version": "2012-10-17",
"Statement": [{
    "Effect": "Allow",
    "Action": [
      "logs:CreateLogGroup",
      "logs:CreateLogStream",
      "logs:PutLogEvents"
    ],
    "Resource": "arn:aws:logs:*:*:*"
},
{
    "Effect": "Allow",
    "Action": [
      "ec2:DescribeImages",
      "ec2:DescribeRegions",
      "ec2:DeregisterImage"
    ],
    "Resource": "*"
```

```
        }
    ]
}
```

8. Click on **Review policy**:

Edit AWSLambdaBasicExecutionRole-2e608e42-2653-4c1c-a7ea-9b1ca71671b   (2)

A policy defines the AWS permissions that you can assign to a user, group, or role. You can create and edit a policy in the visual editor and using JSON. Learn more

| Visual editor | **JSON** | | Import managed policy |

```
1 ▾ {
2       "Version": "2012-10-17",
3 ▾     "Statement": [{
4           "Effect": "Allow",
5 ▾         "Action": [
6               "logs:CreateLogGroup",
7               "logs:CreateLogStream",
8               "logs:PutLogEvents"
9           ],
10          "Resource": "arn:aws:logs:*:*:*"
11      },
```

Character count: 275 of 6,144.   Cancel   **Review policy**

Figure 4.31 – Lambda IAM policy review

9. Click on **Save changes**:

Review policy

Review this policy before you save your changes.

☑ Save as default

Summary

This policy defines some actions, resources, or conditions that do not provide permissions. To grant access, policies must have an action that has an applicable resource or condition. For details, choose **Show remaining.** Learn more

🔍 Filter

Service ▾	Access level	Resource	Request condition
Allow (2 of 235 services) Show remaining 233			
CloudWatch Logs	**Limited**: Write	arn:aws:logs:*:*:*	None
EC2	**Limited**: List, Write	All resources	None

* Required   Cancel   Previous   Save changes

Figure 4.32 – Save Lambda IAM policy

10. Go back to the Lambda console, clean up all the default code, and copy-paste the code from the GitHub link: `https://github.com/PacktPublishing/AWS-for-System-Administrators/tree/master/Chapter4/python/cleanup_unused_ami`. In the next few steps, we are going to take a look at the code step by step:

Figure 4.33 – Lambda code editor console

11. You will then replace this default code with the following Python code shown in the following screenshot:

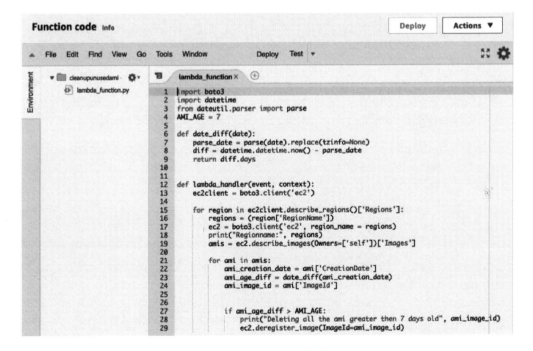

Figure 4.34 – AMI cleanup Python code

12. Now let's understand this code step by step. In the first step, you are importing all the standard modules (`boto3` SDK for Python and `datetime` and `dateutil` to get the current date and date difference when the AMI is created):

```
import boto3
import datetime
from dateutil.parser import parse
```

13. In the next step, you need to create the function that gives us a difference in terms of the date when the AMI was created and the current date:

```
def date_diff(date):
parse_date = parse(date).replace(tzinfo=None)
diff = datetime.datetime.now() - parse_date
return diff.days
```

14. Then you will get the list of all regions (as an AMI is a regional entity and its value—AMI ID—is different based on the region):

```
    for region in ec2client.describe_regions()
['Regions']:
        regions = (region['RegionName'])
        ec2 = boto3.client('ec2', region_name = regions)
        print("Regionname:", regions)
```

15. Moving further, you will get the AMIs that you own (ones you created) and get their creation date and AMI ID. Finally, use the `date_diff` function to find out the difference between when the AMI was created and the current date:

```
    amis = ec2.describe_images(Owners=['self'])
['Images']

    for ami in amis:
        ami_creation_date = ami['CreationDate']
        ami_age_diff = date_diff(ami_creation_date)
        ami_image_id = ami['ImageId']
```

16. In the next step, if the AMI's age is greater than 7 days, then you will deregister that AMI. This depends upon your requirement, and the ideal place to start is at 60 or 90 days, but in this example, I am using 7 days:

```
if ami_age_diff > AMI_AGE:
        print("Deleting all the ami greater then
7 days old", ami_image_id)
        ec2.deregister_image(ImageId=ami_image_id)
```

17. Under **Basic settings** click on **Edit**:

Figure 4.35 – Lambda Basic settings

18. Increase **Timeout** to more than **2 min** from the default value of **3 sec**. The reason behind that is you might have a lot of AMIs in your account and executing your Lambda function in 3 seconds is a very short duration.

Click on **Save**:

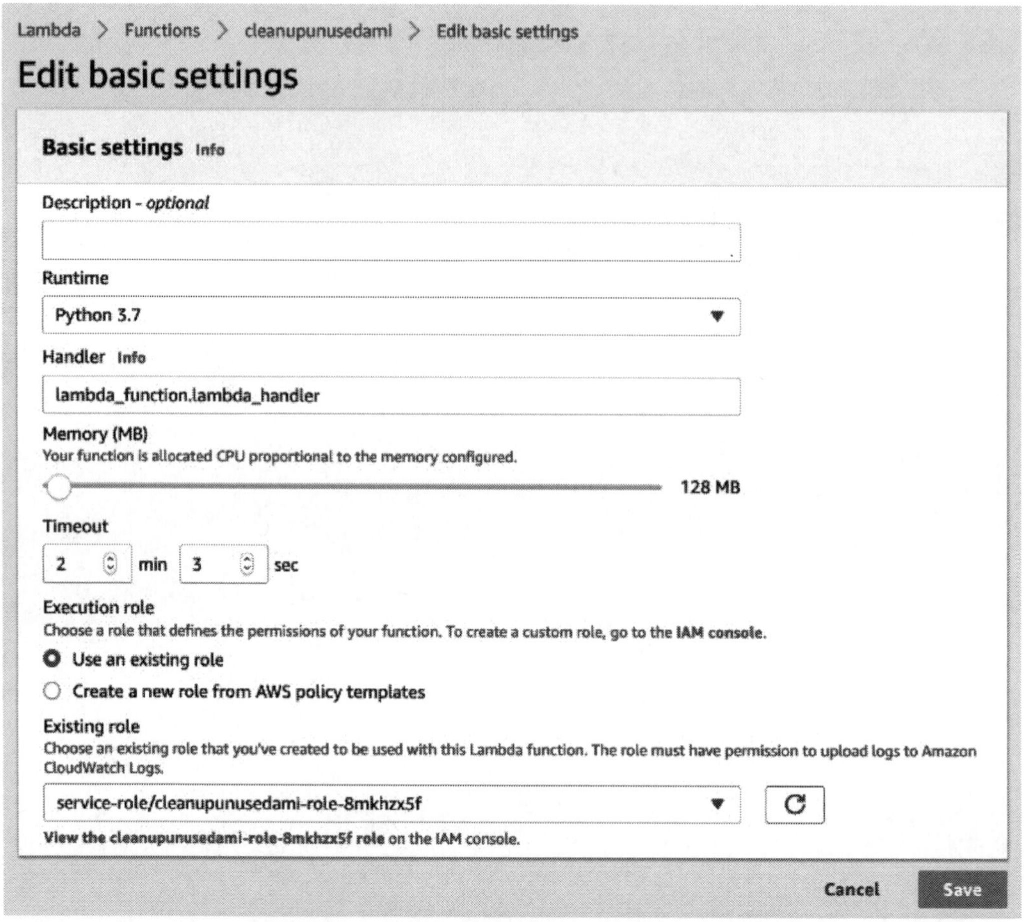

Figure 4.36 – Lambda Timeout settings

19. Click on **Save** at the top of the Lambda function:

Lambda > Functions > cleanupunusedami
ARN - arn:aws:lambda:us-we
nction:cleanupunusedami
cleanupunusedami
Throttle
Qualifiers
Actions
Select a test event
Test
Save
Configuration
Permissions
Monitoring
Designer
Function code Info
Actions
File Edit Find View Go Tools Window
Save Test
Environment
cleanupunusedami
lambda_function.py
lambda_function
import boto3
import datetime
from dateutil.parser import parse
AMI_AGE = 7
def date_diff(date):

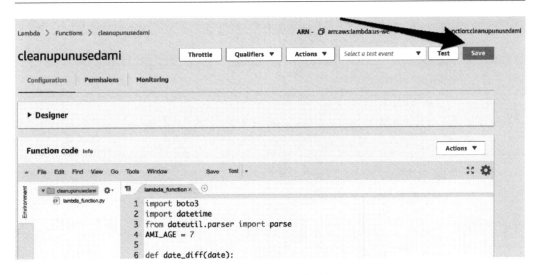

Figure 4.37 – Save Lambda function

Now your Lambda function is ready, to trigger this function, you need to use a CloudWatch event. You can create a rule that self-triggers based on a schedule in CloudWatch events using a cron or rate expression. In this case, you are defining a fixed rate of 1 day that will trigger the Lambda function once a day.

To configure it, you need to follow this series of steps:

1. Go to the CloudWatch console at `https://us-west-2.console.aws.amazon.com/cloudwatch/home` and click on **Rules** and **Create rule**:

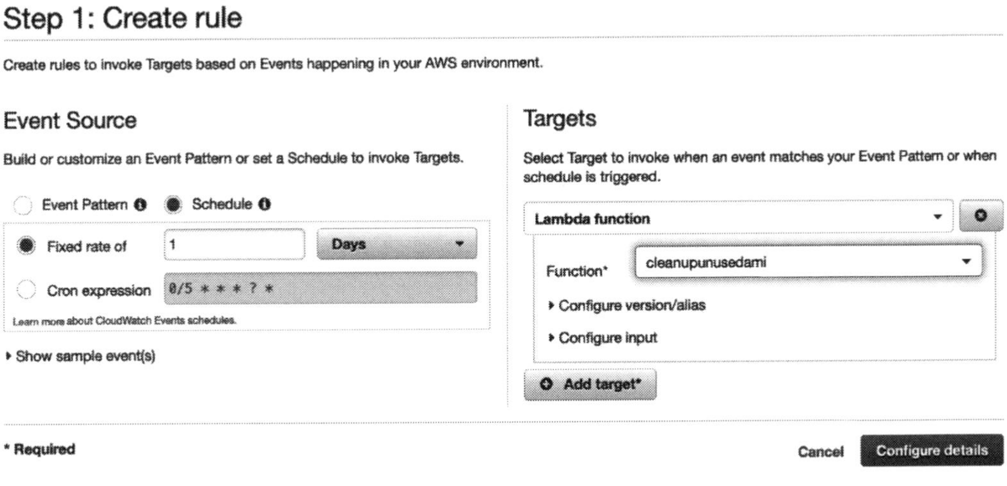

Step 1: Create rule
Create rules to invoke Targets based on Events happening in your AWS environment.
Event Source
Build or customize an Event Pattern or set a Schedule to invoke Targets.
Event Pattern
Schedule
Fixed rate of
1
Days
Cron expression
0/5 * * * ? *
Learn more about CloudWatch Events schedules.
Show sample event(s)
Targets
Select Target to invoke when an event matches your Event Pattern or when schedule is triggered.
Lambda function
Function*
cleanupunusedami
Configure version/alias
Configure input
Add target*
* Required
Cancel
Configure details

Figure 4.38 – CloudWatch event rule

Under **Event Source**, select **Schedule** and then check **Fixed rate of** and enter the value as 1 and the timeline as **Days**. Under **Targets**, from the dropdown, select the Lambda you created in the earlier step (for example, `cleanupunusedami`). Click on **Configure details**.

2.   Under **Configure rule details**, fill in the following parameters:

3.   Give your rule a meaningful name (for example, `amicleanup`) and a description (for example, `Lambda Function to clean up unused ami on daily basis`). Click on **Create rule**:

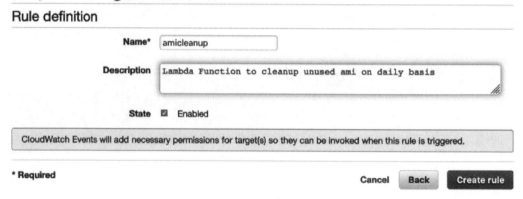

Figure 4.39 – CloudWatch Create rule

Now you have a CloudWatch rule along with a Lambda function configured that will run daily and clean up any AMIs greater than 7 days. This will help us to lower your AWS budget by cleaning up any unused AMIs.

Real-time use case to detach unused EBS volumes

In this section, you will see how you can save costs by cleaning up unused **Elastic Block Storage (EBS)** volumes. EBS costs are always overlooked, as the life cycle of an EBS volume is independent of the instance life cycle, which means that even if you delete an EC2 instance, the EBS volume of it is still there and incurs a cost.

As discussed in the last use case, there are multiple ways to achieve the end goal, but the approach we are going to use is a combination of Lambda and CloudWatch rules. We are following this approach as it gives us a high level of flexibility; for example, you can filter the volume based on whether they are used or unused.

To create a Lambda function, please follow the same steps (1-5) as described in the *Real-time use case to clean up an unused AMI* section. There are a few parameters you need to change:

1. Similar to step 1, in this real-time use case, please change the function name to a new name, for example, `cleanupunattachedebsvol`. The rest of the steps, from steps 2-5, will remain the same, but in step 7 replace the IAM policy with the following IAM policy. The reason we are replacing the default IAM policy is our Python script needs some extra IAM permissions; for example, `DeleteVolume`, which is used to delete the volume not in use; `ec2:DescribeRegions`, to get the list of all AWS regions; and `ec2:DescribeVolumes`, to describe the volume. The IAM permission, which is needed along with default permission, is to create a CloudWatch log group (`logs:CreateLogGroup`), a CloudWatch log stream where Lambda logs are stored (`logs:CreateLogStream`), and finally, the permission to put logs into the CloudWatch logs (`logs:PutLogEvents`):

```
{
    "Version": "2012-10-17",
    "Statement": [{
        "Effect": "Allow",
        "Action": [
            "logs:CreateLogGroup",
            "logs:CreateLogStream",
            "logs:PutLogEvents"
        ],
        "Resource": "arn:aws:logs:*:*:*"
    },
    {
        "Effect": "Allow",
        "Action": [
            "ec2:DeleteVolume",
            "ec2:DescribeRegions",
            "ec2:DescribeVolumes"
        ],
        "Resource": "*"
    }
    ]
}
```

2.   Click on **Review policy**:

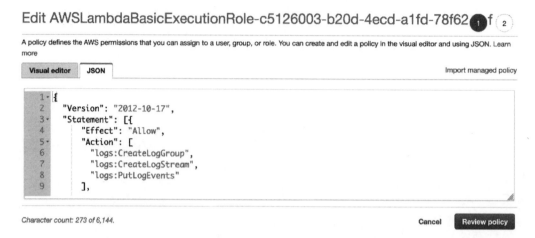

Figure 4.40 – Lambda IAM policy review

3.   Click on **Save changes**:

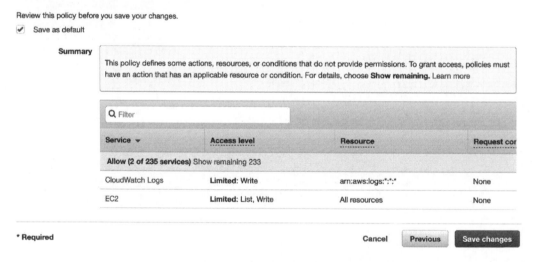

Figure 4.41 – Save Lambda IAM policy

4.   Go back to the Lambda console, clean up all the default code, and copy-paste the code from the GitHub link: `https://github.com/PacktPublishing/AWS-for-System-Administrators/tree/master/Chapter4/python/cleanup_unattached_ebs_vol`. In the next few sections, we are going to look at this code step by step. This is how the complete code will look:

Figure 4.42 – EBS volume cleanup Python code

5.   Now let's understand this code step by step. In the first step, you are importing all the standard modules (the `boto3` SDK for Python):

```
import boto3
```

Then you will get the list of all regions (as you need to find out all the unused EBS volumes present in all the regions):

```
ec2client = boto3.client('ec2')
```

```
for region in ec2client.describe_regions()['Regions']:
regions = (region['RegionName'])
ec2 = boto3.resource('ec2', region_name = regions)
print("Regionname:", regions)
```

Finally, you need to create a filter to find out all the volumes in the available state. For that, you create a filter with Name as `status` and Values as `available`, which only filters volume, which is in available state:

```
unattached_ebs_vol = ec2.volumes.
filter(Filters=[{'Name':'status','Values':
['available']}])
```

```
for vol in unattached_ebs_vol:
```

```
v = ec2.Volume(vol.id)
```

```
print("Cleaning up all the unattached ebs Volumes")
```

```
v.delete()
```

6. If you scroll down, under **Basic settings**, click on **Edit**:

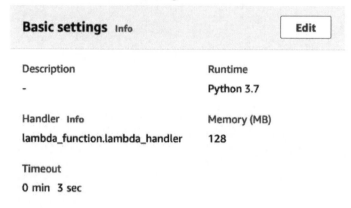

Figure 4.43 – Lambda Basic settings

7. Increase **Timeout** to more than **1 min** from the default value of **3 sec**. The reason behind that is you might have a lot of EBS volume in your account and executing your Lambda function in 3 seconds is a very short duration. Click on **Save**:

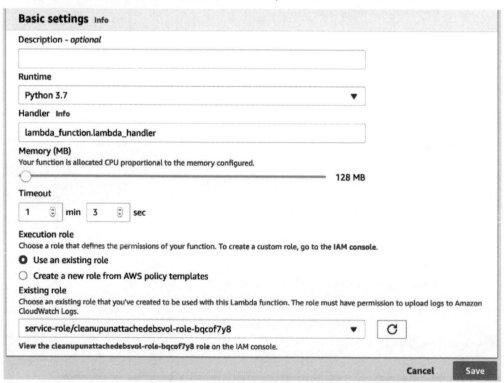

Figure 4.44 – Lambda Timeout settings

8. Click on **Save** at the top of the Lambda function:

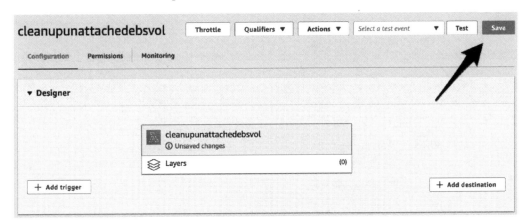

Figure 4.45 – Save the Lambda function

Now our Lambda function is ready, to trigger this function to create a CloudWatch event rule, please follow steps 1-3 from the *Real-time use case to clean up an unused AMI* section. There are a few parameters that you need to change in step 2. In this real-time use case, you need to choose a different Lambda function for targets (for example, `cleanupunattachedebsvol`). Similarly, as defined in step 3, you need to configure rule details, but this time give them a different name, for example, `cleanupunattachedebsvol`.

Now you have a CloudWatch rule along with a Lambda function configured that will run daily and clean up any EBS volumes in an unused state. This will help us to lower our AWS budget by cleaning up any unused EBS volumes.

Real-time use case to shutdown instances on a daily basis

In the next real-time use case, you will see how you can shut down an instance daily to save costs. This is especially useful in a non-production or development environment to shut down instances, for example, at 9 P.M. (or based on your company policy) to save costs.

So far, the use cases we have looked at have used the AWS console. In this use case, you are going to automate the process using Terraform.

These are the steps you need to follow:

1. The first step is to create an IAM role. You need to use a Terraform `aws_iam_role` resource to create a role resource. This policy will give the Lambda function permission to assume the role:

    ```
    "aws_iam_role" "iam_for_lambda" {
      name = "iam_for_lambda"

      assume_role_policy = <<EOF
    {
      "Version": "2012-10-17",
      "Statement": [
        {
          "Action": "sts:AssumeRole",
          "Principal": {
            "Service": "lambda.amazonaws.com"
          },
          "Effect": "Allow",
          "Sid": ""
        }
      ]
    }
    EOF
    }
    ```

2. In the next step, you need to create an IAM policy using the `aws_iam_policy` resource, which will give the Lambda function the necessary permissions to stop/start the instance (`ec2:Stop`/`ec2:Start`), create the CloudWatch log group (`logs:CreateLogGroup` and `logs:CreateLogStream`), and put the logs in that CloudWatch log group using `logs:PutLogEvents`:

    ```
    resource "aws_iam_policy" "lambda_logging" {
      name        = "lambda_logging"
      path        = "/"
      description = "IAM policy for logging from a lambda"
    ```

```
    policy = <<EOF
{
   "Version": "2012-10-17",
   "Statement": [
      {
         "Effect": "Allow",
         "Action": [
            "logs:CreateLogGroup",
            "logs:CreateLogStream",
            "logs:PutLogEvents"
         ],
         "Resource": "arn:aws:logs:*:*:*"
      },
      {
         "Effect": "Allow",
         "Action": [
            "ec2:Start*",
            "ec2:Stop*"
         ],
         "Resource": "*"
      }
   ]
}
EOF
}
```

3. In the last step, you need to attach the IAM policy to the IAM role using the `aws_iam_role_policy_attachment` resource:

```
resource "aws_iam_role_policy_attachment" "lambda_logs" {
   role       = aws_iam_role.iam_for_lambda.name
   policy_arn = aws_iam_policy.lambda_logging.arn
}
```

4. In the next step, we need to zip our Lambda code before uploading it. But before that, let's see what that code is doing.

5. In the first step, we are importing all the standard modules (the `boto3` SDK for Python):

```
import boto3
```

6. In the next step, we are getting the list of all the regions:

```
for region in ec2client.describe_regions()['Regions']:
regions = (region['RegionName'])
ec2 = boto3.resource('ec2', region_name = regions)
print("Regionname:", regions)
```

7. As you only need to stop the instance, which is in the running state, you must need to filter it:

```
running_instances = ec2.instances.
filter(Filters=[{'Name': 'instance-state-name','Values':
['running']}])
```

8. Finally, based on the filter, you will iterate over the instances and stop it:

```
for instance in running_instances:
print("Stopping instance: ", instance.id)
instance.stop()
```

9. Save this Python script in a file, `ec2_stop.py`, and zip it with the name `lambda.zip`:

```
zip lambda.zip ec2_stop.py
adding: ec2_stop.py (deflated 45%)
```

10. In the next step, we need to create our Lambda function using Terraform. To do that, you are going to use `aws_lambda_function` as a resource:

- `filename`: Zip the code file you created in the previous step (`lambda.zip`).

- `function_name`: Give your function a meaningful name (`stop_ec2_nightly`).

- `role`: The IAM role you created in the first step (`aws_iam_role.iam_for_lambda.arn`).

- `handler`: When you create a Lambda function, you need to specify a handler, which is a function in your code that Lambda can invoke when the service executes your code.

- `source_code_hash`: This is used to trigger an update. It must be set to a based64-encoded SHA256 hash of the package file, either specified with `s3_key` or the filename.

- `runtime`: In this example, you are using Python but Lambda supports various runtimes, such as Node.js, Java, Python, .NET Core, Go, Ruby, and a custom runtime:

```
resource "aws_lambda_function" "test_lambda" {
  filename         = "lambda.zip"
  function_name    = "stop_ec2_nightly"
  role             = aws_iam_role.iam_for_lambda.arn
  handler          = "lambda.lambda_handler"
  source_code_hash = base64sha256("lambda.zip")
  runtime          = "python3.7"
}
```

Finally, you need a CloudWatch event to trigger the Lambda function. For that purpose, I am using the `aws_cloudwatch_event_rule` Terraform resource, which is going to trigger this rule at 9 P.M. UTC (you can customize or set a new time based on your requirement), and then using `aws_cloudwatch_event_target`, you will set up the target, which is the Lambda function you created in the last step:

```
resource "aws_cloudwatch_event_rule" "cron_expr" {
  name                = "cron-expression"
  description         = "Fires every day at 9 pm UTC"
  schedule_expression = "cron(0 21 * * ? *)"
}

resource "aws_cloudwatch_event_target" "cron_expr_target"
{
  rule      = aws_cloudwatch_event_rule.cron_expr.name
  target_id = "lambda"
  arn       = aws_lambda_function.test_lambda.arn
}
```

```
resource "aws_lambda_permission" "allow_cloudwatch_to_
call_lambda" {
    statement_id  = "AlloyouxecutionFromCloudWatch"
    action        = "lambda:InvokeFunction"
    function_name = aws_lambda_function.test_lambda.
function_name
    principal     = "events.amazonaws.com"
    source_arn    = aws_cloudwatch_event_rule.cron_expr.arn
}
```

In this way, you can at least save costs in a non-prod environment by stopping your instance on a daily basis. If your company's requirement is to start these instances again at 9 A.M., modify your Lambda code and replace stop with start in instance.start().

Summary

In this chapter, you have learned about one of the most important AWS offerings, EC2. EC2 is the place most users start their AWS journey, by deploying their application/website.

You learned about the AWS compute offering EC2 and how to create instance using the AWS console and CloudFormation. You further learned how it simplifies our capacity management, where you don't need to order any hardware in advance. We further looked at AWS billing and real-time use cases to save billing costs by shutting down or cleaning up any unused AWS resources.

In the next chapter, we will focus on the elastic load balancer and various load balancer offerings by AWS. So far, we have created only a handful of servers, but once our application demand increases, we'll need to add more servers and make sure that the load is evenly distributed, and at the same time, if any node fails, that the traffic is not routed to that particular node. This is where a load balancer comes in handy. We will start by setting up an application load balancer using the AWS console and then via Terraform in the next chapter.

Section 3: Adding Scalability and Elasticity to the Infrastructure

So far, we have built our initial infrastructure. Now, it's time to add elasticity and scalability to it. We add the application load balancer in front of our **Elastic Compute Cloud (EC2)** instances and then add those instances as a part of the Auto Scaling group. Finally, we add the **Amazon Web Services Relational Database Service (AWS RDS)** database (MySQL) to make it a two-tier application.

The following chapters are included in this section:

5

Increasing an Application's Fault Tolerance with Elastic Load Balancing

In the previous chapter, we learned how to set up our instances in AWS using EC2. In this chapter, we will further extend that concept and start placing instances behind a load balancer to distribute the load. Placing an instance behind a load balancer will not only help in distributing the load but also if your instance goes down, the load balancer will stop routing traffic to that instance, which will increase the reliability of your application.

The primary function of a load balancer is to accept the client's connection (as shown in the following diagram) and distribute it to the backend targets, for example, EC2 instances, IP addresses, Lambda functions, and containers:

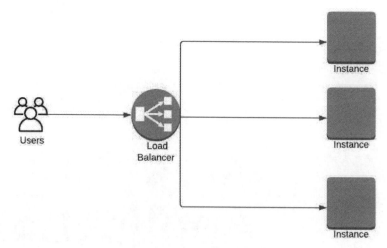

Figure 5.1 – The workings of a load balancer

This chapter will start by looking at various load balancer offerings by AWS and which one to use in which situation. Once we gain theoretical knowledge about load balancers, we will start setting up an application load balancer. The application load balancer is one of the AWS load balancer offerings and provides layer 7 routings. We will set up an application load balancer using the AWS console and then further extend the concept by automating the process using Terraform.

In this chapter, we are going to cover the following main topics:

- Different load balancers offered by AWS
- Setting up the application load balancer
- Automating the application load balancer using Terraform

Technical requirements

To get the most out of this chapter, you should have basic knowledge and awareness of load balancers. Besides that, you should also have basic knowledge of Terraform, which was already covered in *Chapter 1, Setting Up the AWS Environment*. The code for this chapter can be found at the following link:

```
https://github.com/PacktPublishing/AWS-for-System-
Administrators/tree/master/Chapter5
```

Check out the following link to see the Code in Action video:

`https://bit.ly/34VDj8w`

Different load balancers offered by AWS

Before discussing various load balancer offerings by AWS, let's first try to understand what a load balancer is. A load balancer is a device that distributes network and application traffic across multiple servers.

AWS offers three types of load balancers, and they all fulfill a slightly different set of objectives:

- **Classic load balancer**: (Previous generation and now deprecated.) This was initially designed to load balance traffic to multiple EC2 instances. It supports protocols such as HTTP, HTTPS, TCP, and SSL. A common misconception about it is that it acts as a layer 7 (application layer) device, but even if it is a layer 7 device, it doesn't support routing rules based on specific paths (for example, `/test`). This limitation is overcome in the application load balancer.

- **Application load balancer**: This works on layer 7 and supports the HTTP and HTTPS protocols. It allows users to configure and route incoming end user traffic to the application with the support of path- and host-based routing, which lets you route traffic to different target groups. Path-based routing allows you to route a request, such as `/home`, on one set of servers, also known as target groups, and `/contact` on another set. In host-based routing, the application load balancer routes requests based on the domain name specified in the host header, such as `home.example.com` sent to one target group and `contact.example.com` to others. It supports microservice and container-based applications.

- **Network load balancer**: This works on layer 4 (the network layer). It can handle millions of requests per second and is useful for applications where performance is the key metric. It supports static IP (single IP per **availability zone (AZ)**) and is ideal for applications with long-running connections as the network load balancer supports long-running TCP connections.

Out of the three available options, which option to choose is entirely dependent on your requirements. If you are planning to host a web-based application, the application load balancer is recommended. If your application needs a static IP and extreme performance, then a network load balancer is recommended. If you have an existing application built using an EC2 classic network, you should choose a classic load balancer.

Setting up the application load balancer

Before setting up the application load balancer, we need to consider a few points:

- First, we need to decide on two AZs that we will use for our EC2 instance. Generally, we use a public subnet in each AZ and for this example, we are going to use us-west-2a (subnet 10.0.1.0/24) and us-west-2b (subnet 10.0.2.0/24). The reason we are using two subnets is to provide high availability, and we already discussed this in *Chapter 3, Creating a Data Center in the Cloud Using VPC*.

- Now we have decided that we will use two instances. In the next step, we need to install a web server (for example, Apache) on each instance. We already saw, in *Chapter 4, Scalable Compute Capacity in the Cloud via EC2*, as a part of EC2 instance installation, how to use user data to install a web server. To install the second server in different AZs, we will use a Terraform script that will take care of the following step, install Apache RPM, start the Apache service, download the code from the Git repo, and then copy it into the Apache document root (/var/www/html). The Apache document root is the location where the Apache web server looks for your website files. Apache reads this directory and displays the content via a web page.

Before going any further, let's first understand various parameters of Terraform code:

- **VPC security group IDs**: This is the ID of the security group used to filter traffic based on port (in this case, we have opened ports 22 and 80). To get the value of the security group, execute the following command. From the command's output, parse the first column to get the ID, for example, sg-0dabbfc42efb67652, and this is the value we are going to provide to the vpc_security_group_ids parameter. To get the security group's value, we need to use describe-security-groups and then filter the output based on GroupName and GroupId:

```
aws ec2 describe-security-groups --query
"SecurityGroups[*].{Name:GroupName,ID:GroupId}" --output
table
-------------------------------------------------------------
|                    DescribeSecurityGroups                 |
+-----------------------------+-----------------------------+
|             ID              |            Name             |
+-----------------------------+-----------------------------+
|  sg-02c5c861c425409b6       |  default                    |
|  sg-0dabbfc42efb67652       |  vpc-prod-sg                |
+-----------------------------+-----------------------------+
```

- **Subnet ID**: This is the ID of various subnet groups we created during VPC creation. To get the subnet ID, we can use the describe-subnets parameter and then filter the output based on the VPC ID. In this case, to achieve high availability, we are setting our instance in us-west-2b with subnet ID subnet-0e87d62c04db49b80:

```
aws ec2 describe-subnets --filters "Name=vpc-
id,Values=vpc-0e47462967e1b5c57" --query Subnets[].
[AvailabilityZone,SubnetId,VpcId] --output table
----------------------------------------------------------
------------
|                        DescribeSubnets
|
+------------+--------------------------------+------------
-----------+
|   us-west-2a|    subnet-0b0a071bce16f9347    |
vpc-0e47462967e1b5c57    |
|   us-west-2c|    subnet-05c1d5e1541ffbe71    |
vpc-0e47462967e1b5c57    |
|   us-west-2b|    subnet-0e87d62c04db49b80    |
vpc-0e47462967e1b5c57    |
|   us-west-2b|    subnet-0cca9fdeb1b95003c    |
vpc-0e47462967e1b5c57    |
|   us-west-2a|    subnet-07714eb09171b1f7e    |
vpc-0e47462967e1b5c57    |
|   us-west-2c|    subnet-05092c71e8f07167a    |
vpc-0e47462967e1b5c57    |
+------------+--------------------------------+------------
-----------+
```

- **user_data**: For user_data, we are going to use the file function and pass the filename (install_apache.sh). This file is a shell script, which is going to take care of installing and starting Apache, clone the code from GitHub, and copy the code to the Apache document root (/var/www/html):

```
#!/bin/bash
yum -y install httpd git
service httpd start
cd
git clone https://github.com/PacktPublishing/AWS-for-
System-Administrators.git
cd Administrators/tree/master/Chapter4/html
cp -avr work /var/www/html/
```

You can find the complete source code under this link `https://github.com/`
`PacktPublishing/AWS-for-System-Administrators/tree/master/`
`Chapter4/html`

Now that you understand the various parameters of Terraform code, this is what the
Terraform code will look like:

```
resource "aws_instance" "prod_instance" {
  ami = "ami-067f5c3d5a99edc80"
  instance_type = "t2.micro"
  key_name = "vpc-prod"
  vpc_security_group_ids = ["sg-0dabbfc42efb67652"]
  subnet_id = "subnet-0e87d62c04db49b80"
  user_data = file("install_apache.sh")


  tags {
    Name = "prod-server-1"
  }
}
```

Once we have all the prerequisites in place, it's time to execute the code and set up our
second EC2 instance that is being used by the application load balancer:

1. Clone the GitHub repo:

    ```
    git clone https://github.com/PacktPublishing/AWS-for-
    System-Administrators.git
    cd AWS-for-System-Administrators/tree/master/Chapter4/
    html
    ```

2. This will initialize the Terraform working directory or it will download plugins for a
    provider (for example, `aws`):

    ```
    terraform init
    ```

3. The Terraform `plan` command will generate and show the execution plan before
    making the actual changes:

    ```
    terraform plan
    ```

4. To create the EC2 instance, we need to run `terraform apply`:

    ```
    terraform apply
    ```

We have our second instance up and running. In the next step, we will create our application load balancer using the AWS console and place this instance behind the load balancer.

Setting up the application load balancer

The following are the steps to create an application load balancer:

1. To create an application load balancer, go to the EC2 console at `https://console.aws.amazon.com/ec2/`. Under **Load Balancing** in the navigation pane on the left, click on **Load Balancers**:

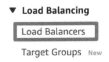

Figure 5.2 – Under Load Balancing, click on Load Balancers

2. On the next screen, click on **Create Load Balancer**:

Figure 5.3 – Creating a load balancer

3. Click on **Create** under **Application Load Balancer**:

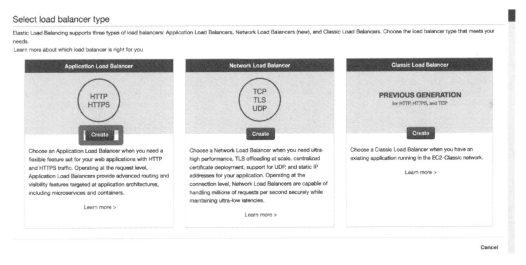

Figure 5.4 – Create under Application Load Balancer

4.   On the **Configure Load Balancer** page, fill in the following details:

- **Name**: Give your load balancer some meaningful name, for example, `prod-alb`.

- **Scheme**: Choose **internet-facing** as the scheme as in our use case, as we need to route client requests over the internet to our target EC2 instance. The other available option is **internal**, which is used for the internal load balancer, and it routes requests from clients to internal private IP addresses.

- **IP address type**: The application load balancer supports **ipv4** or **dualstack** (which are both IPv4 and IPv6). For our use case, we are going with **ipv4**.

- **Listeners**: Keep the default value, port 80, that is, the port used to accept HTTP traffic.

- **Availability Zones**: Select the VPC and AZ from each subnet where we launched our EC2 instance. Please refer to *Chapter 3, Creating a Data Center in the Cloud Using VPC*, if you need more information about AZs.

Next, click on **Next: Configure Security Settings**:

1. Configure Load Balancer	2. Configure Security Settings	3. Configure Security Groups	4. Configure Routing	5. Register Targets	6. Review

Step 1: Configure Load Balancer

Basic Configuration

To configure your load balancer, provide a name, select a scheme, specify one or more listeners, and select a network. The default configuration is an internet-facing load balancer in the selected network with a listener that receives HTTP traffic on port 80.

Name	(i)	prod-alb
Scheme	(i)	⦿ internet-facing ○ internal
IP address type	(i)	ipv4

Listeners

A listener is a process that checks for connection requests, using the protocol and port that you configured.

Load Balancer Protocol	Load Balancer Port	
HTTP	80	⊗

Add listener

Availability Zones

Specify the Availability Zones to enable for your load balancer. The load balancer routes traffic to the targets in these Availability Zones only. You can specify only one subnet per Availability Zone. You must specify subnets from at least two Availability Zones to increase the availability of your load balancer.

VPC	(i)	vpc-0e47462967e1b5c57 (10.0.0.0/16)	prod-vpc
Availability Zones	☑ us-west-2a	subnet-0b0a071bca16f9347 (vpc-prod-us-west-2a)
	IPv4 address (i)	Assigned by AWS
	☑ us-west-2b	subnet-0e67d62c04db49b80 (vpc-prod-us-west-2b)
	IPv4 address (i)	Assigned by AWS
	☐ us-west-2c	Select a subnet

Add-on services

Additional AWS services can be integrated with this load balancer at launch when you enable them below. You can also add these and other services after your load balancer is created by reviewing the

Cancel   **Next: Configure Security Settings**

Figure 5.5 – Configure Load Balancer

5. We don't need to do anything for the **Configure Security Settings** window, but if your listener that is used to accept traffic (HTTP/HTTPS) is listening on port 443 (in our case, it's port 80), you need to configure it. Click on **Next: Configure Security Groups**:

Figure 5.6 – Configure Security Settings

6. You can create a new security group or choose an existing group; in this case, we can select our existing security group. While choosing an existing security group, please ensure that the security group allows communication with instances/register targets on both the listeners and the health check ports (that is, port 80 must be opened under the security group in our use case). In this case, you can select an existing security group (sg-0dabbfc42efb67652) that allows communication on both ports 80 and 22. Click on **Next: Configure Routing**:

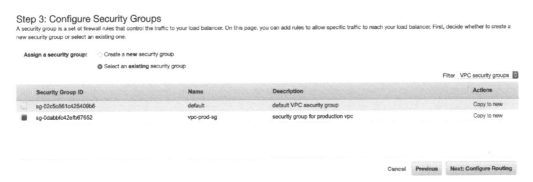

Figure 5.7 – Configure Security Groups

7. In the next step, we need to configure the target group. This is one of the most crucial features, and it's used in request routing. The default rule route requests to register targets in the target groups. The load balancer periodically checks the health of targets in the target group using the defined parameters under the health check settings defined in the target group. To create a target group, fill in the following details:

- **Target group**: We can create a new target group or we can choose an existing target group if one exists.

- **Name**: Please give a meaningful name to your target group.

- **Target type**: The application load balancer supports three target types (**Instance**, which is EC2 and what we are using in this case, **IP**, which is the target IP address, and **Lambda function**, which is the target lambda function).

- **Protocol**: The protocol used by the load balancer to route requests to targets in the target group. It can be **HTTP** or **HTTPS**; in our use case, we are using **HTTP**.

- **Port**: This is the port load balancer used to route traffic to targets in target groups. In this case, I am using the default value of port 80.

- **Health checks**: This is the protocol that the load balancer uses when performing a health check on targets in the target group, and **Path** is the health check path. The default value of the protocol is **HTTP**, but you could use **HTTPS** if you configured your load balancer on port 443. Similarly, the default path is /, but you can give any custom path, such as test.html.

The following screenshot shows all the preceding details filled in:

Step 4: Configure Routing
Target group

Target group	New target group
Name	prod-alb
Target type	● Instance ○ IP ○ Lambda function
Protocol	HTTP
Port	80

Health checks

Protocol	HTTP
Path	/

Figure 5.8 – Configure Routing – Target group

The following details need to be filled in under **Advanced health check settings**:

- **Port**: This is the port load balancer used to perform a check on targets. We can use the default port, or we always have the option to override it.

- **Healthy threshold**: This is the number of consecutive health checks required before considering the unhealthy target as healthy.

- **Unhealthy threshold**: This is the number of consecutive health check failures before considering the target as unhealthy.

- **Timeout**: This is the total amount of time after which if there is no response, it means a failed health check.

- **Interval**: This is the amount of time to do a health check of an individual instance.

- **Success codes**: This is the HTTP code to check the successful response from the target. We can specify multiple values, such as 200, 202, or a range of values, such as 200-299.

The following screenshot shows all the preceding details filled in:

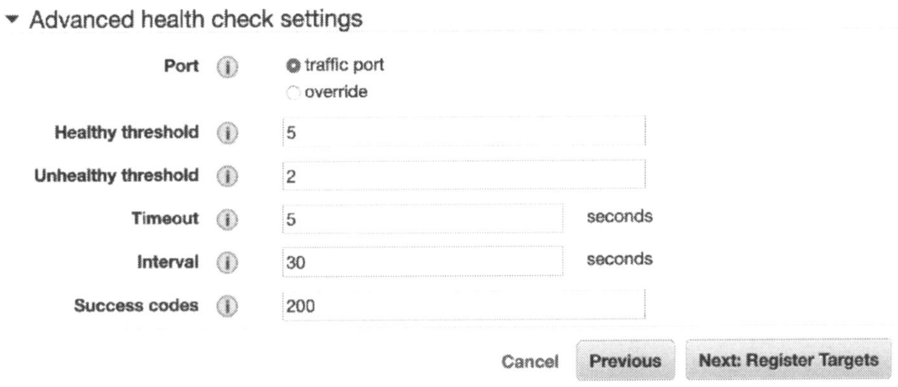

Figure 5.9 – Configure Routing

The load balancer periodically sends health check requests to each registered instance at every interval (**30** seconds by default), as defined under the specified port, protocol, and ping path in the health checks. If the health check exceeds the unhealthy threshold, the load balancer takes the instance out of service. When the health check exceeds the healthy threshold, the load balancer puts the instance back in service. Click on **Next: Register Targets**.

Click on register targets. This will register instances to the target group. Click on **Add to registered** and then click on **Next: Review**:

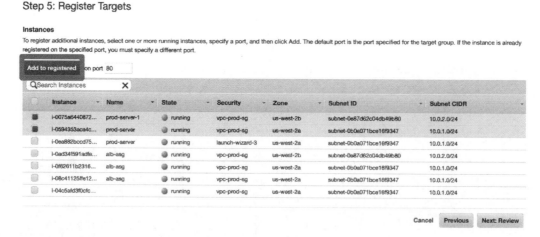

Figure 5.10 – Register Targets

8.   Review all the configuration and click on **Create**:

Figure 5.11 – Review

9.   To verify whether the load balancer was created successfully, go back to the load balancer URL at `https://us-west-2.console.aws.amazon.com/ec2/home?region=us-west-2#LoadBalancers`, and under the **Description** tab, check the **DNS name** value and copy the link into a browser: `http://prod-alb-1183925855.us-west-2.elb.amazonaws.com` (this link is going to be different in your case). If you see **This is the default apache page**, that means your load balancer is working fine:

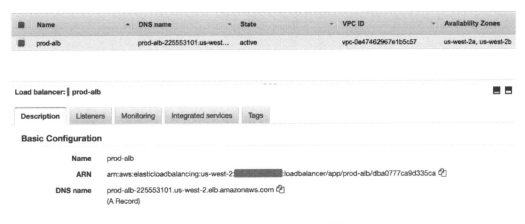

Figure 5.12 – Load balancer URL

10. One more way you can verify whether the load balancer is working is to go back
    to the load balancer URL at `https://us-west-2.console.aws.amazon.`
    `com/ec2/home?region=us-west-2#LoadBalancers` but this time, click on
    Target Groups and then click on **Targets**, and under the **Status** column, the status
    of both the instances must be **healthy**:

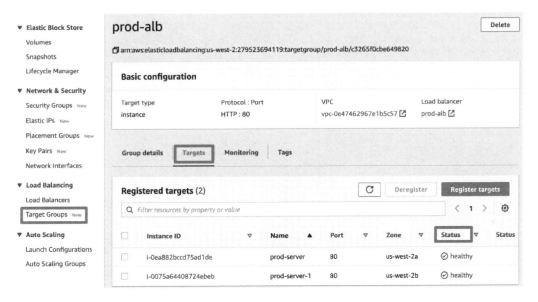

Figure 5.13 – Application load balancer target groups

So far, we have configured the application load balancer. Still, we didn't take advantage
of the new feature of the application load balancer, which supports path- and host-based
routing and lets us route traffic to different target groups.

Modifying listener rules

In this section, we are going to modify the listener rules that will determine how the load balancer routes request the targets in one or more target groups. To add a rule, we perform the following steps:

1. Go back to the load balancer console at `https://us-west-2.console.aws.amazon.com/ec2/home?region=us-west-2#LoadBalancers`, and this time, click on **Listeners** and click on **View/edit rules**:

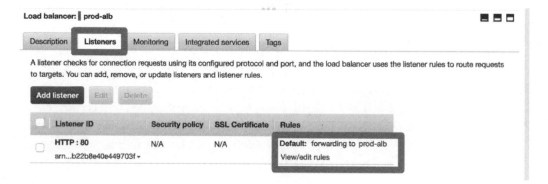

Figure 5.14 – Listeners

2. On the next screen, click on the plus icon (you will see an existing rule that is a default rule or a catch-all rule that is routing all the requests to the `prod-alb` target group):

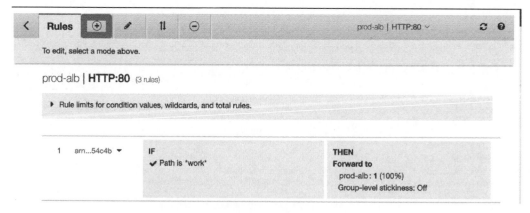

Figure 5.15 – Default listener rule

3. On the next screen, click on **Insert Rule**:

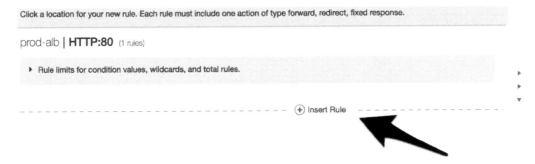

Figure 5.16 – Listeners – Insert Rule

4. Under **IF (all match)**, from the dropdown, select **Path**, and under **is**, use the ***images*** wildcard expression. From the dropdown on the right-hand side, use **Forward to** and under **Target group**, select the **prod-alb** target group we created in the last step. What this is doing is if there is any request coming for images, it will route to the prod-alb target group or the registered target instance behind it. Click on **Save**:

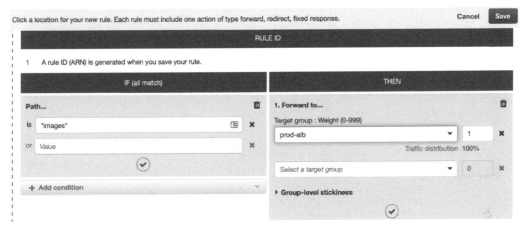

Figure 5.17 – Listener rule

5. We need to perform the same steps for **Path**. As in the *Setting up the application load balancer* section, we have created an instance using `user_data`. We have copied all the images content to the Apache document root. Similarly, in the same section, we created one more instance, and this time we have copied all the work-related content to the Apache document root. Click on the **Save** button:

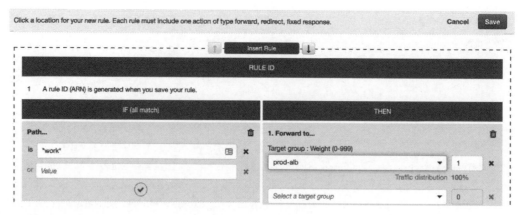

Figure 5.18 – Listener rule

6. To test it, in the browser, type this URL: `http://prod-alb-1183925855.us-west-2.elb.amazonaws.com/images/index.html` (the load balancer URL we created earlier with the `images` directory added to route the request to a particular target group):

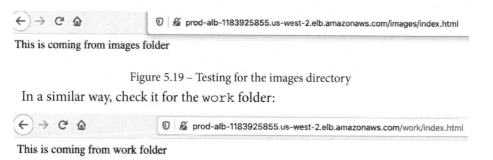

This is coming from images folder

Figure 5.19 – Testing for the images directory

In a similar way, check it for the `work` folder:

This is coming from work folder

Figure 5.20 – Testing for the work directory

At this stage, we know how to create an application load balancer using the AWS console. In the next section, we will see how to automate the entire process using Terraform.

Automating the application load balancer using Terraform

In the last section, we created an application load balancer using the AWS console. In this section, we will see how to automate the entire process using Terraform. These are the steps you need to follow:

1. It always starts with boilerplate syntax where you specify the provider (for example, AWS in our case) and the region (such as us-west-2 in Oregon) where you want to create your resource:

    ```
    provider "aws" {
        region = "us-west-2"
    }
    ```

2. In the next step, we are going to create the application load balancer. Here, we will use the Terraform aws_alb resource to create an application load balancer. To create an application load balancer, we need to pass the following parameters to the aws_alb resource:

    - name: The name of your load balancer. Please provide some meaningful name (for example, prod-alb-new-lb), otherwise Terraform will autogenerate a name beginning with tf-lb.

    - subnets: These are the VPC subnets where you want to host your load balancer.

    - security_groups: This is the security group for your load balancer.

    - internal: If we set this to true, that means your load balancer is internal, that is, not public-facing.

    - tags: This is an optional field but provides labels to your AWS resource.

    The preceding details are as shown in the following code:

    ```
    resource "aws_alb" "alb" {
      name = "prod-alb-new-lb"
      subnets = [
        "${var.subnet1}",
        "${var.subnet2}",
      ]
      security_groups = ["${aws_security_group.my-alb-sg.id}"]
      internal        = "false"
    ```

```
tags = {
    Name = "prod-alb"
  }
}
```

3. In the last step, we created the application load balancer. During creation, we referred to the security group, which we haven't created so far. The security group acts as a virtual firewall and is used to allow traffic on specific ports. Here, we need to use the `aws_security_group` Terraform resource to create a security group named `my-alb-sg` and associate it with the VPC we created in *Chapter 3, Creating a Data Center in the Cloud Using VPC*.

    In this case, we have defined a variable named `vpc_id`, and to reference that variable, we need to create a new file, called `variable.tf`, and specify the VPC ID as described in the following code snippet. We need to use one more resource, such as `aws_security_group_rule`, where we can specify which port to allow for both ingress (network traffic coming to VPC) and egress (traffic leaving VPC). In this case, we are allowing traffic on port `22` (`ssh`) and port `80` (`http`) the same as we had done in the last steps when we created the application load balancer via the console. Similarly, we are allowing all the traffic where `from_port` and `to_port` are set to `0`, which means all the ports, and `-1` means all the protocols for the `egress` rule:

```
resource "aws_security_group" "my-alb-sg" {
  name   = "my-alb-sg"
  vpc_id = "${var.vpc_id}"
}

resource "aws_security_group_rule" "inbound_ssh" {
  from_port         = 22
  protocol          = "tcp"
  security_group_id = "${aws_security_group.my-alb-sg.
id}"
  to_port           = 22
  type              = "ingress"
  cidr_blocks       = ["0.0.0.0/0"]
}

resource "aws_security_group_rule" "inbound_http" {
  from_port         = 80
  protocol          = "tcp"
  security_group_id = "${aws_security_group.my-alb-sg.
id}"
```

```
    to_port              = 80
    type                 = "ingress"
    cidr_blocks          = ["0.0.0.0/0"]
}

resource "aws_security_group_rule" "outbound_all" {
    from_port            = 0
    protocol             = "-1"
    security_group_id = "${aws_security_group.my-alb-sg.
id}"
    to_port              = 0
    type                 = "egress"
    cidr_blocks          = ["0.0.0.0/0"]
}
```

```
variables.tf
variable "vpc_id" {
    default = "vpc-XXXXXXXX"
}
```

4. In the following code section, we are creating a target group. We already discussed
    the target group when we created it via the AWS console. We are doing precisely the
    same thing, but this time via Terraform. We are defining the name of the target groups
    (for example, `alb-prod-tg`), the port where the target group receives the traffic
    (for example, `80`), the protocol to use for routing traffic to the target's `vpc_id`, which
    is the VPC where we want to create the target group, and the series of health checks to
    declare the instance under the load balancer as healthy or unhealthy:

```
resource "aws_alb_target_group" "alb_target_group" {
    name      = "alb-prod-tg"
    port      = "80"
    protocol = "HTTP"
    vpc_id    = var.vpc_id
    tags = {
        name = "alb-prod-tg"
    }
    health_check {
        healthy_threshold   = 3
        unhealthy_threshold = 10
        timeout             = 5
```

```
        interval            = 10
        path                = "/"
        port                = "80"
    }
}
```

5. So far, we have created a load balancer, target, and security group. In this step, we will create a listener that will act as a point to listen to the load balancer request. In this, we will specify the port (80) and protocol (such as HTTP) in which the load balancer is going to listen:

```
resource "aws_alb_listener" "alb_listener" {
    load_balancer_arn = "${aws_alb.alb.arn}"
    port              = "80"
    protocol          = "HTTP"

    default_action {
        target_group_arn = "${aws_alb_target_group.alb_
target_group.arn}"
        type             = "forward"
    }
}
```

6. Then, we will specify the listener rule, similar to what we did when we defined the load balancer using the AWS console. When the request reaches the images pattern, redirect to the image URL, and if the request is for the work pattern, redirect to the work URL:

```
resource "aws_alb_listener_rule" "listener_rule" {
    depends_on    = ["aws_alb_target_group.alb_target_
group"]
    listener_arn = aws_alb_listener.alb_listener.arn
    action {
        type             = "forward"
        target_group_arn = aws_alb_target_group.alb_target_
group.id
    }
    condition {
        path_pattern {
            values = ["*images*"]
```

```
      }
    }
  }

resource "aws_alb_listener_rule" "listener_rule1" {
  depends_on   = ["aws_alb_target_group.alb_target_
group"]
  listener_arn = aws_alb_listener.alb_listener.arn
  action {
    type             = "forward"
    target_group_arn = aws_alb_target_group.alb_target_
group.id
  }
  condition {
    path_pattern {
      values = ["*work*"]
    }
  }
}
```

7. In the final part, we will specify the instance that we will add as a target to this load balancer. For that, we will use aws_lb_target_group_attachment and specify the target group ARN, the instance ID of the EC2 instance, and finally, the port in which these instances are running:

```
resource "aws_lb_target_group_attachment" "my-alb-target-
group-attachment1" {
  target_group_arn = "${aws_alb_target_group.alb_target_
group.arn}"
  target_id        = "${var.instance1_id}"
  port             = 80
}

resource "aws_lb_target_group_attachment" "my-alb-target-
group-attachment2" {
  target_group_arn = "${aws_alb_target_group.alb_target_
group.arn}"
  target_id        = "${var.instance2_id}"
  port             = 80
}
```

At this stage, we understand how our Terraform code is structured to create an application load balancer. Now, it's time to execute the code:

1. The `terraform init` command will initialize the Terraform working directory or it will download plugins for a provider (for example, `aws`):

    ```
    terraform init
    ```

2. The `terraform plan` command will generate and show the execution plan before making the actual changes:

    ```
    terraform plan
    ```

3. To create the application load balancer, we need to run `terraform apply`:

    ```
    terraform apply
    ```

Now you understand how to automate the creation of an application load balancer using Terraform. This is helpful if you have a large-scale AWS deployment, and you need to create a load balancer frequently.

Summary

In this chapter, we learned about the various load balancers offered by AWS and which one to use under which condition. We further looked at creating an application load balancer via the AWS console and then automated the entire process using Terraform. A load balancer is a handy resource to provide high availability and reduce downtime as it will only route requests to healthy nodes and remove the unhealthy nodes from the pool by performing a series of health checks.

In the next chapter, we will focus on auto-scaling, a feature that provides agility to your AWS infrastructure by spinning up and down nodes based on demand.

6

Increasing Application Performance Using AWS Auto Scaling

In the previous chapter, you learned how to set up your application load balancer. This chapter will further extend that concept and see how to use a load balancer with an AWS Auto Scaling group.

AWS Auto Scaling is used to scale your application up or down based on demand. If the demand increases, then Auto Scaling will launch a new instance, and if the demand decreases, it will scale down or terminate instances.

This chapter will start by looking at Auto Scaling and how to set it up. We will further look at various Auto Scaling policies and which one to use under which circumstances. Then, we will look at how to scale your application based on demand using Auto Scaling. We will wrap up this chapter by automating the Auto Scaling process using Terraform.

In this chapter, we are going to cover the following main topics:

- Setting up Auto Scaling
- Understanding Auto Scaling policies
- Scaling an application based on demand
- Creating an Auto Scaling group using Terraform

Technical requirements

To gain the most from this chapter, you should have basic knowledge and awareness of EC2 and load balancers. Besides that, you should have basic knowledge of Terraform, which was covered in *Chapter 1, Setting Up the AWS Environment*.

The code files for this chapter can be downloaded from the following link:

```
https://github.com/PacktPublishing/AWS-for-System-
Administrators/tree/master/Chapter6
```

Check out the following link to see the Code in Action video:

```
https://bit.ly/3rEC1s5
```

Setting up Auto Scaling

Before we add our application to the Auto Scaling group, review your application thoroughly, and consider the following points:

- What are the existing resources your application will use, for example, **Amazon Machine Images** (**AMIs**) or security groups?
- Is your application spread across multiple Availability Zones?
- Do you need to scale in (decrease capacity) or scale out (increase capacity), or does your application always run with a steady load?
- What metrics are relevant for your application's performance?
- How long will it take to configure and launch your server?

Once you have reviewed all of the preceding points and decided that Auto Scaling is appropriate for your application, it's time to create a new launch template.

Creating a launch template

To configure EC2 instances launched by an Auto Scaling group, we need to create a launch template. A launch template contains information about AMIs, security groups, instance types, key pairs, and the user data that you are going to use while creating an Auto Scaling group.

To create a launch template, perform the following steps:

1. Go to the EC2 console at `https://console.aws.amazon.com/ec2/`. Under **Instances**, click on **Launch Templates**:

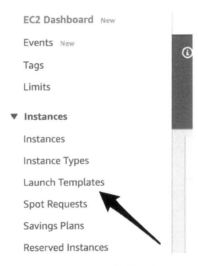

Figure 6.1 – Launch Templates

2. Click on **Create launch template**:

Figure 6.2 – Create launch template

3. In the next section, fill the following details:

    - **Launch template name**: Give a meaningful name to your template; for example, `launch-template-asg`.

    - **Template version description**: Give a meaningful description to your template; for example, `Production launch template for auto scaling group`:

Create launch template

Creating a launch template allows you to create a saved instance configuration that can be reused, shared and launched at a later time. Templates can have multiple versions.

Launch template name and description

Launch template name - *required*

```
launch-template-asg
```

Must be unique to this account. Max 128 chars. No spaces or special characters like '&', '*', '@'.

Template version description

```
Production launch template for auto scaling group
```

Max 255 chars

Auto Scaling guidance   Info
Select this if you intend to use this template with EC2 Auto Scaling
☐ Provide guidance to help me set up a template that I can use with EC2 Auto Scaling

▶ **Template tags**

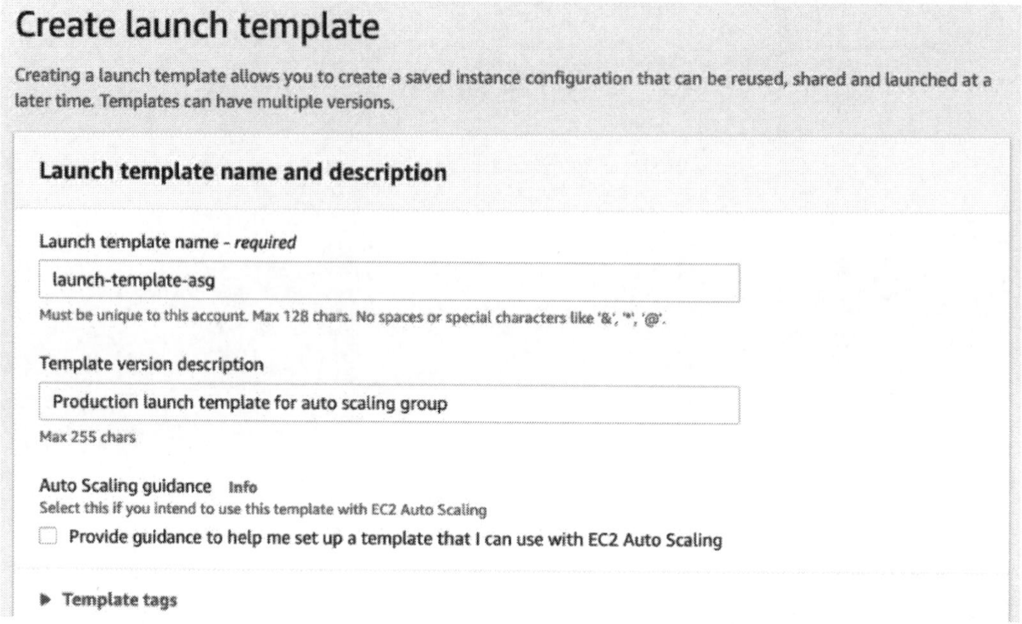

Figure 6.3 – Create launch template details

- **Amazon machine image**: From the dropdown, choose **Amazon Linux AMI 2018.03.0 (HVM)**, which is the latest at the time of writing this book.

- **Instance type**: From the dropdown, choose **t2.micro**:

Launch template contents

Specify the details of your launch template below. Leaving a field blank will result in the field not being included in the launch template.

Amazon machine image (AMI)   Info

AMI

Amazon Linux AMI 2018.03.0 (HVM), SSD Volume Type
ami-0a07be880014c7b8e
Catalog: Quick Start   architecture: 64-bit (x86)   virtualization: hvm

Instance type   Info

Instance type

t2.micro   Free tier eligible   Instance types ↗
Family: General purpose   1 vCPU   1 GiB Memory

Figure 6.4 –Choosing the AMI and instance type

- **Key pair name**: From the dropdown, choose **vpc-prod** (the same key pair we have created in *Chapter 4, Scalable Compute Capacity in the Cloud via EC2.*

- **Network settings**: For **Security groups**, from the dropdown, choose **vpc-prod-sg**:

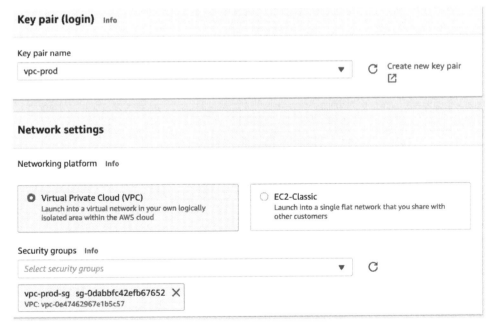

Key pair (login)   Info

Key pair name

vpc-prod   ↻   Create new key pair ↗

Network settings

Networking platform   Info

◉ Virtual Private Cloud (VPC)   ◯ EC2-Classic
Launch into a virtual network in your own logically   Launch into a single flat network that you share with
isolated area within the AWS cloud   other customers

Security groups   Info

Select security groups   ↻

vpc-prod-sg sg-0dabbfc42efb67652 ✕
VPC: vpc-0e47462967e1b5c57

Figure 6.5 – Choosing a key pair and network

4. Keep all the settings as default for **Storage (volumes)**, **Resource tags**, and **Network interfaces**:

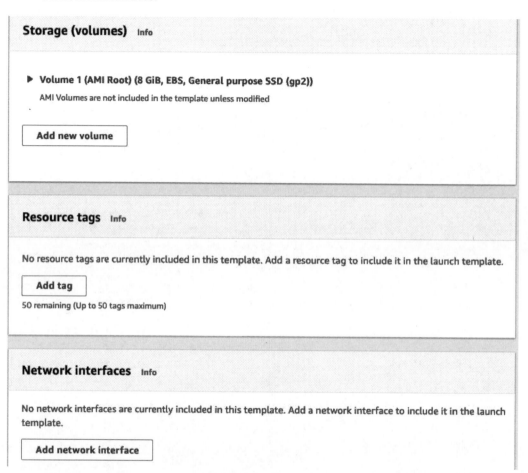

Figure 6.6 – Different settings

5. Click on **Advanced details** and then **User data**, copy the same script we used in *Chapter 4, Scalable Compute Capacity in the Cloud via EC2*, at `https://github.com/PacktPublishing/AWS-for-System-Administrators/blob/master/Chapter4/html/install_apache.sh`, and click on **Create launch template**:

▼ Advanced details   Info

User data   Info

```
#!/bin/bash
yum -y install httpd git
service httpd start
echo "This is coming from default apache page" >> /var/www/html/index.html
cd
git clone https://github.com/PacktPublishing/Mastering-AWS-System-
Administration.git
cd Mastering-AWS-System-Administration/Chapter4-Scalable-compute-capacity-in-
the-cloud-via-EC2/html/
cp -avr work /var/www/html/
```

☐   User data has already been base64 encoded

Cancel   **Create launch template**

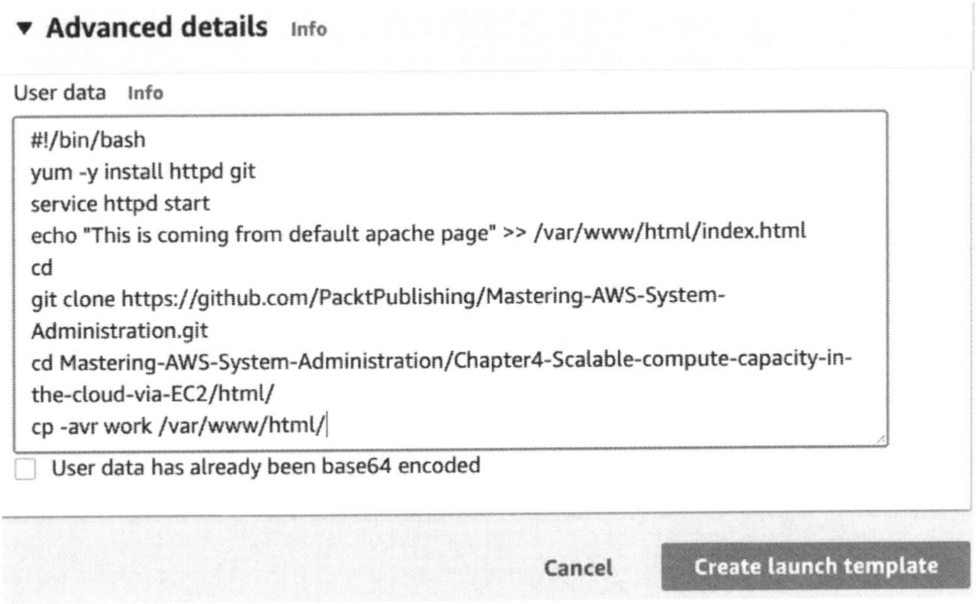

Figure 6.7 – User data script

We have the launch template ready at this stage, which we will use to launch an Auto Scaling group. In the next step, you will learn how to create an Auto Scaling group.

Creating an AWS Auto Scaling group

Now that we have our launch configuration ready, in this step, we are going to create an Auto Scaling group. These are the steps we need to follow:

1. Go to the EC2 console at `https://console.aws.amazon.com/ec2/` and under **AUTO SCALING**, click on **Auto Scaling Groups**:

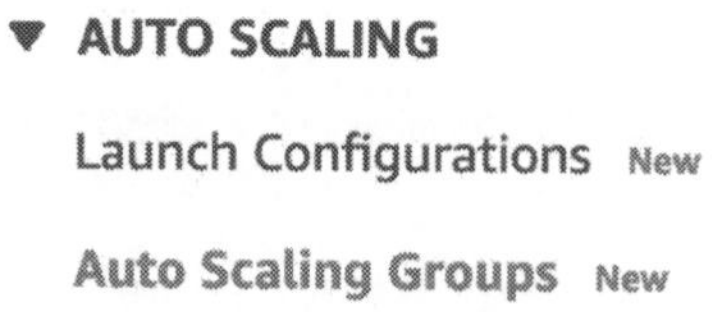

    ▼ AUTO SCALING

    Launch Configurations New

    Auto Scaling Groups New

    Figure 6.8 – Auto Scaling Groups

2. On the next screen, click on **Create Auto Scaling group**:

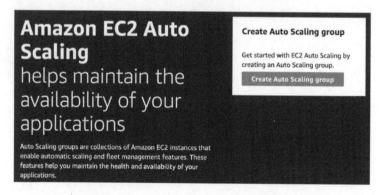

Figure 6.9 – Create Auto Scaling group

3. On the next screen, fill in the following details:

    - **Name**: Give your Auto Scaling group a meaningful name (for example, `prod-asg`).

    - **Launch template**: From the dropdown, select the launch template created in the last step (for example, **launch-template-asg**). Click on **Next**:

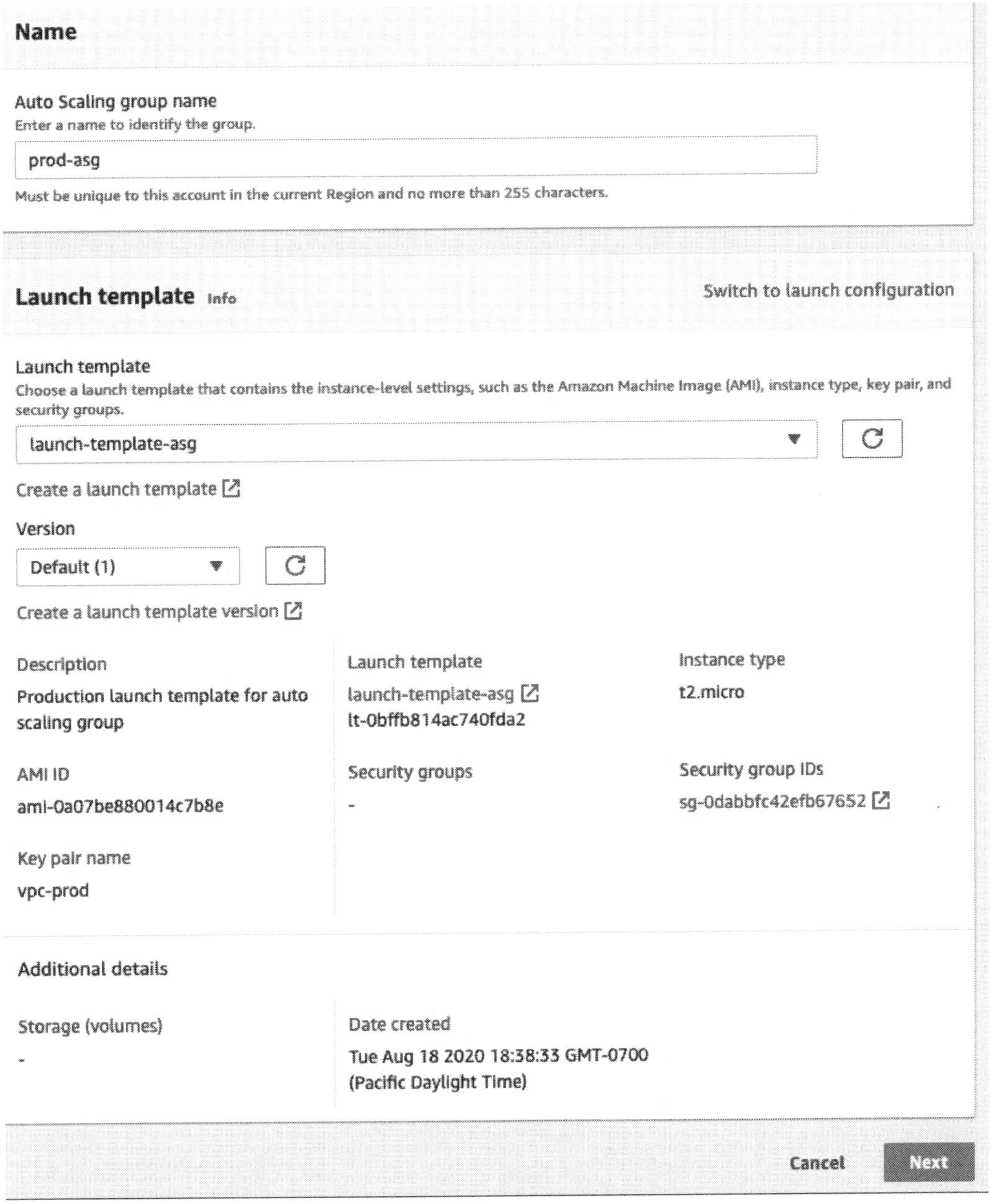

Name

Auto Scaling group name
Enter a name to identify the group.

```
prod-asg
```

Must be unique to this account in the current Region and no more than 255 characters.

Launch template Info   Switch to launch configuration

Launch template
Choose a launch template that contains the instance-level settings, such as the Amazon Machine Image (AMI), instance type, key pair, and security groups.

```
launch-template-asg                                          ▼        C
```

Create a launch template [↗]

Version

```
Default (1)        ▼        C
```

Create a launch template version [↗]

Description	Launch template	Instance type
Production launch template for auto scaling group	launch-template-asg [↗] lt-0bffb814ac740fda2	t2.micro
AMI ID	**Security groups**	**Security group IDs**
ami-0a07be880014c7b8e	-	sg-0dabbfc42efb67652 [↗]
Key pair name		
vpc-prod		

Additional details

Storage (volumes)	Date created
-	Tue Aug 18 2020 18:38:33 GMT-0700 (Pacific Daylight Time)

Cancel   Next

Figure 6.10 – Auto Scaling groups Details

- **VPC**: From the dropdown, choose the VPC you created in *Chapter 3, Creating a Data Center in the Cloud Using VPC* (for example, **prod-vpc**).

- **Subnets**: Choose the subnets where you want to launch your instances (for example, **us-west-2a** and **us-west-2b**). In this case, you need to choose public subnets as we want our web instance to be accessible via the internet. Click on **Next**:

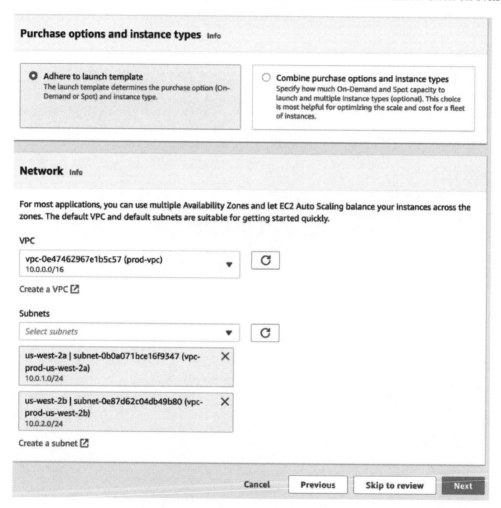

Figure 6.11 – Choosing a network

4. Click on **Enable load balancing** and choose **Application Load Balancer or Network Load Balancer**, and from the dropdown, select the application load balancer (**prod-alb**) that we created in *Chapter 5, Increasing Applications' Fault Tolerance with Elastic Load Balancing*. After enabling the load balancing option, we can launch the EC2 instance behind a load balancer. When we attach the load balancer, it automatically registers the instance. When the load balancer receives traffic, it will automatically distribute it to the instance in the Auto Scaling group.

Set **Health check type** to **ELB** (the default is **EC2**; when the instance reaches an impaired state, the Auto Scaling group terminates that instance and replaces it with a new instance). With health check set to ELB, Auto Scaling gracefully detaches the instance from the load balancer. Then, launch the new instance and attach it back to the load balancer. Click on **Next**:

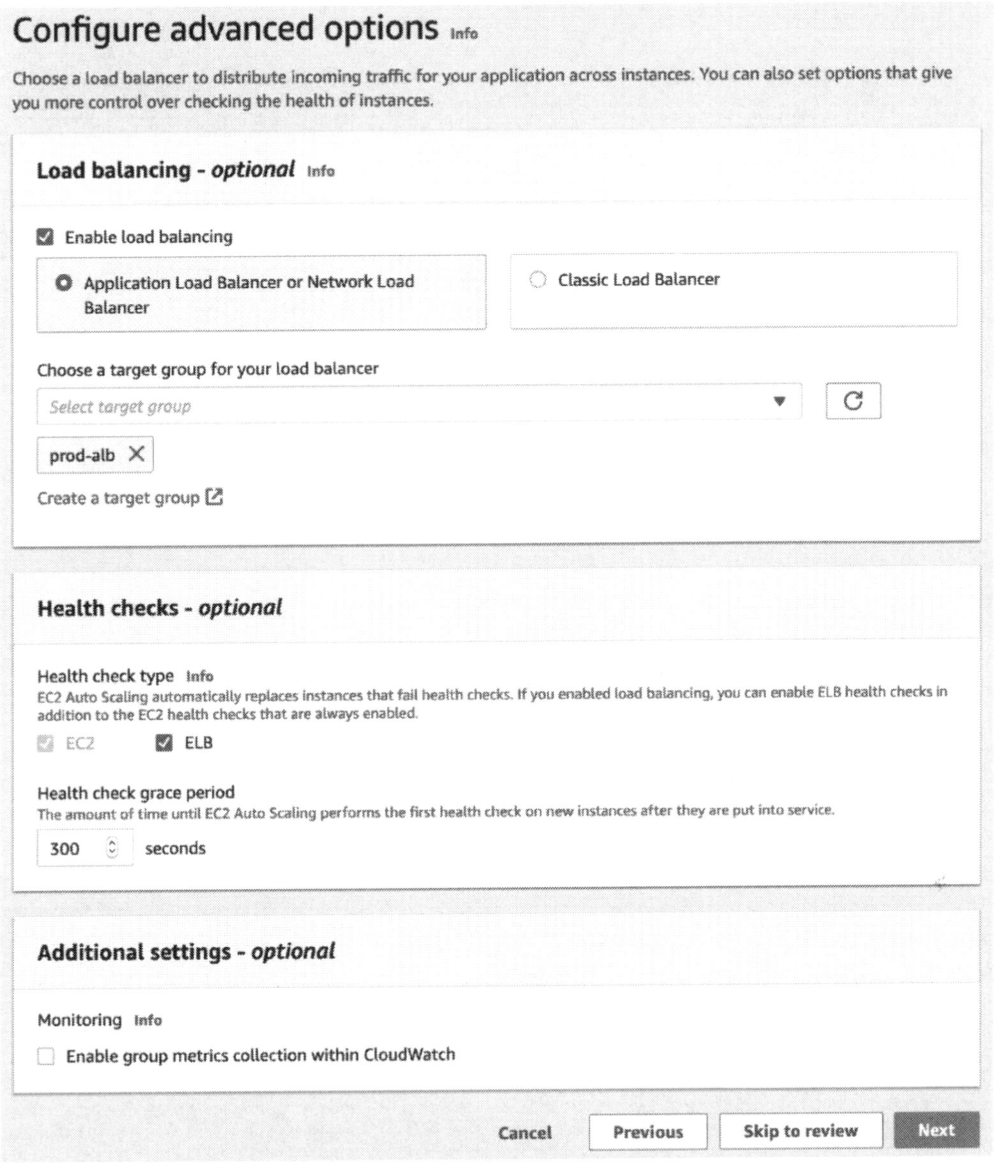

Figure 6.12 – Selecting the load balancer

5. Set **Desired capacity** to **2**, which sets the number of EC2 instances which the Auto Scaling group will attempt to launch and maintain. Set **Minimum capacity** to **1** and **Maximum capacity** to **3**, which sets the minimum and maximum number of instances that the Auto Scaling group will attempt to launch. Click on **Next**:

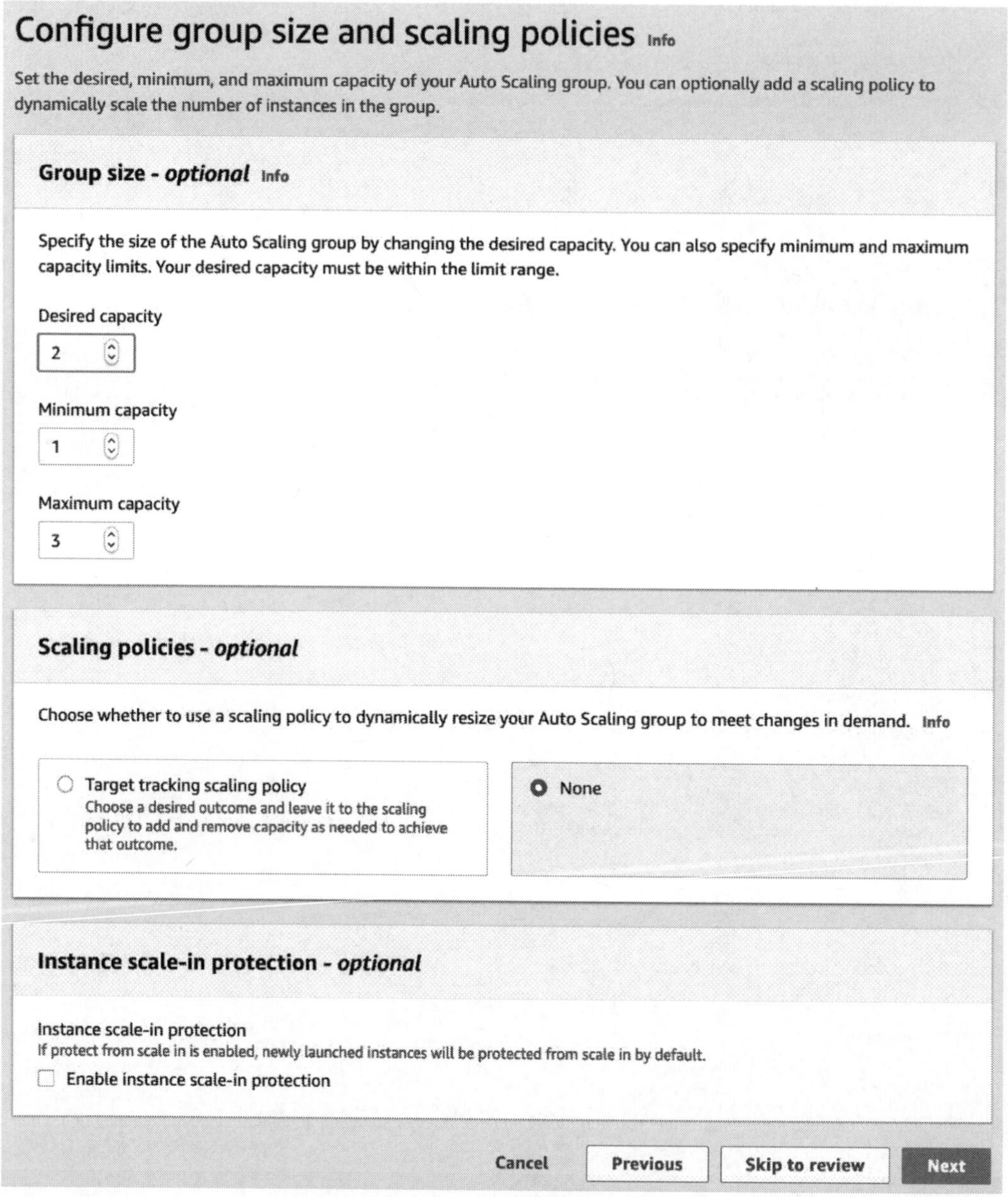

Configure group size and scaling policies Info

Set the desired, minimum, and maximum capacity of your Auto Scaling group. You can optionally add a scaling policy to dynamically scale the number of instances in the group.

Group size - *optional* Info

Specify the size of the Auto Scaling group by changing the desired capacity. You can also specify minimum and maximum capacity limits. Your desired capacity must be within the limit range.

Desired capacity

> 2

Minimum capacity

> 1

Maximum capacity

> 3

Scaling policies - *optional*

Choose whether to use a scaling policy to dynamically resize your Auto Scaling group to meet changes in demand. Info

○ **Target tracking scaling policy**
    Choose a desired outcome and leave it to the scaling
    policy to add and remove capacity as needed to achieve
    that outcome.

● **None**

Instance scale-in protection - *optional*

Instance scale-in protection
If protect from scale in is enabled, newly launched instances will be protected from scale in by default.

☐ Enable instance scale-in protection

Cancel   Previous   Skip to review   Next

Figure 6.13 – Selecting scaling policies

6. For this example, I don't want to set any SNS notifications. If we set SNS notifications, we will receive an alert when a particular event occurs, such as the Auto Scaling group terminating an instance or launching a new one. Click **Next**:

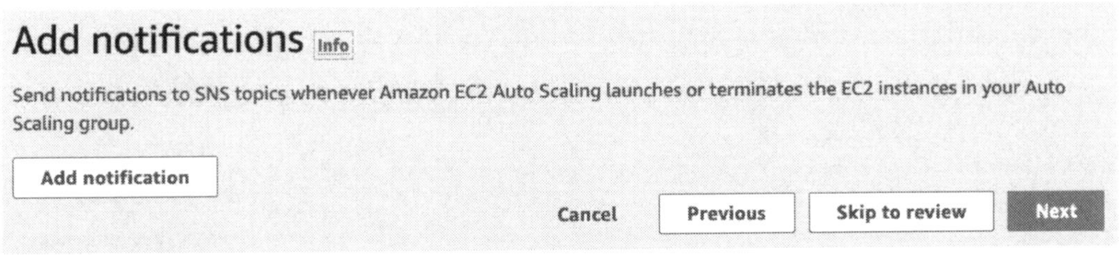

Add notifications Info

Send notifications to SNS topics whenever Amazon EC2 Auto Scaling launches or terminates the EC2 instances in your Auto Scaling group.

Add notification

Cancel   Previous   Skip to review   Next

Figure 6.14 – SNS notifications

7. We can add tags, which will assign labels to launched EC2 instances and EBS volumes. Click **Next**:

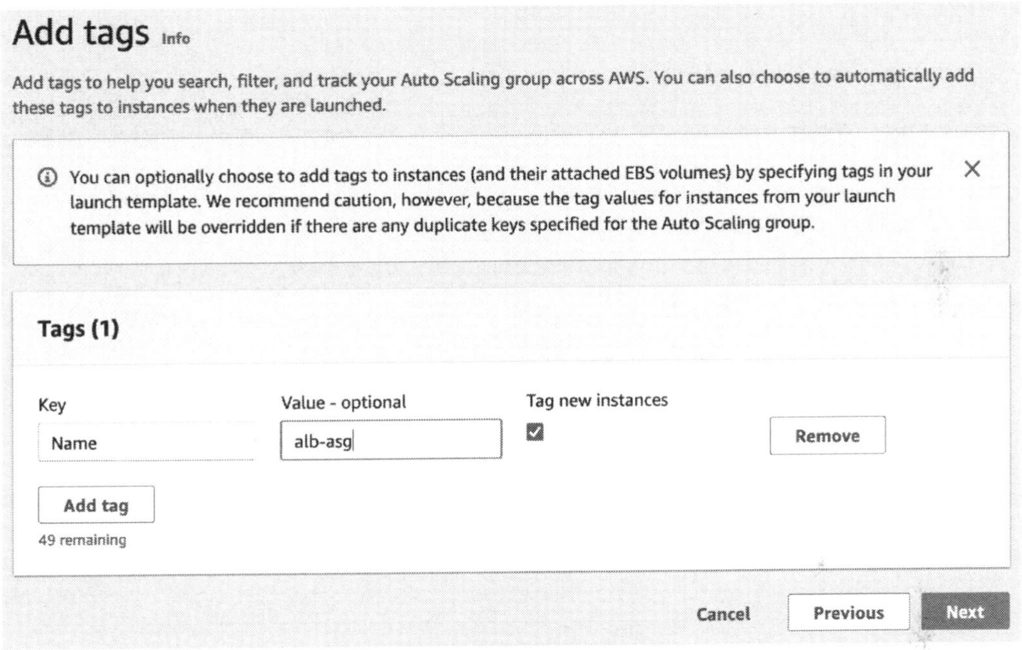

Add tags Info

Add tags to help you search, filter, and track your Auto Scaling group across AWS. You can also choose to automatically add these tags to instances when they are launched.

ⓘ You can optionally choose to add tags to instances (and their attached EBS volumes) by specifying tags in your   ✕
launch template. We recommend caution, however, because the tag values for instances from your launch template will be overridden if there are any duplicate keys specified for the Auto Scaling group.

Tags (1)

Key	Value - optional	Tag new instances	
Name	alb-asg	☑	Remove

Add tag

49 remaining

Cancel   Previous   Next

Figure 6.15 – Adding tags

8. On the **Review** page, verify the configuration and click on **Create Auto Scaling group**.

At this stage, we have the Auto Scaling group up and running. The next step is to verify the configuration.

Verifying an Auto Scaling group

At this stage, we have created an Auto Scaling group; as a next step, we can now verify whether it has launched an EC2 instance:

1. Go to the EC2 console at `https://console.aws.amazon.com/ec2/` and under **AUTO SCALING**, click on **Auto Scaling Groups**. You will see a newly created Auto Scaling group, **prod-asg**. Click on it:

Figure 6.16 – Verify the Auto Scaling group

2. On the next screen, click on the **Activity** tab and at the bottom, under **Activity history**, you will see the status of the instance. Make sure the status is **Successful**:

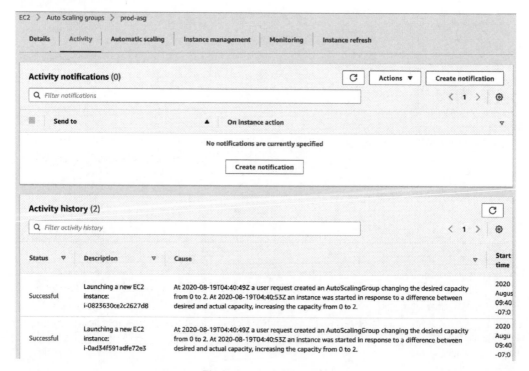

Figure 6.17 – Activity tab

3. Click on the **Instance management** tab and check the second column, **Lifecycle**; when the instance is ready to receive traffic, its state should be **InService**:

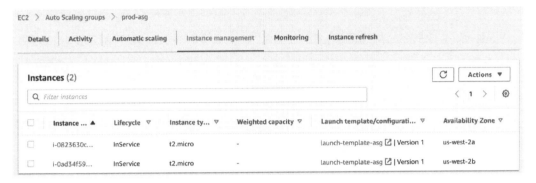

Figure 6.18 – Instance management tab

Now you know how to create an Auto Scaling group using the AWS console. Later in this chapter, we will look at how to automate the entire process using Terraform.

Understanding Auto Scaling policies

Let's revisit the concept of scaling once more. Scaling refers to the increasing or decreasing of the compute capacity of your application. It usually starts with a scaling action or an event that tells an Auto Scaling group to either launch a new instance or terminate existing ones.

AWS provides a bunch of ways to scale your Auto Scaling group. Let's look at these scaling policies one by one:

- **Scale manually**: This is the most basic way to scale your resources. You only need to specify the minimum, maximum, or desired capacity of your Auto Scaling group. We used a manual scaling policy in *Figure 6.14*, where we manually specify the desired, minimum, and maximum capacity.

- **Scale based on demand/dynamic scaling**: This is an advanced scaling policy where we can define the parameter that controls our scaling process in response to changing demand. For example, so far, we only have two EC2 web instances to handle the application load, but we can define a policy that says that when the CPU utilization reaches higher than 70%, add one more instance. We can also define a scale-down policy that says that when the CPU utilization goes lower than 40%, remove one instance. This is useful to handle traffic spikes while, at the same time, reducing the number of idle resources. Later on in this chapter, we will see how to do this.

- **Scheduled scaling**: Scheduled scaling allows you to set up scaling based on a schedule. It's useful for applications where the traffic pattern is predictable. For example, if the traffic in your web application increases on Monday, remains high on Tuesday, and start to decrease on Wednesday, then you can set automatic scaling as a function of time and date.

Now you know about the various Auto Scaling policies. Choosing the right policy is the key to reducing costs and optimizing performance.

Scaling an application based on demand

In this section, we are going to see some real-time dynamic scaling. In this example, you will see how to dynamically scale by modifying an existing scaling group. These are the steps you need to follow:

1. Go back to the Auto Scaling console and click on an existing auto-scaling group (for example, **prod-asg**):

Figure 6.19 – Auto Scaling groups

2. Click on **Automatic scaling** and then **Add policy**:

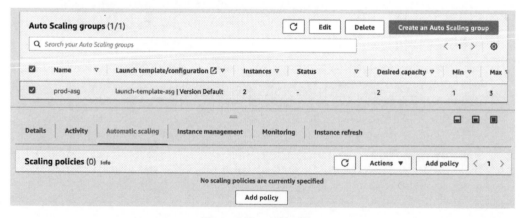

Figure 6.20 – Add policy

3.   In the next step, we need to create a scaling policy that will add an additional instance based on demand. Fill in the following details:

- **Policy type**: From the dropdown, select **Step scaling**.

- **Scaling policy name**: Give a meaningful name to your policy (for example, `asg-scale-in`).

- **CloudWatch alarm**: We are going to come back to this shortly.

- **Take the action**: From the dropdown, select **Add** and in the box, choose **1** (this is going to add one instance based on the CloudWatch trigger):

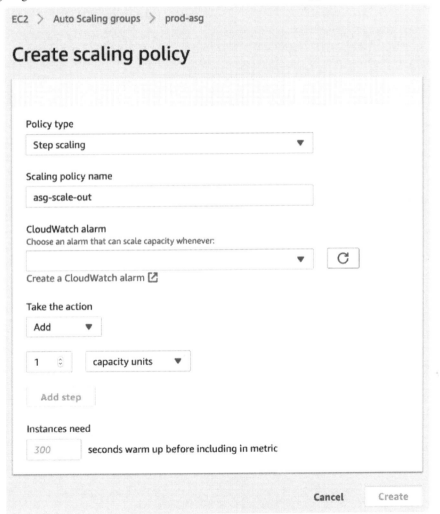

Figure 6.21 – Create scaling policy

4. Click on **Create a CloudWatch alarm** and click on **Select metric**: a CloudWatch alarm will trigger an Auto Scaling group based on a transition to an alarm state, such as **ok** or **alarm**. If CloudWatch is in an **alarm** state, it will spin up more instances and bring down these instances once it reaches the **ok** state:

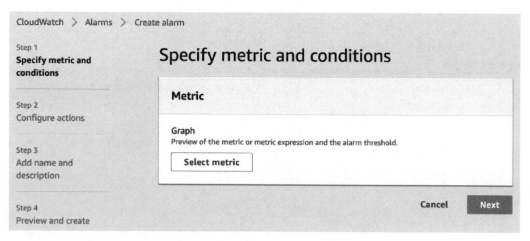

Figure 6.22 – Specify metric and conditions

5. On the next screen, select **EC2**:

Figure 6.23 – Select EC2

6. Now select **By Auto Scaling Group**:

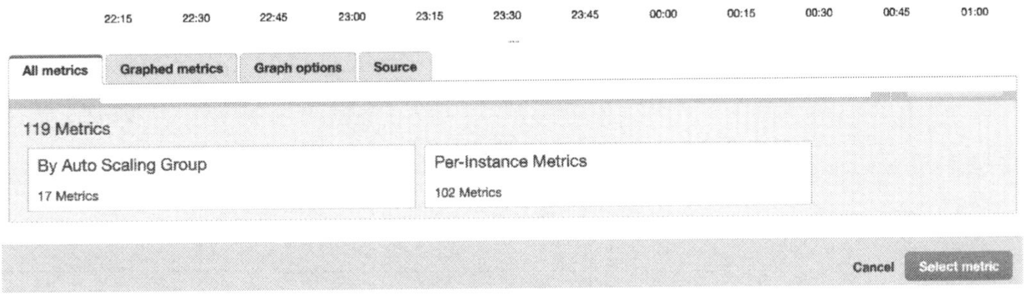

Figure 6.24 – Select By Auto Scaling Group

7. Select **CPUUtilization** and click **Select metric**:

Figure 6.25 – Select CPUUtilization

8. On the next screen, under **Conditions**, set the values as their defaults. This is going to trigger an alarm when the CPU utilization goes higher than 70%. Click on **Next**:

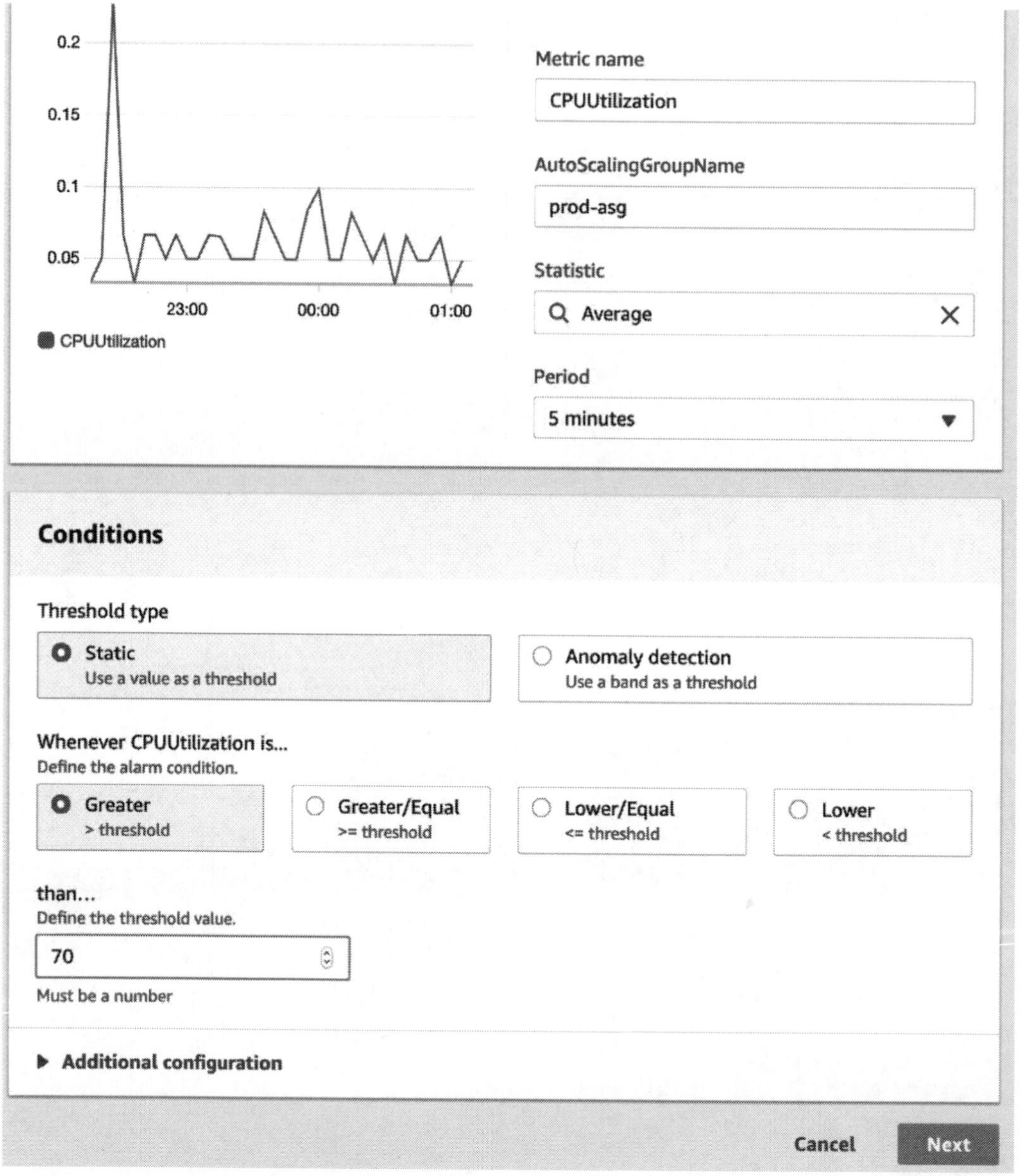

Figure 6.26 – Selecting a threshold value

9. On the next screen, under **Send a notification to...**, select the topic we created in the earlier chapter (**my-topic**). This going to send a notification to the email ID that is subscribed to this topic; click on **Next**:

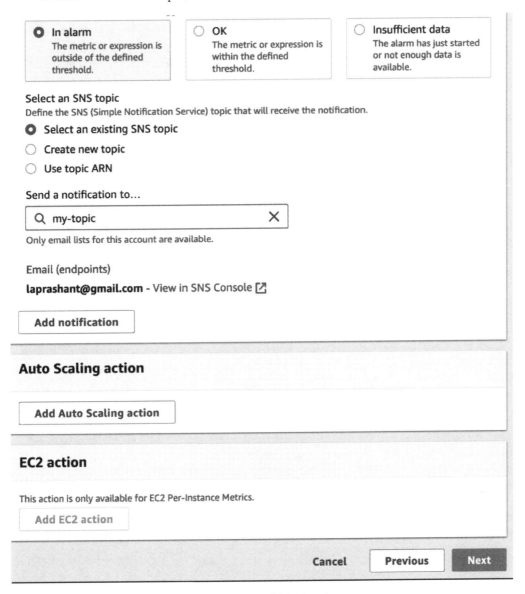

Figure 6.27 – Add SNS topic

10. Give your CloudWatch alarm name and description. Click on **Next**:

   - **Alarm name**: Give your alarm a unique name (for example, `asg-cloudwatch-alarm`).

   - **Alarm description**: Give your alarm a unique description (for example, `CloudWatch alarm for auto-scaling group`):

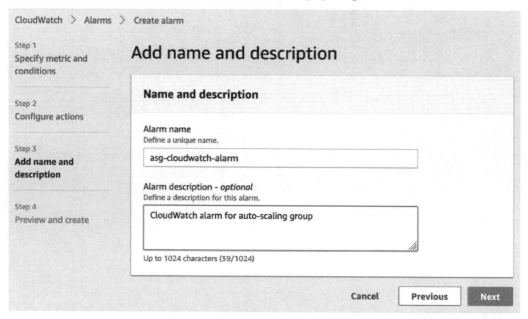

Figure 6.28 – Adding a name and description for your alarm

11. Review all the settings and click on **Create alarm**:

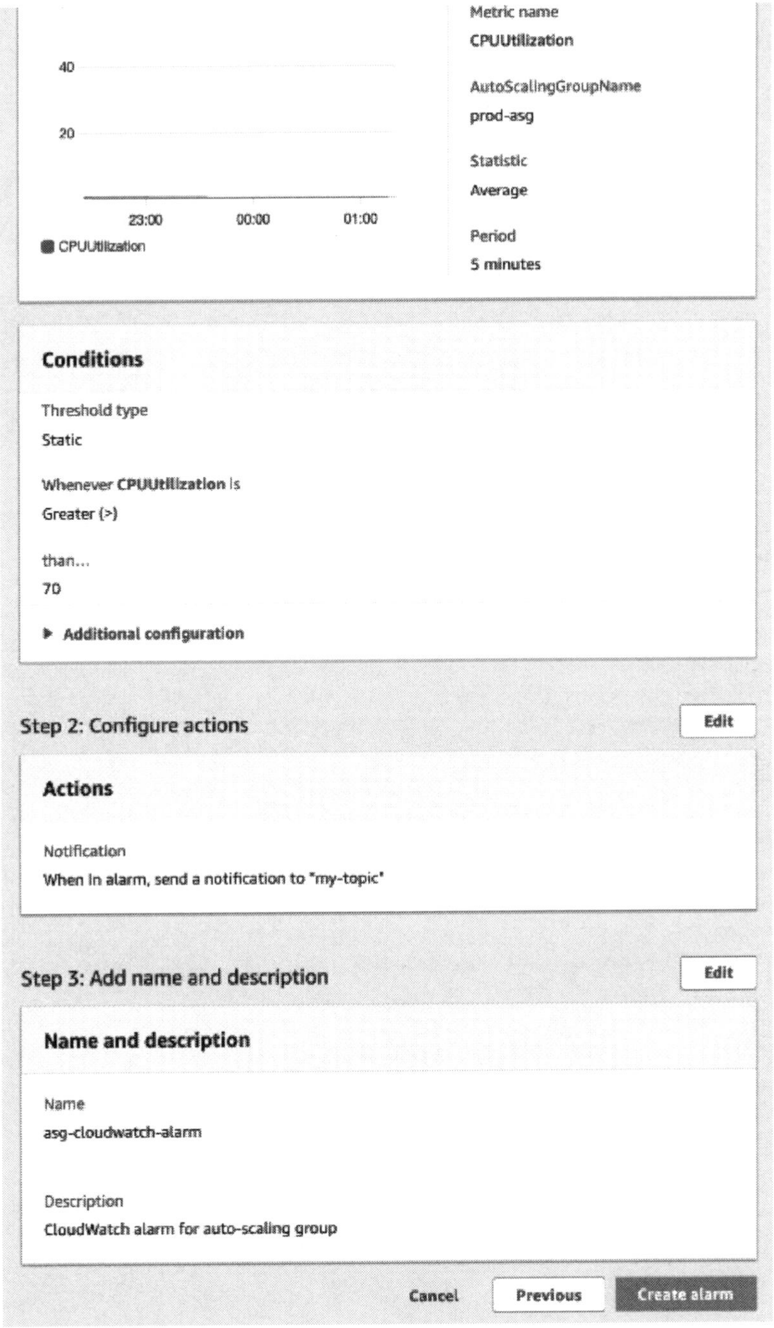

40

20

23:00   00:00   01:00
■ CPUUtilization

Metric name
CPUUtilization

AutoScalingGroupName
prod-asg

Statistic
Average

Period
5 minutes

Conditions

Threshold type
Static

Whenever **CPUUtilization** is
Greater (>)

than...
70

▶ **Additional configuration**

Step 2: Configure actions   Edit

Actions

Notification
When in alarm, send a notification to "my-topic"

Step 3: Add name and description   Edit

Name and description

Name
asg-cloudwatch-alarm

Description
CloudWatch alarm for auto-scaling group

Cancel   Previous   Create alarm

Figure 6.29 – Reviewing the settings

12. Now select the CloudWatch alarm we created in the previous step. Click on **Create**:

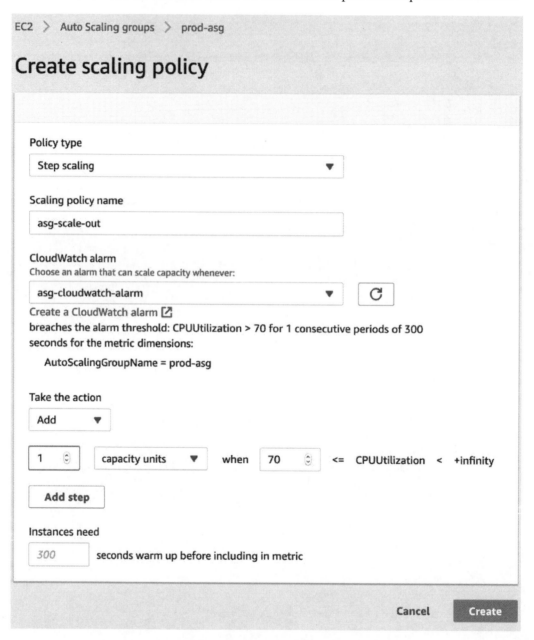

Figure 6.30 – Create scaling policy

Similarly, we can create a scale-down policy where when the CPU utilization goes below 40% it will start terminating EC2 instances to save costs. We need to repeat the same procedure but, in this case, I will only show you what we do differently:

1. Again, go back to the Auto Scaling console at `https://us-west-2.console.aws.amazon.com/ec2autoscaling` and click on **Add policy**:

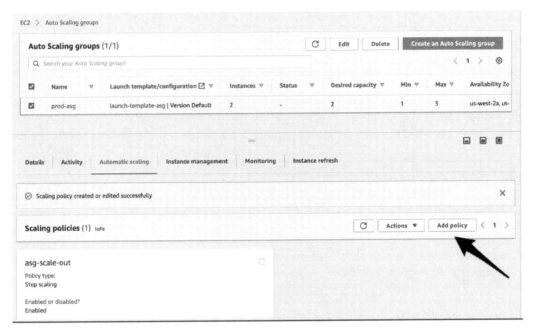

Figure 6.31 – Existing Auto Scaling groups

2. This time, we are going to make some slight changes. For example, **Scaling policy name** will be `asg-scale-in`, and this time, under **Take the action**, from the dropdown, choose **Remove**:

    - **Policy type**: From the dropdown, select **Step scaling**.

    - **Scaling policy name**: Give a meaningful name to your policy (for example, `asg-scale-in`).

- **CloudWatch alarm**: We are going to create a CloudWatch alarm in the next step.

- **Take the action**: From the dropdown, select **Add** and, in the box, choose **1** (this is going to remove one instance based on the CloudWatch trigger):

Figure 6.32 – New scale-in policy

3. The other difference is that while creating the CloudWatch alarm, for the threshold value, choose **40**. The rest of the steps are exactly the same as they were in the last section:

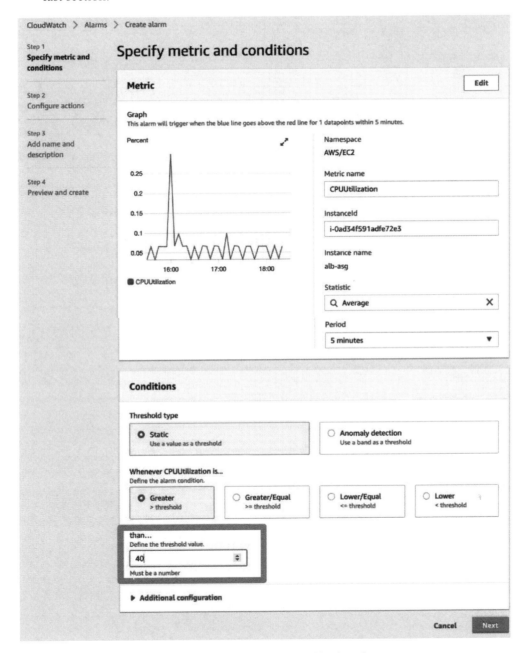

Figure 6.33 – Selecting a threshold value of 40

Once the CloudWatch alarm is created, select the alarm and click on **Create**:

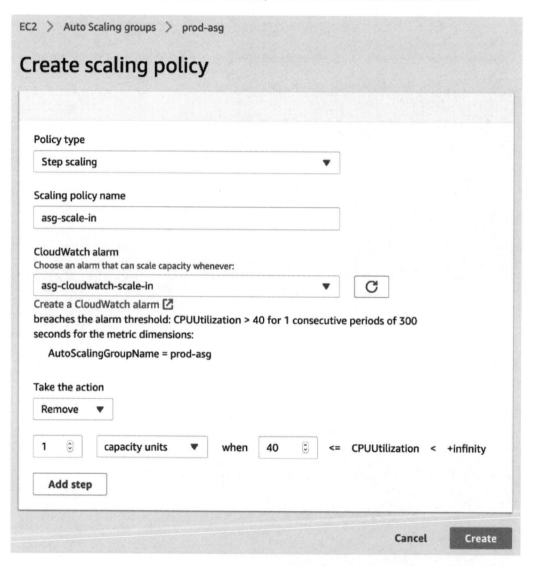

Figure 6.34 – Create scaling policy

4. Now we have two scaling policies, one for scale-out events (adding instances) and the other for scale-in events (removing instances):

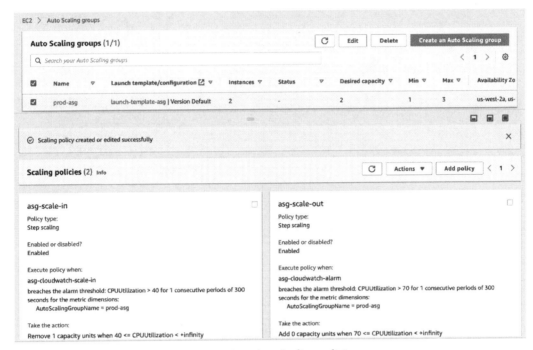

Figure 6.35 – Auto Scaling policies

Now that we have an Auto Scaling policy in place, the next step is to test it.

Testing the Auto Scaling group

In order to test the Auto Scaling policy we created in the last step, these are the steps we need to follow:

1. Log in to any of the instances that were created as part of the Auto Scaling group:

```
ssh -i <public key> ec2-user@<public ip of the instance>
```

2. Install the `stress` package. This package is a utility that is used to impose load on test systems:

```
yum -y install stress
```

3. Now to add a load on one CPU, we can use the following command; this command will time out after 300 seconds (5 minutes):

```
stress --cpu 1 --timeout 300&
```

4. If you go back to the **Activity** tab in the Auto Scaling console, you will see that Auto Scaling will start spinning up a new instance:

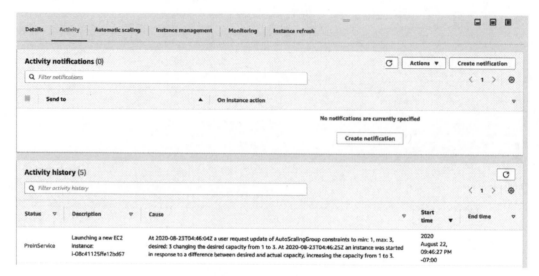

Figure 6.36 – Activity tab

Now you know how an Auto Scaling group adds or terminates instances based on the scaling policy.

Creating an Auto Scaling group using Terraform

So far, we have created Auto Scaling groups manually, but as we did in other chapters, we will also see how to automate the process of Auto Scaling group creation using Terraform. These are the steps that we need to follow:

1. The first step is to create the launch configuration. For that purpose, we are going to use the aws_launch_configuration resource. This is going to specify how to configure each EC2 instance's parameters, such as the image ID (AMI), instance type, security group, and user data.

2. The new parameter that is defined here is the life cycle (`create_before_destroy`). This is always going to involve creating a resource before destroying it. For example, in the case of an EC2 instance, before terminating any instance, it always creates a new one, waits for it to come up, and then removes the old EC2 instance:

```
resource "aws_launch_configuration" "my-asg-launch-config" {
    image_id         = "ami-0a07be880014c7b8e"
    instance_type    = "t2.micro"
    security_groups  = ["sg-0dabbfc42efb67652"]


    user_data = <<-EOF
                #!/bin/bash
                yum -y install httpd
                echo "Hello, from auto-scaling group" > /
var/www/html/index.html
                service httpd start
                chkconfig httpd on
                EOF


    lifecycle {
        create_before_destroy = true
    }
}
```

3. The next step is to define the Auto Scaling group using the `aws_autoscaling_group` resource. We discussed all these parameters while configuring Auto Scaling using the AWS console:

```
resource "aws_autoscaling_group" "example" {
    name                  = "prod-asg-terraform"
    launch_configuration  = aws_launch_configuration.my-asg-launch-config.name
    vpc_zone_identifier   = ["${var.subnet1}", "${var.subnet2}"]
    target_group_arns     = ["${var.target_group_arn}"]
    health_check_type     = "ELB"
```

```
min_size        = 1
max_size        = 3
desired_capacity = 2

tag {
  key                = "Name"
  value              = "my-test-asg"
  propagate_at_launch = true
  }
}
```

> **Information note**
> You can refer to this code at `https://github.com/`
> `PacktPublishing/AWS-for-System-Administrators/`
> `tree/master/Chapter6/terraform`.

At this stage, we understand how the Terraform code needs to be structured to create an Auto Scaling group. Now, it's time to execute the code:

1. The following command initializes the Terraform working directory, or it will download plugins for a provider (for example, `aws`):

    ```
    terraform init
    ```

2. The `terraform plan` command will generate and show the execution plan before making the actual changes:

    ```
    terraform plan
    ```

3. To create the application load balancer, we need to run the `terraform apply` command:

    ```
    terraform apply
    ```

Now you understand how to automate the creation of Auto Scaling groups using Terraform. This is helpful if you have a large-scale AWS deployment and you need to create Auto Scaling groups frequently.

Summary

In this chapter, you have learned about one of the most popular features of AWS, Auto Scaling. Auto Scaling is a powerful and great way to reduce costs while maximizing your application's performance by intelligently scaling your environment based on demand.

In this chapter, we learned how to set up Auto Scaling both via the AWS console and via Terraform. We learned the importance of Auto Scaling and how it makes your infrastructure reliable and scalable. We also saw one real-world example of how Auto Scaling helps give us a consistent performance when demand increases and tears down instances once the load decreases. This is helpful in cases where you want to save costs.

In the next chapter, we will focus on databases and use an AWS managed database service known as Amazon **Relational Database Service** (**RDS**). We will see how by using RDS, AWS will take care of all the heavy lifting (such as patching, backup, and recovery). We will start by setting up an RDS MySQL database via the AWS console and then via Terraform.

7

Creating a Relational Database in the Cloud using AWS Relational Database Service (RDS)

In the last chapter, you learned how to use the Auto Scaling group to scale in and scale down your resources based on demand.

In this chapter, we'll look at AWS **Relational Database Service (RDS)**, to manage database service by using AWS. Using AWS RDS, it's easier to set up and manage databases in the cloud. When you use AWS RDS to create your database, AWS will take care of some of the heavy lifting, including the following:

- Automated patching

- Automatic failover

- Backup and recovery

- The point-in-time recover

In this chapter, we will look at various RDS offerings, and then we deep dive into the offering covering MySQL. We will start with setting up MySQL in multiple Availability Zones, which is useful in case of disaster recovery. Then we will further look at setting up a read-only replica, which takes away all the heavy read load from the master. We will wrap up this chapter by automating the RDS MySQL creation using Terraform.

We are going to cover the following database topics:

- The different database offerings in AWS RDS

- Setting up AWS RDS in high availability mode

- Setting up a MySQL read replica

- Automating AWS RDS MySQL creation using Terraform

Technical requirements

To gain the most from this chapter, you should have basic knowledge and awareness of both AWS and databases. You should be familiar with terms such as *relational database*. Besides this, you should also have basic knowledge of Terraform.

The GitHub link for the solution scripts for this chapter can be found at
`https://github.com/PacktPublishing/AWS-for-System-Administrators/tree/master/Chapter7`.

Check out the following video to see the Code in Action:

`https://bit.ly/3n6Big8`

The different database offerings in AWS RDS

AWS RDS is a portfolio of managed relational database services that AWS offers to its customers. AWS provides a range of options, from commercial databases (for example, Oracle and Microsoft SQL Server) created by other vendors to the most popular open source database types (MySQL, MariaDB, and PostgreSQL). AWS also owns a cloud-native engine (Amazon Aurora), which is MySQL- and PostgreSQL-compatible. Using AWS RDS, you can manage these databases from one centralized console, the AWS CLI, or via API calls. Using this managed service has other advantages, such as the fact that all the administrative tasks including setting up the database, backups, and patching are already automated. There are a variety of use cases for AWS RDS:

- **Mobile and web application**: It provides high availability and scalability for enterprise applications.

- **E-commerce applications**: It provides the security and PCI compliance needed for e-commerce websites or applications.

- **Online games**: It provides high throughput and availability to make sure that online games are responsive to players at all times.

With such a wide portfolio of database offerings from AWS, which database solution we choose depends entirely upon our application and requirements. In the next section, we will set up a MySQL database across multiple Availability Zones using AWS RDS.

Setting up AWS RDS in high availability mode

In this section, we will see how to create a MySQL database in AWS RDS across multiple Availability Zones. AWS RDS provides high availability and failover support for database instances using Multi-AZ deployments. In a Multi-AZ deployment, AWS RDS automatically provisions and maintains a synchronous standby replica in a different Availability Zone. The primary database synchronously replicates data across the Availability Zone to provide data redundancy and high availability in case of failure.

We need to follow this series of steps to do so:

1. Go to the AWS management console at `https://console.aws.amazon.com/console/home` and click on **RDS** under **Database**:

Figure 7.1 – AWS RDS

2. In the next step, we will create a MySQL database instance by selecting **Create database**:

Figure 7.2 – Creating an RDS database

3. In the next section, keep all the values as their defaults (**Standard Create** and **Edition**), select the MySQL icon, and select the **Dev/Test** template, as we want to create an RDS instance in high availability mode:

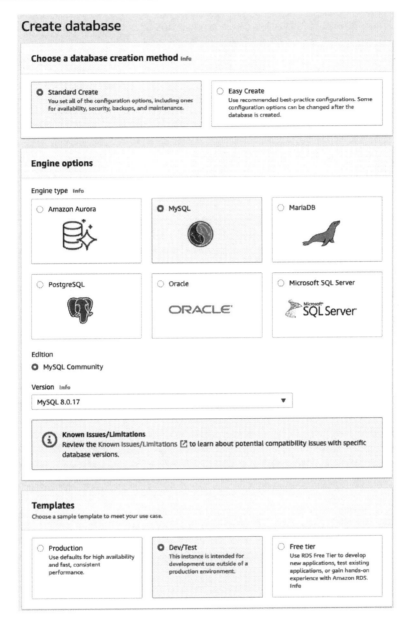

Figure 7.3 – Creating an RDS database using Dev/Test

4. In the next section, you need to configure your database instance. Please fill in all the details as follows:

    - **DB instance identifier**: Type a unique name of your database instance – it should be unique to your account, for example, `prod-db`.

- **Master username**: Type a username you want to use to log in to the database instance; for example, admin.

- **Master password**: Type a password for your master username.

- **Confirm password**: Retype your password to confirm it.

- **DB Instance class**: From the dropdown, select **db.t2.micro**, which provides 1 vCPU and 1 GiB of RAM:

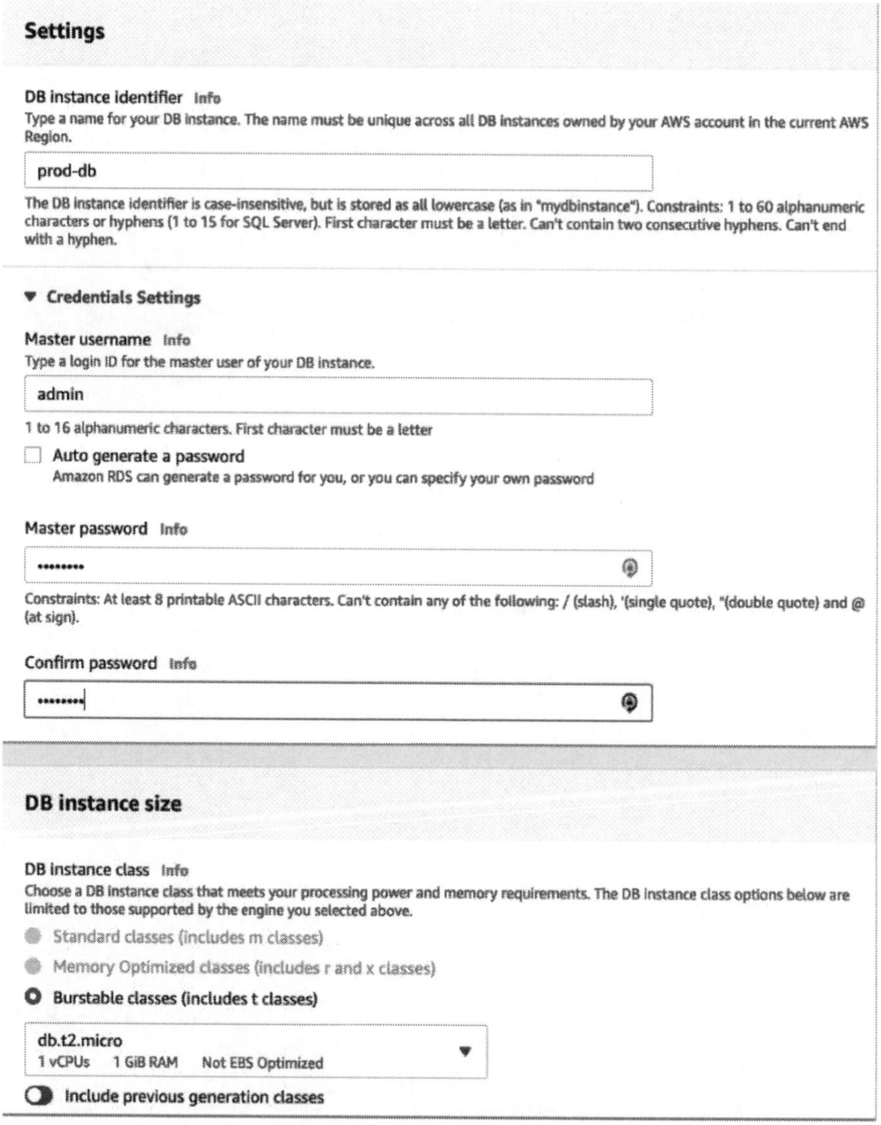

Settings

DB instance identifier Info
Type a name for your DB instance. The name must be unique across all DB instances owned by your AWS account in the current AWS Region.

> prod-db

The DB instance identifier is case-insensitive, but is stored as all lowercase (as in "mydbinstance"). Constraints: 1 to 60 alphanumeric characters or hyphens (1 to 15 for SQL Server). First character must be a letter. Can't contain two consecutive hyphens. Can't end with a hyphen.

▼ **Credentials Settings**

Master username Info
Type a login ID for the master user of your DB instance.

> admin

1 to 16 alphanumeric characters. First character must be a letter

☐ Auto generate a password
Amazon RDS can generate a password for you, or you can specify your own password

Master password Info

> •••••••

Constraints: At least 8 printable ASCII characters. Can't contain any of the following: / (slash), '(single quote), "(double quote) and @ (at sign).

Confirm password Info

> •••••••

DB instance size

DB instance class Info
Choose a DB instance class that meets your processing power and memory requirements. The DB instance class options below are limited to those supported by the engine you selected above.

◉ Standard classes (includes m classes)

◉ Memory Optimized classes (includes r and x classes)

◉ Burstable classes (includes t classes)

> db.t2.micro
> 1 vCPUs   1 GiB RAM   Not EBS Optimized   ▼

◯ Include previous generation classes

Figure 7.4 – Setting the parameters for the RDS database

5. In the next section, please type/select all the storage and availability-related details as follows:

- **Storage type**: Select **General Purpose (SSD)**. We already discussed the storage options in *Chapter 4, Scalable Compute Capacity in the Cloud via EC2*.

- **Allocated storage**: Select **20** (the default value) to allocate 20 GB to your database. In the case of MySQL, you can scale up to 64 TB as required.

- **Enable storage autoscaling**: You can enable dynamic scaling in cases where your workload is unpredictable or dynamic. Once enabled, your storage will be scaled automatically when needed.

- **Multi-AZ deployment**: Select **Create a standby instance**. This will automatically provision a standby replica in a different Availability Zone:

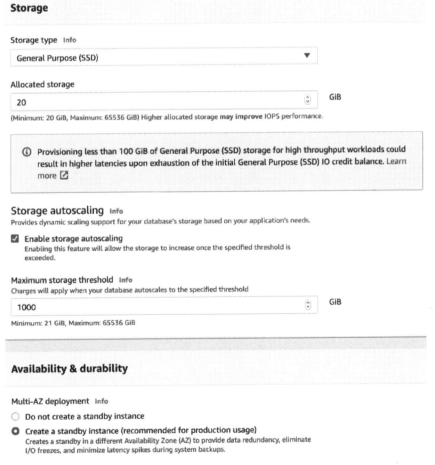

Figure 7.5 – Choosing storage for the RDS database

6.   In the **Connectivity** section, you need to provide information to connect to the database. Please fill in all the details as follows:

- **Virtual private cloud (VPC)**: Choose the **prod-vpc (vpc-0e47462967e1b5c57)** VPC that we created in *Chapter 3*, *Creating a Data Center in the Cloud Using VPC*.

- **Subnet group**: This will define the subnet and IP range a database instance can use in the VPC you choose.

- **Public access**: Set it to **No**, as we don't want our database instance to be connected over the internet.

- **Existing VPC security groups**: In this case, we will choose the default security group created during the VPC creation. In this security group, port 3306 is required to connect to MySQL but is not opened for inbound connections, so once the database creation is done, we need to modify the security group:

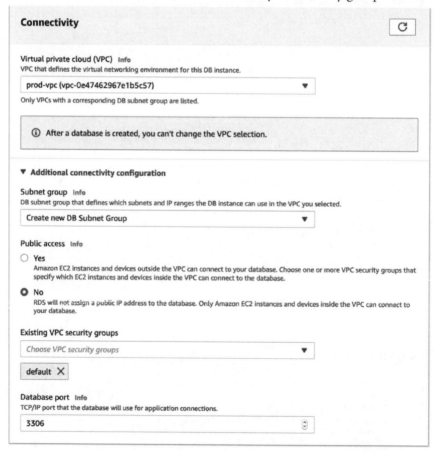

Figure 7.6 – Choosing the networking configuration for the RDS database

7. Under the **Additional configuration** section, fill in the following details:

- **Initial database name**: Type the name of the database (for example, `proddb`).

- **DB parameter group**: Keep the default value (for example, **default.mysql8.0**).

- **Option group**: Keep the default value (for example, **default.mysql-8-0**).

- **Backup retention period**: You can choose the amount of days you want to keep the backup. For this example, we will choose the default value of **7 days**:

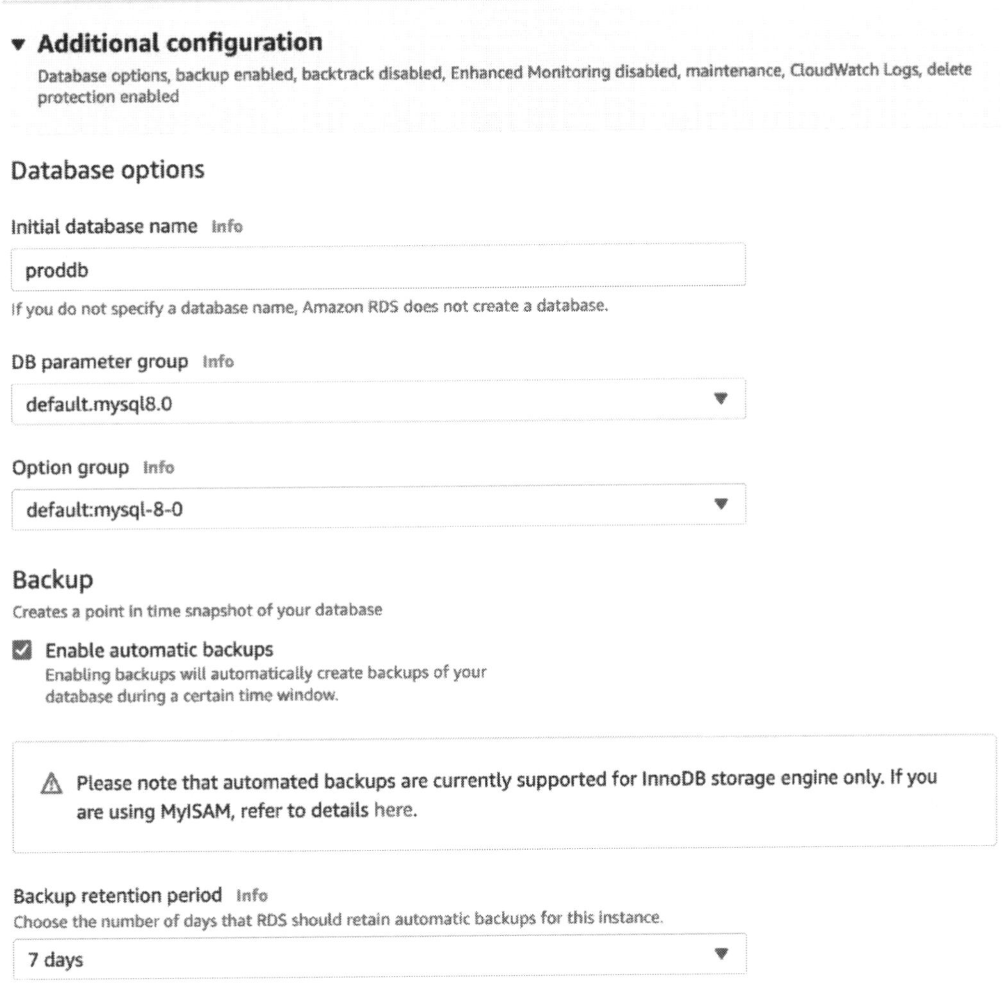

▼ **Additional configuration**

Database options, backup enabled, backtrack disabled, Enhanced Monitoring disabled, maintenance, CloudWatch Logs, delete protection enabled

Database options

Initial database name Info

proddb

If you do not specify a database name, Amazon RDS does not create a database.

DB parameter group Info

default.mysql8.0	▼

Option group Info

default:mysql-8-0	▼

Backup

Creates a point in time snapshot of your database

☑ **Enable automatic backups**

Enabling backups will automatically create backups of your database during a certain time window.

⚠ Please note that automated backups are currently supported for InnoDB storage engine only. If you are using MyISAM, refer to details here.

Backup retention period Info

Choose the number of days that RDS should retain automatic backups for this instance.

7 days	▼

Figure 7.7 – Choosing database options for the RDS database

8.   In the next section, fill in the following details:

- **Backup window**: You can select your own window (in the UTC time zone) or select **No preference**. This is the window in which AWS RDS will create automated backups.

- **Enable Enhanced monitoring**: This will give you access to the real-time operating system metrics of your database instance. To stay within the free tier, I am not enabling this option. If you want to enable it, click on the box next to **Enable Enhanced monitoring**, but this will incur an extra charge.

- **Enable auto minor version upgrade**: This will automatically upgrade the minor version of the operating system during the maintenance window:

Backup window Info
Select the period you want automated backups of the database to be created by Amazon RDS.

○ Select window

◉ No preference

☑ Copy tags to snapshots

Monitoring

☐ Enable Enhanced monitoring
Enabling Enhanced monitoring metrics are useful when you want to see how different processes or threads use the CPU

Log exports

Select the log types to publish to Amazon CloudWatch Logs

☐ Error log

☐ General log

☐ Slow query log

IAM role
The following service-linked role is used for publishing logs to CloudWatch Logs.

RDS service-linked role

ⓘ Ensure that General, Slow Query, and Audit Logs are turned on. Error logs are enabled by default.
Learn more

Maintenance

Auto minor version upgrade Info

☑ Enable auto minor version upgrade
Enabling auto minor version upgrade will automatically upgrade to new minor versions as they are released. The automatic upgrades occur during the maintenance window for the database.

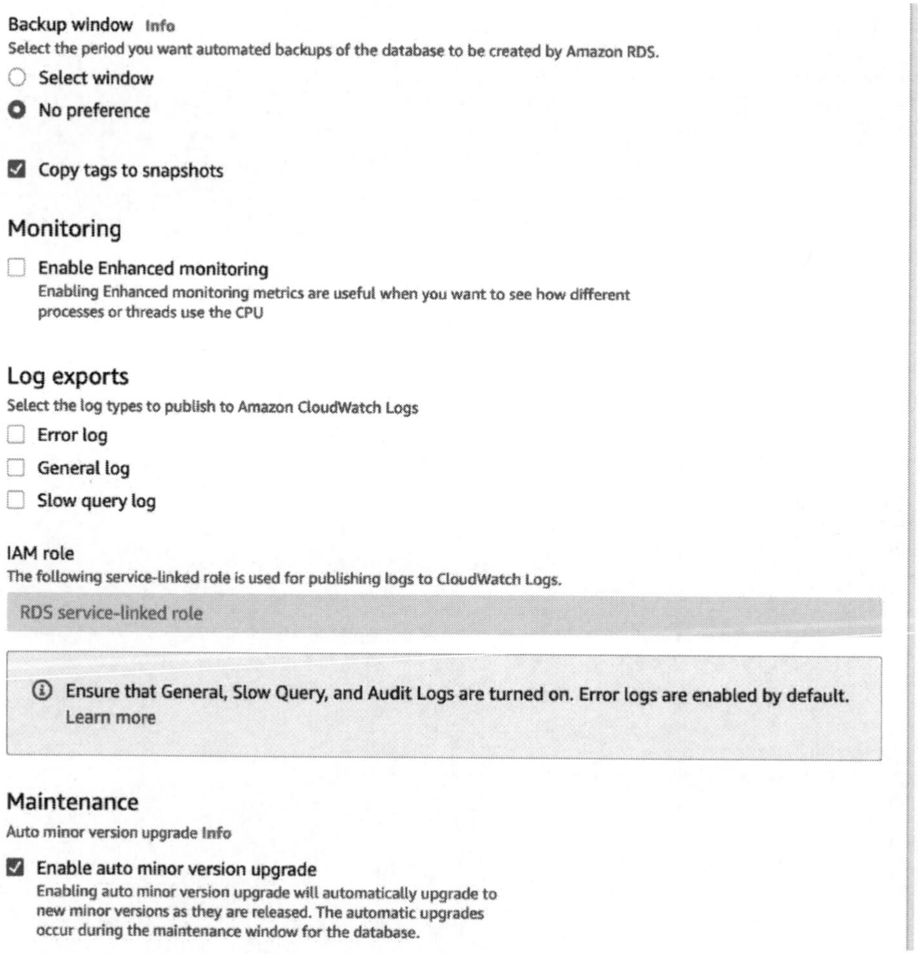

Figure 7.8 – Choosing the backup window for the RDS database

9. In the next section, fill the following details:

- **Maintenance window**: This is the period where all the pending modifications will be applied. For example, this could include patching the database instance or changing the instance family.

- **Enable deletion protection**: This will prevent anyone from accidentally deleting your database.

Now, click **Create database**:

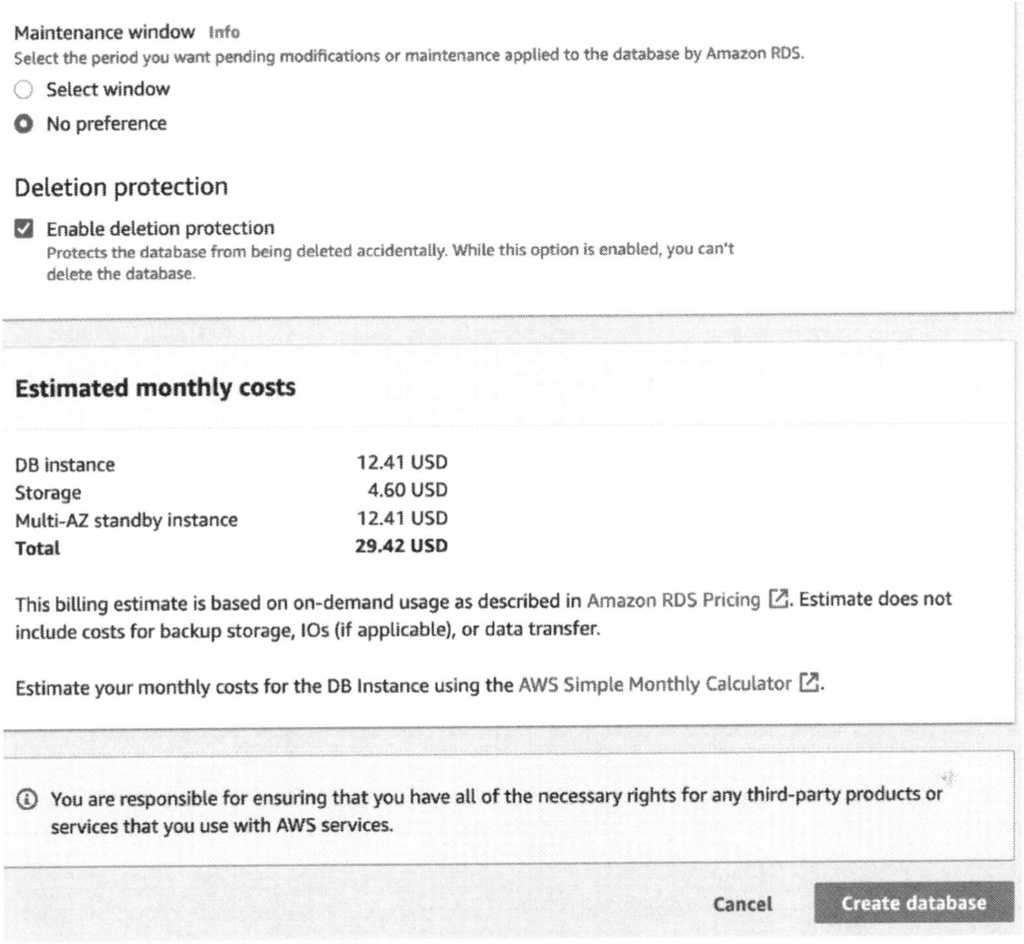

Maintenance window Info
Select the period you want pending modifications or maintenance applied to the database by Amazon RDS.

◯ Select window

◉ No preference

Deletion protection

☑ Enable deletion protection
Protects the database from being deleted accidentally. While this option is enabled, you can't delete the database.

Estimated monthly costs

DB instance	12.41 USD
Storage	4.60 USD
Multi-AZ standby instance	12.41 USD
Total	**29.42 USD**

This billing estimate is based on on-demand usage as described in Amazon RDS Pricing ☒. Estimate does not include costs for backup storage, IOs (if applicable), or data transfer.

Estimate your monthly costs for the DB Instance using the AWS Simple Monthly Calculator ☒.

ⓘ You are responsible for ensuring that you have all of the necessary rights for any third-party products or services that you use with AWS services.

Cancel   **Create database**

Figure 7.9 – Creating the database

10. Once the database instance creation is complete, you will see the **Status** is **Available**:

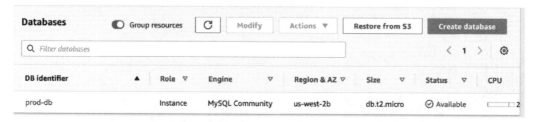

Figure 7.10 – The database console once the database creation is complete

11. Click on **prod-db**, and under **Endpoint & port** you will see **Endpoint**. This is what you will use to connect to the MySQL database (this is going to be different in your case):

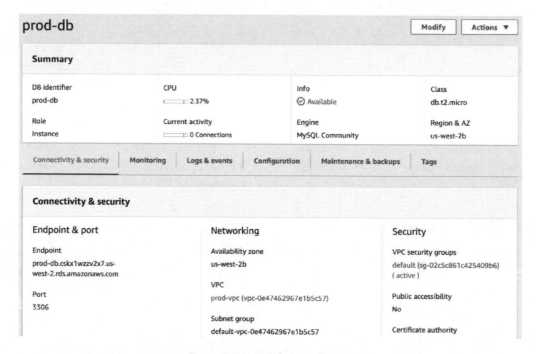

Figure 7.11 – Database endpoint

12. Before we connect to this endpoint, we need to make changes to our security group. Go back to VPC console at `https://us-west-2.console.aws.amazon.com/vpc/home` and from the dropdown, select the **prod-vpc** VPC, then click on **Security Groups** on the left pane. Select the default security group, click on the **Inbound rules** tab, and then **Edit Inbound rules**:

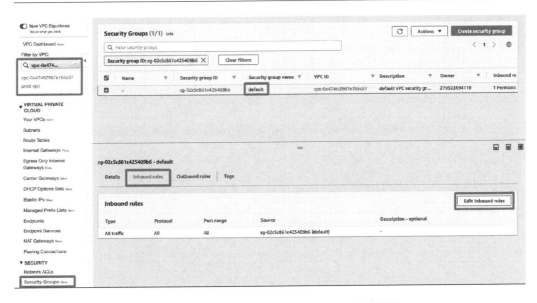

Figure 7.12 – Changing the security group for RDS

13. In the next window, click on **Add rule**. From the dropdown, select **MYSQL/Aurora** and in the **Source** field, add the custom IP of VPC, that is, 10.0.0.0/16. Click on **Save rules**:

Figure 7.13 – Adding the MySQL port

14. Once the database creation is complete, you can connect to the database using any of the SQL clients, but before doing that, connect to any of the EC2 instances you created in *Chapter 4, Scalable Compute Capacity in the Cloud via EC2*. The public key and public IP are going to be different in your case. To connect to the instance, use ssh by inputting the public key and IP of the server:

```
ssh -i <public key> ec2-user@<public ip of the server>
```

The following is an example:

```
ssh -i vpc-prod.pem ec2-user@52.13.17.115
```

Install the MySQL client by running the following command:

```
yum -y install mysql55-5.5.62-1.23.amzn1.x86_64
```

Connect to the MySQL database (where the username is admin, which we selected during database creation, and –h is the endpoint we got once the database was created, as shown in *Figure 7.11*):

```
mysql -u admin -h prod-db.cskxlwzzv2x7.us-west-2.rds.
amazonaws.com -p
Enter password:
Welcome to the MySQL monitor.  Commands end with ; or \g.
Your MySQL connection id is 88
Server version: 8.0.17 Source distribution
Copyright (c) 2000, 2018, Oracle and/or its affiliates.
All rights reserved.
Oracle is a registered trademark of Oracle Corporation
and/or its affiliates. Other names may be trademarks of
their respective owners.
Type 'help;' or '\h' for help. Type '\c' to clear the
current input statement.
mysql>
```

You have learned how to create, and have now connected to, the MySQL database with AWS RDS. RDS makes it easy to create, manage, and scale databases in the cloud. Later in this chapter (in the *Automating AWS RDS MySQL creation using Terraform* section), you will learn how to automate the AWS RDS creation process using Terraform.

Setting up a MySQL read replica

The main purpose of a read-only replica is to serve read-only traffic, so that the load (namely, read-only load) from the primary database will be reduced. Read-only replicas can also be used as a disaster recovery solution because we can promote the read-only replica to the master if our master instance happened to fail. In order to create a read-only replica for MySQL, please follow this series of steps:

1. Go back to the RDS console at `https://console.aws.amazon.com/rds/`. In the left navigation pane, click on **Databases**, choose the database you have created in the last step (**prod-db**), and then, from the **Actions** dropdown, select **Create read replica**:

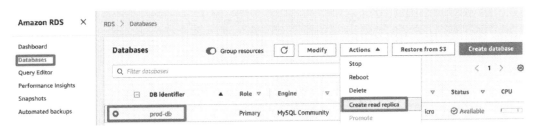

Figure 7.14 – Setting up the read replica

2. Here, keep all the settings as their defaults, except under **Settings**: make sure to give the **DB instance identifier** some meaningful name. This is used to uniquely identify your database instance (for example, `prod-db-replica`). One of the primary reasons to keep all the settings as their defaults is because in the case of disaster recovery, if we need to promote the read-only replica to be the master, then it should be of the same configuration as the master. However, please feel free to modify the settings based on your requirements (we have already discussed all the settings in the *Setting up AWS RDS in high availability mode* section):

Settings

Read replica source
Source DB instance Identifier

```
prod-db                                                        ▼
```

DB instance identifier
DB Instance identifier. This is the unique key that identifies a DB Instance. This parameter is stored as a lowercase string (e.g. mydbinstance).

```
prod-db-replica
```

Figure 7.15 – Setting up the database instance identifier for the read replica

3. Scroll down all the way and click on **Create read replica**:

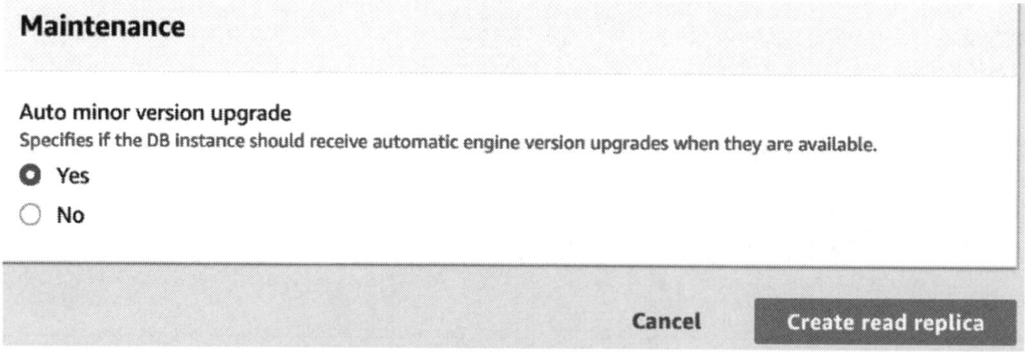

Maintenance

Auto minor version upgrade
Specifies if the DB instance should receive automatic engine version upgrades when they are available.

🔘 Yes
⭘ No

Cancel   **Create read replica**

Figure 7.16 – Creating the read replica

Creating a read replica is a great way to reduce the load on your primary instance and defer all the read-only queries to the replica instead.

Automating AWS RDS MySQL creation using Terraform

So far, we have created a MySQL database using the AWS console. In this section, we will learn how to automate the entire process using Terraform. The whole process is divided into four steps:

1. We will start with the boilerplate syntax where we specify aws as `provider`, and the region where we want to create this database (for example, us-west-2, which is in Oregon):

```
provider "aws" {
    region = "us-west-2"
}
```

2. In the next step, you need to specify the database subnet group. This is the subnet group that MySQL uses to create the database instance:

    - name: This is the name of the subnet group. For example, you could use rds-db-subnet. If you omit this, Terraform will randomly assign some unique name for you.

- `subnet_ids`: Here you specify the list of subnet IDs (for example, `subnet-07714eb09171b1f7e` and `subnet-0cca9fdeb1b95003c` – these are the subnet IDs from `prod-vpc`):

```
resource "aws_db_subnet_group" "rds-db-subnet" {
  name         = "rds-db-subnet"
  subnet_ids = ["${var.rds_subnet1}", "${var.rds_subnet2}"]
}
```

3. In this step, you need to define the security group to allow incoming and outgoing connections to the database. For that purpose, you need to use the `aws_security_group` resource to create the security group and `aws_security_group_rule` to create the actual rules. In this case, we are allowing port `3306` (`from_port` and `to_port`), which is the MySQL port for inbound traffic, and port `0` (`from_port` and `to_port`), which means all ports for outbound traffic. Entering `-1` in the `protocol` field means *all protocols*:

```
resource "aws_security_group" "rds-sg" {
  name   = "rds-sg"
  vpc_id = var.vpc_id
}
resource "aws_security_group_rule" "rds-sg-rule" {
  from_port         = 3306
  protocol          = "tcp"
  security_group_id = aws_security_group.rds-sg.id
  to_port           = 3306
  type              = "ingress"
  cidr_blocks       = ["0.0.0.0/0"]
}
resource "aws_security_group_rule" "rds-outbound-rule" {
  from_port         = 0
  protocol          = "-1"
  security_group_id = aws_security_group.rds-sg.id
  to_port           = 0
  type              = "egress"
  cidr_blocks       = ["0.0.0.0/0"]
}
```

4. Finally, we will create database using the `aws_db_instance` resource. We already discussed all these parameters when we created a database using the AWS console in the *Automating AWS RDS MySQL creation using Terraform* section:

```
resource "aws_db_instance" "rds-mysql" {
    instance_class              = var.db_instance
    engine                      = "mysql"
    engine_version              = "8.0.17"
    multi_az                    = true
    storage_type                = "gp2"
    allocated_storage           = 20
    name                        = "rdsmysqlinstance"
    username                    = "admin"
    password                    = "admin123"
    apply_immediately           = "true"
    backup_retention_period = 10
    backup_window               = "09:46-10:16"
    db_subnet_group_name    = aws_db_subnet_group.rds-db-
subnet.name
    vpc_security_group_ids  = ["${aws_security_group.
rds-sg.id}"]
}
```

At this stage, we have all our code ready to create our AWS RDS MySQL database using Terraform. Now, it's time to execute the code:

1. We start off by cloning the Git repo:

```
https://github.com/PacktPublishing/AWS-for-System-
Administrators
```

Go the directory where the Terraform code is located:

```
cd AWS-for-System-Administrators/tree/master/Chapter7/
terraform
```

2. The following command will initialize the Terraform working directory, or it will download the necessary plugins for a provider (for example, `aws`) and then initialize it:

```
$ terraform init
Initializing the backend...
Initializing provider plugins...
```

```
- Checking for available provider plugins...
- Downloading plugin for provider "aws" (hashicorp/aws)
3.4.0...
The following providers do not have any version
constraints in configuration, so the latest version was
installed.
To prevent automatic upgrades to new major versions that
may contain breaking changes, it is recommended to add
version = "..." constraints to the corresponding provider
blocks in configuration, with the constraint strings
suggested below.
* provider.aws: version = "~> 3.4"


Terraform has been successfully initialized!


You may now begin working with Terraform. Try running
"terraform plan" to see any changes that are required for
your infrastructure. All Terraform commands should now
work.


If you ever set or change modules or backend
configuration for Terraform, rerun this command to
reinitialize your working directory. If you forget,
other commands will detect it and remind you to do so if
necessary.
```

3. The `terraform plan` command will generate and show the execution plan before making the actual changes:

```
$ terraform plan
Refreshing Terraform state in-memory prior to plan...
The refreshed state will be used to calculate this plan,
but will not be persisted to local or remote state
storage.
------------------------------------------------------------
----------------
An execution plan has been generated and is shown below.
Resource actions are indicated with the following
symbols:
  + create
```

```
Terraform will perform the following actions:

  # aws_db_instance.rds-mysql will be created
  + resource "aws_db_instance" "rds-mysql" {
      + address                        = (known
after apply)
      + allocated_storage              = 20
      + apply_immediately              = true
      + arn                            = (known
after apply)
      + auto_minor_version_upgrade     = true
      + availability_zone              = (known
after apply)
      + backup_retention_period        = 10
      + backup_window                  = "09:46-
10:16"


Plan: 5 to add, 0 to change, 0 to destroy.


------------------------------------------------------------
---------------


Note: You didn't specify an "-out" parameter to save this
plan, so Terraform
can't guarantee that exactly these actions will be
performed if
"terraform apply" is subsequently run.
```

4. To create the AWS RDS MySQL database, we need to run the `terraform apply` command:

```
$ terraform apply
An execution plan has been generated and is shown below.
Resource actions are indicated with the following
symbols:
  + create
```

```
Terraform will perform the following actions:

  # aws_db_instance.rds-mysql will be created
  + resource "aws_db_instance" "rds-mysql" {
      + address                             = (known
after apply)
      + allocated_storage                   = 20
      + apply_immediately                   = true
      + engine                              = "mysql"
      + engine_version                      = "8.0.17"
      + hosted_zone_id                      = (known
after apply)
      + id                                  = (known
after apply)


aws_db_instance.rds-mysql: Still creating... [15m30s
elapsed]
aws_db_instance.rds-mysql: Creation complete after 15m36s
[id=terraform-20200830004343229900000001]


Apply complete! Resources: 5 added, 0 changed, 0
destroyed.
```

Automating the creation of an AWS RDS MySQL database using Terraform is helpful where we to want to create a similar database in the future. At this point, having completed this chapter, you now have a firm knowledge of the different components of AWS RDS MySQL and how to create such a database via both the AWS console and Terraform.

Summary

Databases are always a critical component of any infrastructure. Using the AWS RDS managed service, AWS will take care of most of the heavy lifting, such as patching and backups, so your team can focus on writing business logic rather than managing database tasks. In this chapter, you have learned how to increase your database's availability by setting it up in high availability mode and creating and using read replicas.

In the next chapter, we will look at the monitoring solutions provided by AWS and how to set them up.

Section 4: The Monitoring, Metrics, and Backup Layers

In the last part of the book, to add robustness to the infrastructure, we start to add the monitoring layer by using CloudWatch to monitor any high CPU, memory, and **input/output (I/O)** usage. We then look at how to push logs to the remote location (CloudWatch logs) and then transfer them to Elasticsearch/Kibana to get meaningful metrics out of these logs. Finally, we add the most critical piece, which is the backup layer, to make sure that we have data to restore in the event of a disaster.

The following chapters are included in this section:

- *Chapter 8, Monitoring AWS Services Using CloudWatch and SNS*
- *Chapter 9, Centralizing Logs for Analysis*
- *Chapter 10, Centralizing Cloud Backup Solution*
- *Chapter 11, AWS Disaster Recovery Solutions*
- *Chapter 12, AWS Tips and Tricks*

8
Monitoring AWS Services Using CloudWatch and SNS

Amazon CloudWatch is a monitoring service used to monitor your resources and applications running in **Amazon Web Services (AWS)**. CloudWatch can monitor things such as **Elastic Compute Cloud (EC2)** instances, **Elastic Block Store (EBS)** volumes, **Relational Database Service (RDS)** databases, and **Simple Queue Service (SQS)** queues.

To get a complete list of services that publish CloudWatch metrics, please refer to the following link:

```
https://docs.aws.amazon.com/AmazonCloudWatch/latest/
monitoring/aws-services-cloudwatch-metrics.html
```

The chapter will start by setting up CloudWatch monitoring. We will further examine how to push custom metrics—such as swap, network, and disk space utilization—to CloudWatch. Then, we will look at SNS and how it's tightly coupled with CloudWatch to provide you with a seamless notification experience. We will further tighten our monitoring by looking at how to use CloudWatch Events to search for events—for example, EC2 instance state change (stop and start). Finally, we explore newly emerging fields such as ChatOps, where we integrate AWS services such as **Simple Notification Service (SNS)** to Slack using AWS Lambda.

In this chapter, we're going to cover the following main topics:

- CloudWatch monitoring

- Monitoring custom metrics using CloudWatch

- Introduction to SNS

- Introduction to CloudWatch Events

- Automating alarm notification using email and Slack channel

Technical requirements

To gain the most from this chapter, you should have a basic knowledge and awareness of monitoring and notification.

Check out the following link to see the code in action:

`https://bit.ly/3rFoFMj`

CloudWatch monitoring

Let's take a look at some of the metrics published by CloudWatch. To view those metrics, go to the EC2 instance **Uniform Resource Locator (URL)** at `https://us-west-2.console.aws.amazon.com/ec2/v2/home?region=us-west-2#Instances`, and then select one of the instances (created during *Chapter 4, Scalable Compute Capacity in the Cloud via EC2*) and click on **Monitoring**. In this case, we see metrics sent by EC2 to CloudWatch. These are host-level metrics that consist of the following:

- CPU utilization, CPU credit usage, and balance

- Network packets/data in and out

- Disk read/write

- Status check (instance/system)

We can see some of these metrics (for example, CPU utilization, disk read/write, and network packets) in the following screenshot:

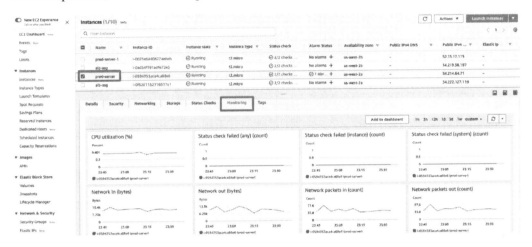

Figure 8.1 – AWS CloudWatch dashboard for EC2 instance

By default, EC2 monitoring takes 5 minutes, but if you enable **Detailed Monitoring**, you will get data in 1 minute. Enabling detailed monitoring will incur an extra charge.

Memory utilization, free disk space, and process count are all custom metrics. An EC2 service is a **virtual machine (VM)** emulating physical hardware, such as CPU, disk, and **random-access memory (RAM)**. The operating system controls how memory is allocated, so it's not possible to determine the memory utilization by looking at virtual hardware. To get these metrics, we need to run something on the operating system to extract these metrics and send them to CloudWatch, and we can do that with the help of the CloudWatch agent.

Monitoring custom metrics using CloudWatch

This section will show how to install the CloudWatch agent to monitor custom metrics (memory and disk utilization). To achieve this, we need to follow a series of steps.

Downloading and installing the CloudWatch agent

Firstly, we need to download and install the CloudWatch agent package. To do so, we perform the following steps:

1. Log in to the EC2 instance by running the following command with your details filled in:

   ```
   ssh -i vpc-prod.pem ec2-user@<server public ip>
   ```

2. Download the CloudWatch agent with the following command:

   ```
   wget https://s3.amazonaws.com/amazoncloudwatch-agent/
   amazon_linux/amd64/latest/amazon-cloudwatch-agent.rpm
   ```

3. Install the CloudWatch agent using the following command:

   ```
   sudo rpm -ivh amazon-cloudwatch-agent.rpm
   Preparing...                              ##################
   ############# [100%]
   create group cwagent, result: 0
   create user cwagent, result: 0
   Updating / installing...
      1:amazon-cloudwatch-
   agent-1.247345.############################### [100%]
   ```

4. Install the `collectd` **RPM Package Manager** (**RPM**) if you want to collect custom metrics from your application. `collectd` is a daemon that is used to collect application and system performance metrics on a periodic basis. Here is the code to install it:

   ```
   sudo yum -y install collectd
   ```

At this point, we have all the necessary RPM installed. We will configure the **Identity and Access Management** (**IAM**) role in the next step, giving the CloudWatch agent the required permission to write to CloudWatch.

Creating an IAM role used by CloudWatch agent

Next, we need to create an IAM role that will give the CloudWatch agent the necessary permissions to write metrics to CloudWatch. To do so, we perform the following steps:

1. Go to the IAM console at `https://console.aws.amazon.com/iam/home#/home`. In the navigation bar, click on **Roles** and then **Create role**.

2. Under **Select type of trusted entity**, make sure **AWS service** is selected. For **Common use cases**, we choose **EC2**. Then, click on **Next: Permissions**, as illustrated in the following screenshot:

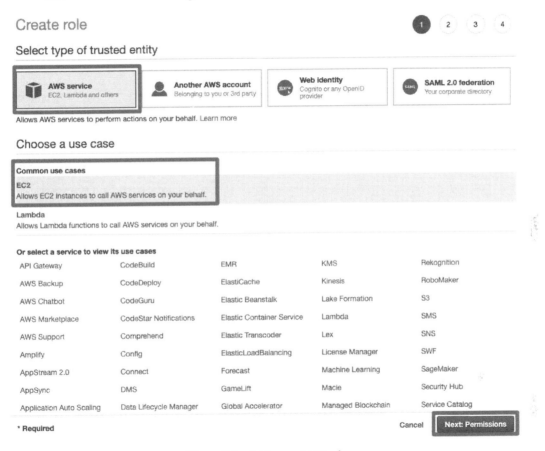

Figure 8.2 – Setting up IAM role

3. In the search bar, search for `CloudWatchAgentServerPolicy` and click on **Next: Tags**, as illustrated in the following screenshot:

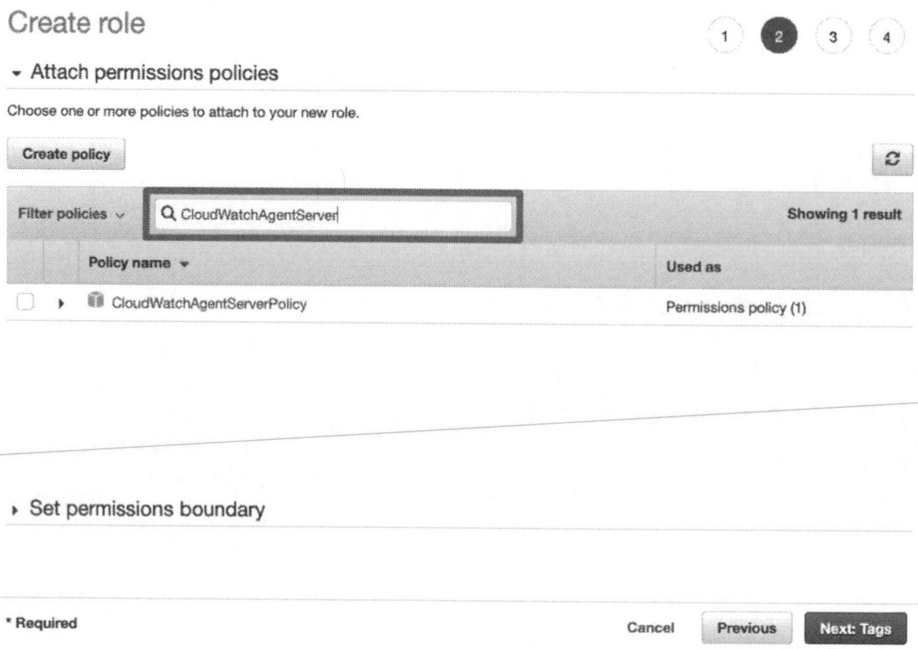

Figure 8.3 – Attaching policy to IAM role

4. Leave the page as default and click on **Next: Review**, as illustrated in the following screenshot:

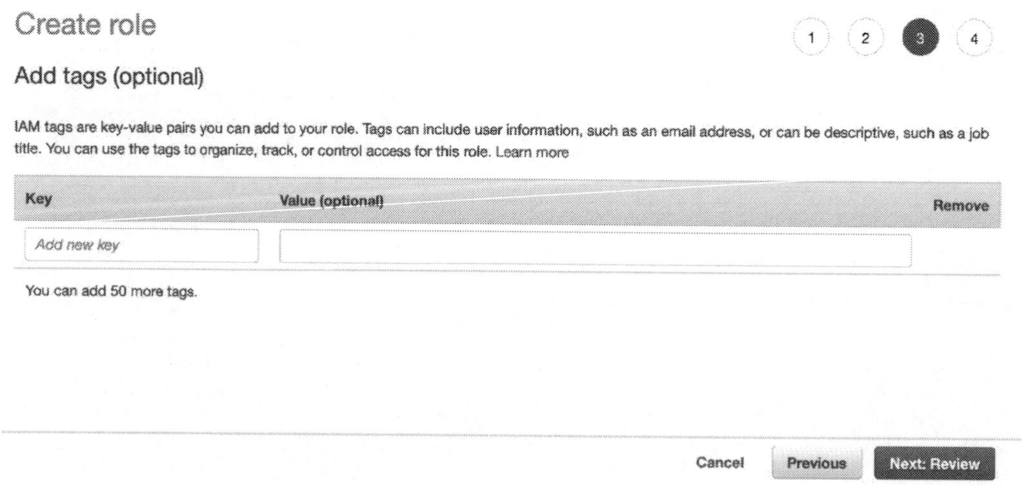

Figure 8.4 – Setting up tags is an optional for an IAM role

5. Give your role some meaningful name (for example, `CloudWatchAgentRole`) and click on **Create role**, as illustrated in the following screenshot:

Create role
1
2
3
4
Review
Provide the required information below and review this role before you create it.
Role name*
CloudWatchAgentRole
Use alphanumeric and '+=,.@-_' characters. Maximum 64 characters.
Role description
Allows EC2 instances to call AWS services on your behalf.
Maximum 1000 characters. Use alphanumeric and '+=,.@-_' characters.
Trusted entities
AWS service: ec2.amazonaws.com
Policies
Policies not attached
Permissions boundary
Permissions boundary is not set
No tags were added.
* Required
Cancel
Previous
Create role

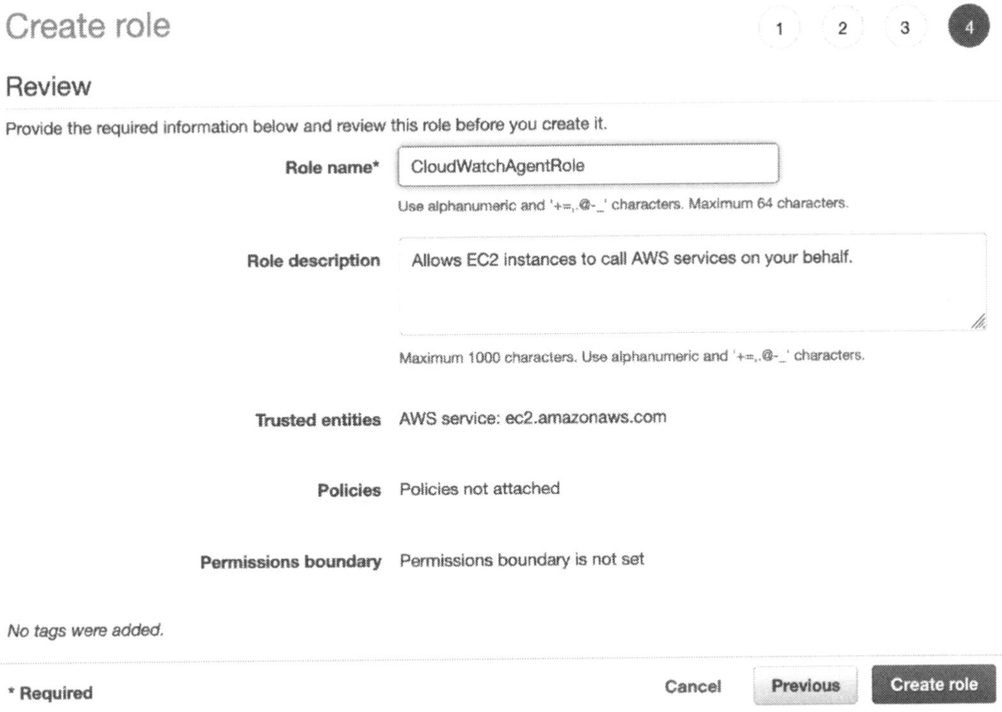

Figure 8.5 – Creating an IAM role

6. Once the IAM role is created, attach it to the instance. To do that, go back to the EC2 console at `https://us-west-2.console.aws.amazon.com/ec2/v2/home`, select the instance (for example, `prod-server`), click on **Actions**, and then, under **Instance settings**, click on **Modify IAM role**, as illustrated in the following screenshot:

Instances (1/10)
Actions
Launch instances
Attach to Auto Scaling Group
Modify IAM role
Change termination protection
Change shutdown behavior
Edit user data
Change credit specification
View details
Connect
Create template from instance
Launch more like this
Manage tags
Instance state
Instance settings
Networking
Image
Monitoring
Name
Instance ID
Instance state
Instance type
Status check
PacktPub
prod-server-1
alb-asg
prod-server
Running
t2.micro

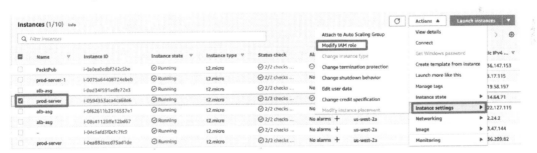

Figure 8.6 – Selecting an IAM role for an EC2 instance

7. From the IAM role dropdown, select `CloudWatchAgentRole` as created in *Step 5* and click on **Save**, as illustrated in the following screenshot:

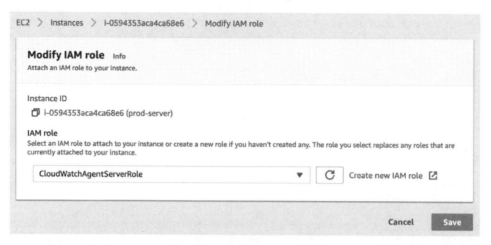

Figure 8.7 – Attaching an IAM role

At this point, we have the necessary IAM role attached to the EC2 instance. In the next step, we will start the CloudWatch agent, which will start pushing metrics to CloudWatch.

Running the CloudWatch agent on your server

In the next step, we need to create an agent configuration file that specifies the metrics you want to push to CloudWatch from your EC2 instance. To do that, you need to run an `amazon-cloudwatch-agent-config-wizard` wizard, as shown here:

1. In the following wizard, you need to choose the default option based on your requirement (for example, `On which OS are you planning to use the agent?`). In this case, as we are running the agent on Linux, you need to choose the default option `1`. The only time you should avoid choosing the default option is for `Which default metrics config do you want?`. In this case, choose `3. Advanced` as we need metrics such as memory, disk space, and swap memory, which are only available under the **Advanced** option). The code for this process is illustrated in the following code block:

```
$ sudo /opt/aws/amazon-cloudwatch-agent/bin/amazon-
cloudwatch-agent-config-wizard

==============================================================
====
= Welcome to the AWS CloudWatch Agent Configuration
Manager =
```

```
================================================================
====
On which OS are you planning to use the agent?
1. linux
2. windows
default choice: [1]:
1
Trying to fetch the default region based on ec2
metadata...
Are you using EC2 or On-Premises hosts?
1. EC2
2. On-Premises
default choice: [1]:
1
Which user are you planning to run the agent?
1. root
2. cwagent
3. others
default choice: [1]:

Do you want to turn on StatsD daemon?
1. yes
2. no
default choice: [1]:

Which port do you want StatsD daemon to listen to?
default choice: [8125]

What is the collect interval for StatsD daemon?
1. 10s
2. 30s
3. 60s
default choice: [1]:

What is the aggregation interval for metrics collected by
StatsD daemon?
1. Do not aggregate
```

```
2. 10s
3. 30s
4. 60s
default choice: [4]:


Do you want to monitor metrics from CollectD?
1. yes
2. no
default choice: [1]:


Do you want to monitor any host metrics? e.g. CPU,
memory, etc.
1. yes
2. no
default choice: [1]:


Do you want to monitor cpu metrics per core? Additional
CloudWatch charges may apply.
1. yes
2. no
default choice: [1]:


Do you want to add ec2 dimensions (ImageId, InstanceId,
InstanceType, AutoScalingGroupName) into all of your
metrics if the info is available?
1. yes
2. no
default choice: [1]:


Would you like to collect your metrics at high resolution
(sub-minute resolution)? This enables sub-minute
resolution for all metrics, but you can customize for
specific metrics in the output json file.
1. 1s
2. 10s
3. 30s
4. 60s
```

```
default choice: [4]:


Which default metrics config do you want?
1. Basic
2. Standard
3. Advanced
4. None
default choice: [1]:
3  <-----------------------------------------------------
----
Current config as follows:
{
    "agent": {
        "metrics_collection_interval": 60,
        "run_as_user": "root"
    },
            "swap": {
                "measurement": [
                    "swap_used_percent"
                ],
                "metrics_collection_interval": 60
            }
        }
    }
}
```

Are you satisfied with the above config? Note: it can be manually customized after the wizard completes to add additional items.

```
1. yes
2. no
default choice: [1]:
1
```

Do you have any existing CloudWatch Log Agent (http://docs.aws.amazon.com/AmazonCloudWatch/latest/logs/AgentReference.html) configuration file to import for migration?

```
1. yes
```

```
2. no
default choice: [2]:


Do you want to monitor any log files?
1. yes
2. no
default choice: [1]:
2
Saved config file to /opt/aws/amazon-cloudwatch-agent/
bin/config.json successfully.
Current config as follows:
{
    "agent": {
        "metrics_collection_interval": 60,
        "run_as_user": "root"
    },
            "swap": {
                "measurement": [
                    "swap_used_percent"
                ],
                "metrics_collection_interval": 60
            }
        }
    }
}
Please check the above content of the config.
The config file is also located at /opt/aws/amazon-
cloudwatch-agent/bin/config.json.
Edit it manually if needed.
Do you want to store the config in the SSM parameter
store?
1. yes
2. no
default choice: [1]:
2
Program exits now.
```

2. To validate and start the CloudWatch agent, run the following command:

```
$ sudo /opt/aws/amazon-cloudwatch-agent/bin/amazon-
cloudwatch-agent-ctl -a fetch-config -m ec2 -c file:/opt/
aws/amazon-cloudwatch-agent/bin/config.json -s
```

```
/opt/aws/amazon-cloudwatch-agent/bin/config-downloader
--output-dir /opt/aws/amazon-cloudwatch-agent/etc/
amazon-cloudwatch-agent.d --download-source file:/opt/
aws/amazon-cloudwatch-agent/bin/config.json --mode ec2
--config /opt/aws/amazon-cloudwatch-agent/etc/common-
config.toml --multi-config default
```

```
Successfully fetched the config and saved in /opt/aws/
amazon-cloudwatch-agent/etc/amazon-cloudwatch-agent.d/
file_config.json.tmp
```

```
Start configuration validation...
```

```
/opt/aws/amazon-cloudwatch-agent/bin/config-translator
--input /opt/aws/amazon-cloudwatch-agent/etc/amazon-
cloudwatch-agent.json --input-dir /opt/aws/amazon-
cloudwatch-agent/etc/amazon-cloudwatch-agent.d --output /
opt/aws/amazon-cloudwatch-agent/etc/amazon-cloudwatch-
agent.toml --mode ec2 --config /opt/aws/amazon-
cloudwatch-agent/etc/common-config.toml --multi-config
default
```

```
2020/09/14 00:22:42 Reading json config file path: /
opt/aws/amazon-cloudwatch-agent/etc/amazon-cloudwatch-
agent.d/file_config.json.tmp ...
```

```
Valid Json input schema.
```

```
I! Detecting runasuser...
```

```
No csm configuration found.
```

```
No log configuration found.
```

```
Configuration validation first phase succeeded
```

```
/opt/aws/amazon-cloudwatch-agent/bin/amazon-cloudwatch-
agent -schematest -config /opt/aws/amazon-cloudwatch-
agent/etc/amazon-cloudwatch-agent.toml
```

```
Configuration validation second phase succeeded
```

```
Configuration validation succeeded
```

```
amazon-cloudwatch-agent start/running, process 31816
```

Once the wizard creation is complete, it will create a configuration file and store it in `/opt/aws/amazon-cloudwatch-agent/bin/config.json`.

3. To verify if the CloudWatch agent has been started successfully, run the following command:

```
# ps aux|grep -i amazon-cloudwatch-agent
root      31816  0.2  3.6 759712 37276 ?          Ssl
00:22   0:00 /opt/aws/amazon-cloudwatch-agent/bin/amazon-
cloudwatch-agent -config /opt/aws/amazon-cloudwatch-
agent/etc/amazon-cloudwatch-agent.toml -envconfig /opt/
aws/amazon-cloudwatch-agent/etc/env-config.json -pidfile
/opt/aws/amazon-cloudwatch-agent/var/amazon-cloudwatch-
agent.pid
```

4. In order to view these custom metrics, go back to the CloudWatch console at `https://us-west-2.console.aws.amazon.com/cloudwatch/home` and click on **Metrics**. You will now see **CWAgent** under **Custom Namespaces**, as illustrated in the following screenshot:

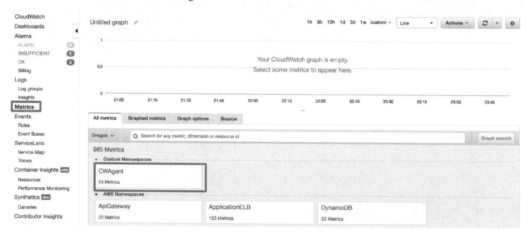

Figure 8.8 – CloudWatch metrics

5. Click on **CWAgent**, and then on the next screen, click on any metric (for example, **ImageId, InstanceId, InstanceType**), as illustrated in the following screenshot:

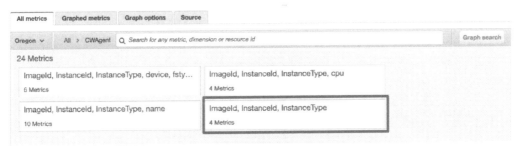

Figure 8.9 – CloudWatch custom metrics

6. You will see metrics such as mem_used_percent and swap_used_percent that were not displayed earlier, as illustrated in the following screenshot:

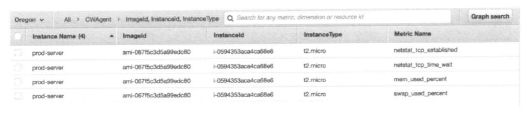

Figure 8.10 – CloudWatch custom metrics such as memory and network metrics

7. If you want to stop the CloudWatch agent, run the following code:

```
sudo /opt/aws/amazon-cloudwatch-agent/bin/amazon-
cloudwatch-agent-ctl -m ec2 -a stop
amazon-cloudwatch-agent stop/waiting
```

We have the CloudWatch agent up at this stage, and it starts pushing custom metrics (for example, memory and disk space) to CloudWatch. In the next section, we will begin exploring SNS, which will automate the sending of notifications.

Introduction to SNS

SNS is a web service that helps you automate sending an email or text message notifications based on events (for example, stopping an EC2 instance or deleting a **Simple Storage Service (S3)** bucket) that happen in your AWS account. It's a fully managed **publish/subscribe (pub/sub)** messaging service that lets you send messages to many recipients at once, using topics.

AWS SNS has the following two major components:

- **Publisher (producers)**: The publisher's responsibility is to produce and send a message to the topic, which acts as a logical access point.

- **Subscriber (consumers)**: The consumer consumes or receives the message or notification over one of the supported protocols (for example, email, SNS, SQS, or Lambda) when they are subscribed to the topic.

Now, you understand what SNS is. To get started with SNS, you need to follow this series of steps:

1. Go to the SNS console at `https://us-west-2.console.aws.amazon.com/sns/v3/home` and click on **Topics** and then **Create topic**, as illustrated in the following screenshot:

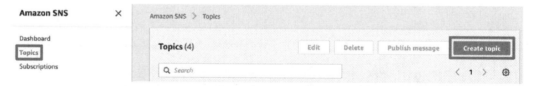

Figure 8.11 – AWS SNS

2. In the **Create topic** section, fill in the following details:

    - **Name**: Give your topic some meaningful name (for example, `my-topic`).

    - **Display name**: If you want to use this topic with an SMS subscription, enter a display name; its first 10 characters will be displayed in an SMS message.

Click on **Create topic**, as illustrated in the following screenshot:

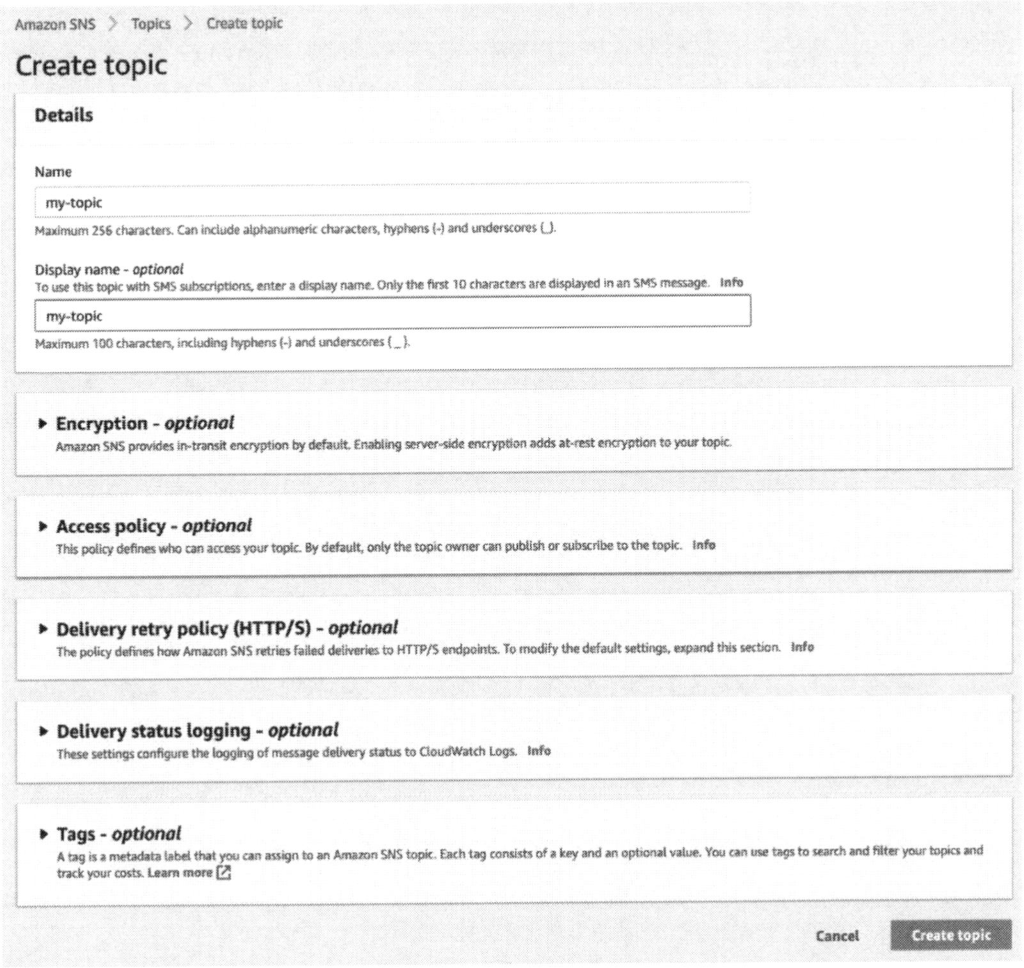

Figure 8.12 – Creating SNS topic

3. Once the topic is created, you need to create a subscription. To do this, click on **Create subscription**, as illustrated in the following screenshot:

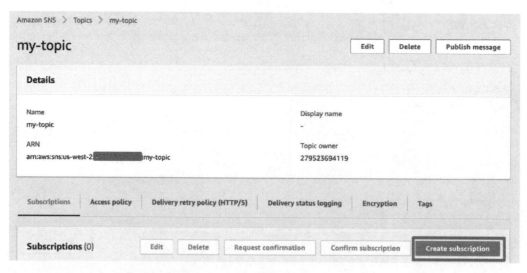

Figure 8.13 – Creating SNS topic subscription

4. In the **Create subscription** dialog box, select the protocol (for example, **Email**) and enter the email ID for where you want to deliver this email, then click on **Create subscription**, as illustrated in the following screenshot:

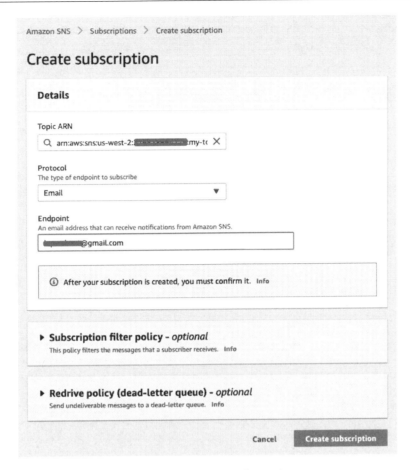

Figure 8.14 – Creating subscription

5. You will receive an email in your inbox whereby you need to **Confirm subscription**, as illustrated in the following screenshot:

Figure 8.15 – Confirming topic notification

Now, we have created the SNS topic. In the next section, we will see how to integrate it with CloudWatch Events to get the instance state change notification.

Introduction to CloudWatch Events

AWS CloudWatch Events are similar to alarms but instead of configuring alarms or thresholds, they match event patterns. These event patterns can relate to EC2 state change, a file upload to an S3 bucket, **Key Management Service (KMS)** key deletion, and so on. You can create CloudWatch Events rules that match the event pattern and take actions in response to those patterns. The following events are some of those supported by CloudWatch Events:

- EC2 state change

- **Application programming interface (API)** call reported by CloudTrail

CloudWatch Events provide a near-real-time stream of system events, and to configure it, we need to follow this series of steps:

1. Go back to the CloudWatch console at `https://us-west-2.console.aws.amazon.com/cloudwatch/home`, then click on **Rules** and **Create rule**, as illustrated in the following screenshot:

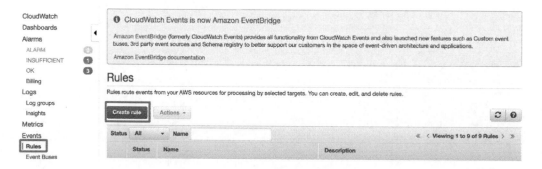

Figure 8.16 – AWS CloudWatch Events

CloudWatch Events rules are used to trigger events emitted by the AWS service—in this case, EC2. Configure the rule as follows:

- **Service Name**: From the dropdown, choose **EC2**.

- **Event Type**: From the dropdown, choose **EC2 Instance State-change Notification**.

- **Targets**: Choose the SNS topic (for example, **my-topic** we created in the earlier chapter).

Click on **Configure details**.

The process is illustrated in the following screenshot:

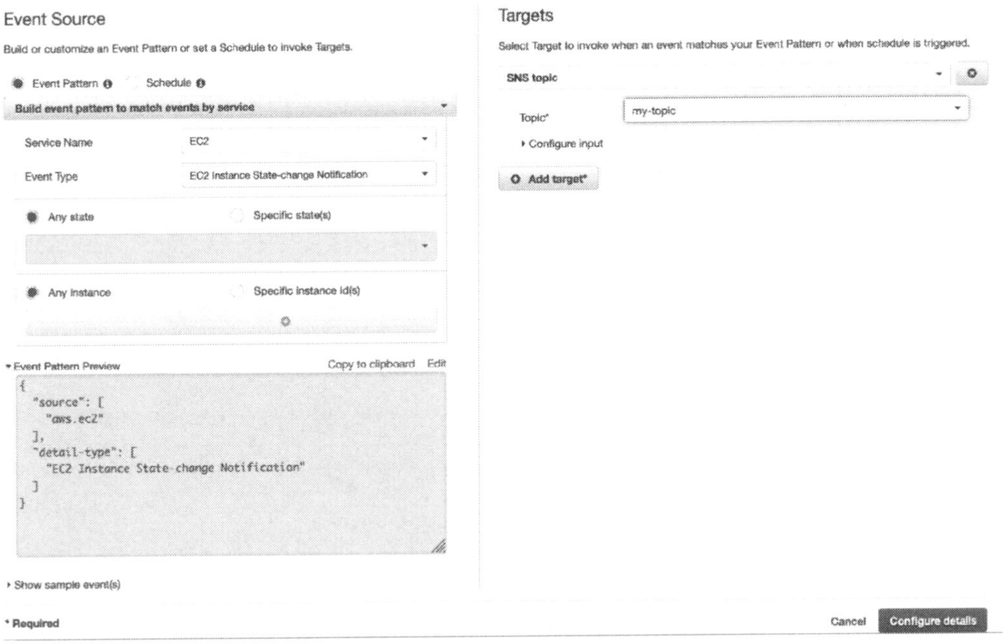

Figure 8.17 – CloudWatch Events configuration

2. Under **Configure rule details**, fill in the following details:

    - **Name**: Give your rule some meaningful name (for example, `ec2-state-change`).

    - **Description**: Give it some meaningful description (for example, `ec2 instance state change notification`).

    Click on **Create rule**.

    The process is illustrated in the following screenshot:

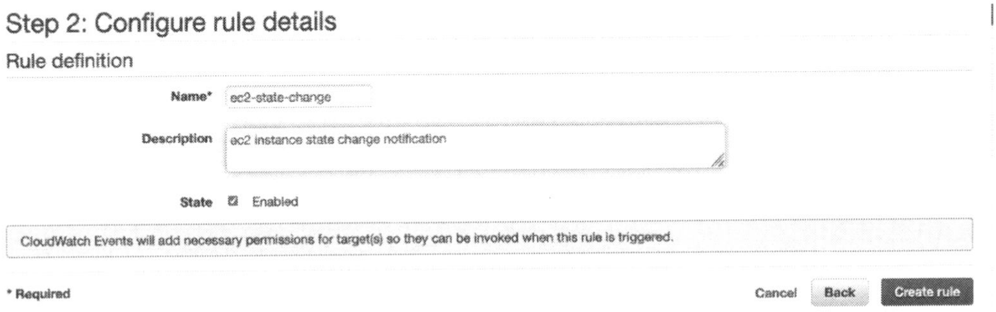

Figure 8.18 – CloudWatch Events rules

3. In order to test it, go back to the EC2 console at `https://us-west-2.console.aws.amazon.com/ec2/v2/home` and select the instance (for example, **prod-server**). Then, under **Actions**, go to **Instance state** and then **Stop instance**, as illustrated in the following screenshot:

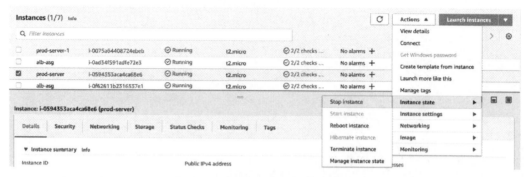

Figure 8.19 – Stopping EC2 instance

4. In your mailbox, you will receive a notification like this:

Figure 8.20 – SNS notification

AWS SNS is one of the critical components of your infrastructure monitoring as it will help to receive any alert in the form of an email, an SMS message, and more, so that you take action based on the notification. In the next section, we will see how to integrate it with CloudWatch Events to notify us if the EC2 instance state changes—for example, stop, start, reboot, and so on.

Automating alarm notification using email and a Slack channel

So far, we have discussed CloudWatch for monitoring and SNS for alerting. But nowadays, a newly emerging field is ChatOps, whereby your DevOps/System team can receive a notification on a collaboration platform such as Slack. Unfortunately, SNS doesn't support out-of-the-box Slack integration, so we need to use AWS Lambda for that.

The way the whole integration works is that CloudWatch will trigger an alarm that sends messages to SNS topics when certain events occur—in this case, when CPU utilization goes beyond 40%. A Lambda function will get invoked in response to SNS, and it will then call the Slack API to post the message to the Slack channel.

Configuring Slack

To configure Webhooks in Slack for CloudWatch Alarms, we perform the following steps:

1. As a first step, we need to create a Slack app. To do that, go to this URL at `https://api.slack.com/apps/new` and fill in the following details:

   - **App Name**: Give your app some meaningful name (for example, `cloudwatch-sns-to-slack-integration`).

   - **Development Slack Workspace**: Select your Slack workspace.

   Click on **Create App**, as illustrated in the following screenshot:

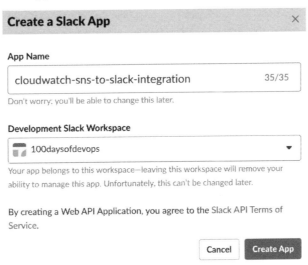

Figure 8.21 – Creating a Slack app

2. Now, click on **Incoming Webhooks**, as illustrated in the following screenshot:

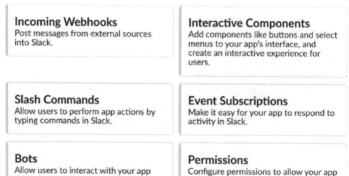

Figure 8.22 – Slack Incoming Webhooks

3. Set **Activate Incoming Webhooks** to **On**, as illustrated in the following screenshot:

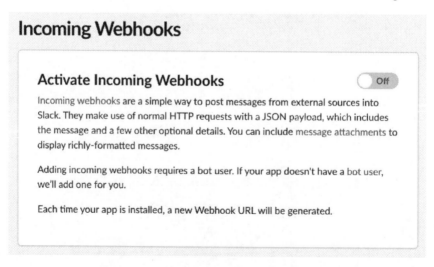

Figure 8.23 – Configuring Incoming Webhooks

4. Scroll down and click on **Add New Webhook to Workspace**, as illustrated in the following screenshot:

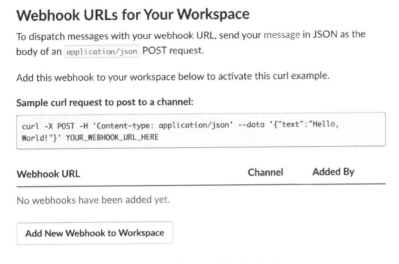

Figure 8.24 – Webhook URL for Workspace

5. Choose the channel where the message will be sent (for example, the **slacktest** channel in my case) and click on **Allow**, as illustrated in the following screenshot:

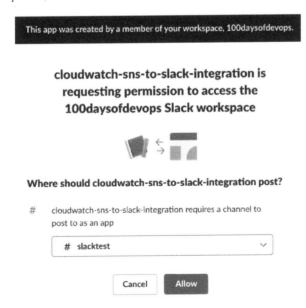

Figure 8.25 – Choosing the Slack channel to deliver notification

6. Please make a note of the Webhook URL, as shown in the following screenshot:

Webhook URL	Channel	Added By
https://hooks.slack.com/services/TP [Copy]	#slacktest	Prashant Lakhera Sep 15, 2020

Figure 8.26 – Slack Webhook URL

We have created the Slack-incoming Webhook, an endpoint where we can post a message to the Slack channel. In the next step, we will configure CloudWatch and integrate it with SNS.

Configuring CloudWatch

In this step, we will configure CloudWatch and integrate it with SNS. In the CloudWatch console, we can define the threshold hold—for example, 40%—that is responsible for triggering an SNS notification once that limit is reached. To configure that, we need to follow this series of steps:

1. Go to the EC2 console at `https://us-west-2.console.aws.amazon.com/ec2/v2/home` and select the instance where you want to configure the CloudWatch alarm, then copy its instance ID (for example, **i-0594353aca4ca68e6**), as illustrated in the following screenshot:

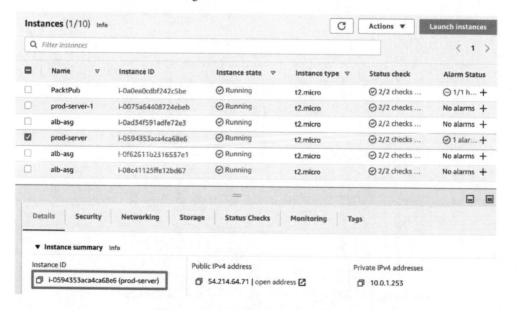

Figure 8.27 – Configuring CloudWatch

2. Go to the CloudWatch console at `https://us-west-2.console.aws.amazon.com/cloudwatch`, click on **Metrics** and then on **EC2**, as illustrated in the following screenshot:

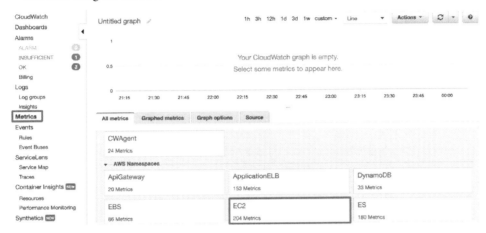

Figure 8.28 – CloudWatch metrics

3. Click on **Per-Instance Metrics**, as illustrated in the following screenshot. This is going to display all the metrics (CPU, disk, **input/output (I/O)**) for the instances:

Figure 8.29 – CloudWatch per-instance metrics

4. In the search bar, paste the instance ID (we copied this in *Step 1*) and check the **CPUUtilization** metric, as illustrated in the following screenshot:

Figure 8.30 – CloudWatch CPUUtilization metric

5. Click on **Graphed metrics** and then the bell icon, as shown in the following screenshot:

Figure 8.31 – Creating CloudWatch notification

6. In the next screen, keep all the values as default but change the threshold to **40**, and then click on **Next**, as illustrated in the following screenshot:

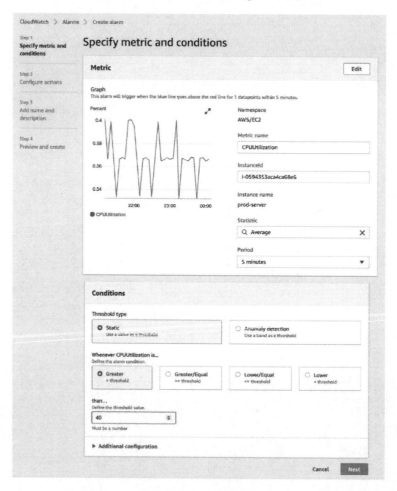

Figure 8.32 – Defining CloudWatch threshold

7. Under **Select an SNS topic**, choose **Create new topic** and fill in the following details:

    - **Create new topic**: Give your topic some meaningful name (for example, `sns-to-slack`).

    - **Email endpoints that will receive the notification**: The email ID where you want to receive the notification.

    Click **Create topic** and then click **Next**, as illustrated in the following screenshot:

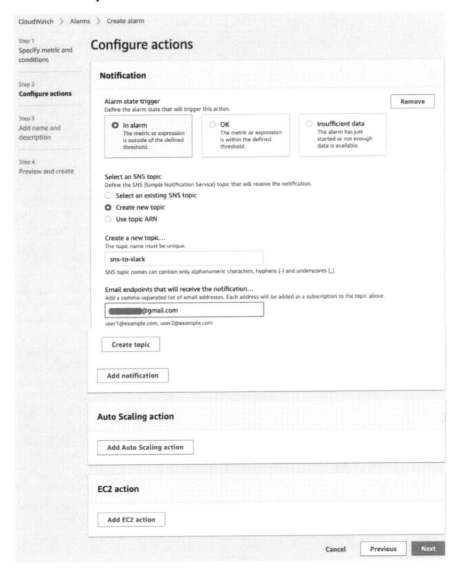

Figure 8.33 – Creating SNS topic

8. Add a name and description to your CloudWatch alert, as follows:

    - **Alarm name**: Give some meaningful name to your alarm (for example, `High-cpu-slack-alert`).

    - **Alarm description – optional**: Add some meaningful description to your alarm (for example, `Slack Alert When CPU Utilization goes more than 40 % to slacktest channel`).

    Click **Next**.

    The process is illustrated in the following screenshot:

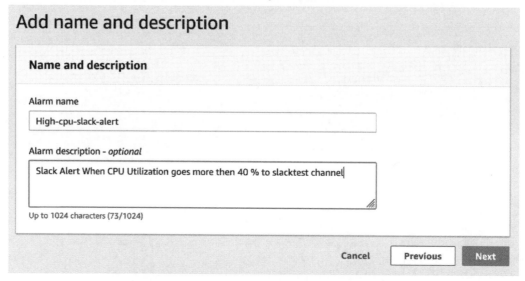

Figure 8.34 – Adding name and description to SNS topic

9. Under the **Preview and create** configuration page review your configuration, and then click on **Create alarm**, as illustrated in the following screenshot:

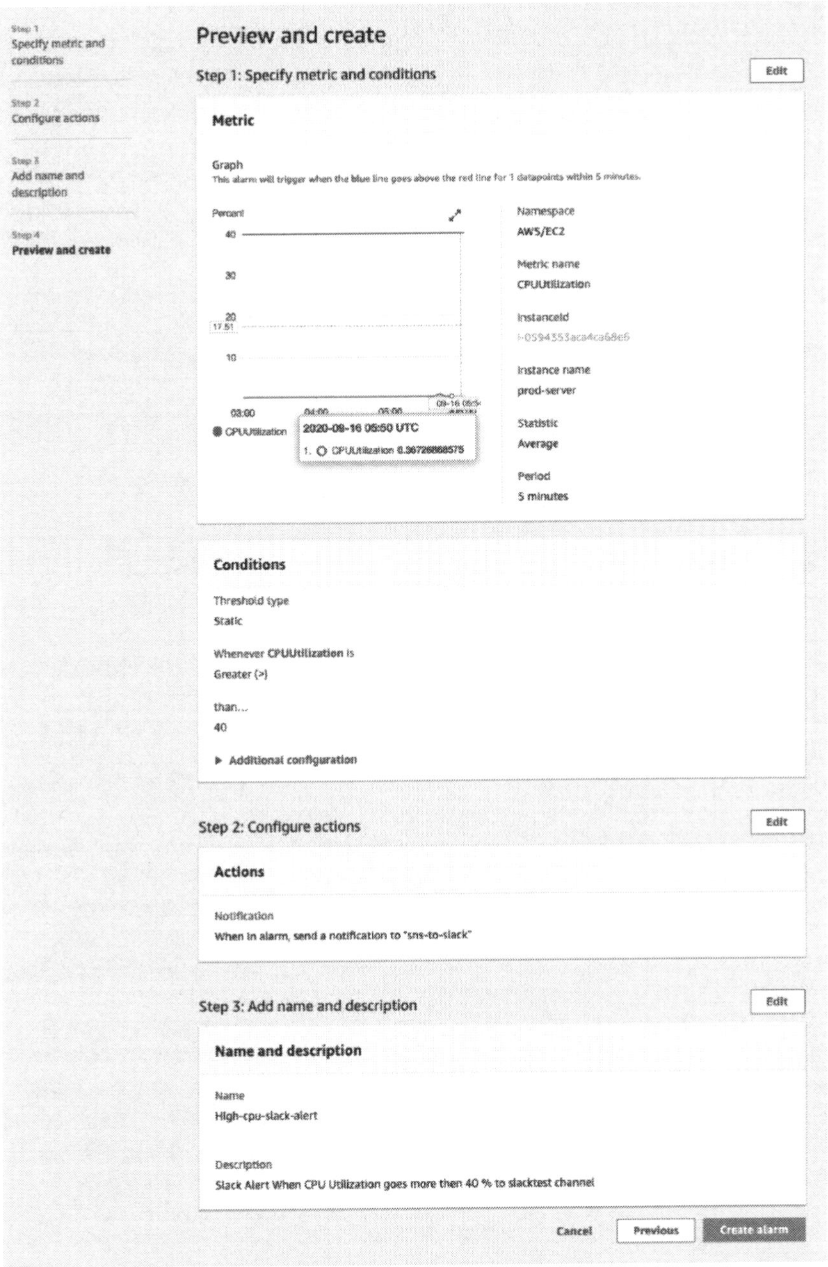

Figure 8.35 – Review and create alarm

So far, we have configured a Slack-incoming Webhook and integrated CloudWatch with SNS. As SNS doesn't provide any out-of-the-box Slack integration, we need to use an AWS-provided Lambda function.

Creating a Lambda function

To create a Lambda function that provides integration between SNS and Slack, we need to follow this series of steps:

1. Go back to the Lambda console `https://us-west-2.console.aws.amazon.com/lambda/home` and click on **Create function**, as illustrated in the following screenshot:

Figure 8.36 – Lambda function

2. Under **Create function**, select **Author from scratch** and then fill in the following details:

    - **Function name**: Give your function some meaningful name (for example, `sns-to-slack-function`).

    - **Runtime**: Choose **Python 3.8**.

    Click on **Create function**.

    The process is illustrated in the following screenshot:

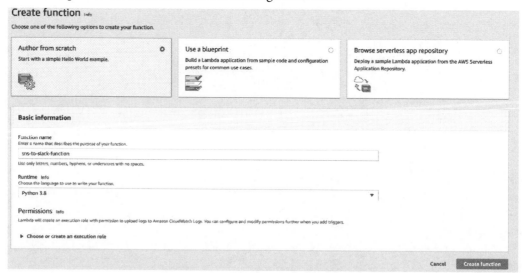

Figure 8.37 – Create Lambda function

3. Now, under the Lambda console (`https://aws.amazon.com/ premiumsupport/knowledge-center/sns-lambda-webhooks-chime- slack-teams/`), copy and paste the code provided by AWS after modifying a few parameters. These modified parameters are as follows:

- `url`: This is the Webhook URL we created in *Step 6 (Configuring Slack)*.

- `channel`: The Slack channel where we want to send the message.

You can see an example of Lambda code being added in the following screenshot:

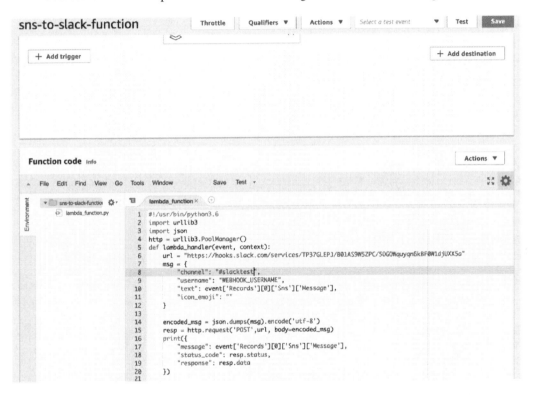

Figure 8.38 – Adding Lambda code

4.   Now, click on **Add trigger**, as illustrated in the following screenshot:

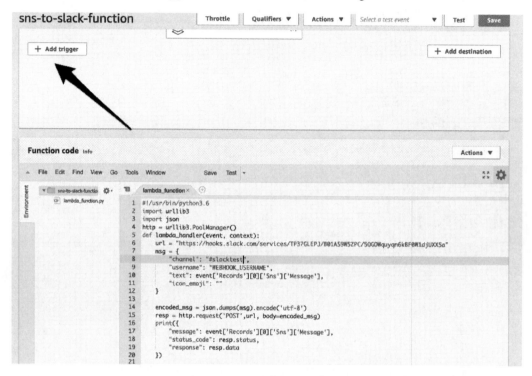

Figure 8.39 – Adding Lambda trigger

5.   Under **Add trigger** select **SNS**, and for **SNS topic**, select the SNS topic we created under *step 7* (in the *Configuring CloudWatch* section):

Figure 8.40 – Adding SNS Lambda trigger

6.   Click on **Save**, as illustrated in the following screenshot:

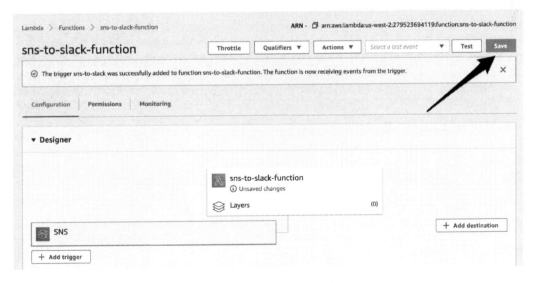

Figure 8.41 – Save your Lambda function

At this stage, we have all the components (CloudWatch, SNS, Lambda, and Slack) integrated. In the next step, we will test this full integration by stressing our instance, by invoking a bunch of dd commands.

Testing the integration

To test this integration, we first need to log in to the EC2 instance. The invocation of multiple dd commands increases CPU utilization beyond 40%. This will invoke the CloudWatch alarm, which in turn sends an SNS notification. SNS triggers an event to the Lambda function, which will then send a notification to Slack.

To test the integration, we need to follow these steps:

1. Log in to the instance where we set up the CloudWatch alarm, as follows:

```
ssh -i <key name> ubuntu@<public ip>
```

2. Try to generate some load by executing the dd command multiple times, like this:

```
ubuntu@ip-172-31-23-196:~$ dd if=/dev/zero of=/dev/null &
[6] 21955
ubuntu@ip-172-31-23-196:~$ dd if=/dev/zero of=/dev/null &
[7] 21956
ubuntu@ip-172-31-23-196:~$ dd if=/dev/zero of=/dev/null &
[8] 21957
ubuntu@ip-172-31-23-196:~$ dd if=/dev/zero of=/dev/null &
[9] 21958
ubuntu@ip-172-31-23-196:~$ dd if=/dev/zero of=/dev/null &
[10] 21959
```

3. You will see an alarm like this, under the Slack channel:

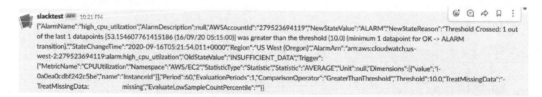

Figure 8.42 – Slack notification when alarm triggered

In this section, we learned how to integrate AWS services with Slack. A Slack notification is a great way to notify your team in the case there's an incident and resolve issues quickly.

Summary

Monitoring is always a critical part of any infrastructure. With a dynamic environment such as AWS, CloudWatch provides lots of features to monitor your infrastructure, but it's not a replacement of full-fledged monitoring solutions such as Nagios or Prometheus.

In this chapter, we have learned how to set up CloudWatch and the default metrics (CPU, disk, and network) we can monitor using it. In most production scenarios, we need to monitor additional metrics such as memory, and we have learned how to push these additional custom metrics to CloudWatch. We learned that with monitoring, we need an alerting service that will notify us in the case of issues, and to solve that, AWS provides a service called SNS. We further integrated SNS with CloudWatch Events to provide near-real-time monitoring. Finally, we looked at how we integrate SNS with Slack via Lambda to enhance our notification capabilities further.

In the next chapter, we will look at AWS's centralized log monitoring solution known as CloudWatch Logs. Logs are the first place where we look in the case of any system, performance, or security issue, but nowadays, applications are generating **terabytes** (**TB**) to **petabytes** (**PB**) of data. We need some solution through which we can quickly search inside these logs, and for that, AWS provides a solution called AWS Elasticsearch. We will learn how to configure it, and then, to analyze these logs, we will use a solution such as Kibana.

9
Centralizing Logs for Analysis

Log analysis is a critical piece of any infrastructure. The log is the first place that we usually start debugging. In a dynamic environment such as the cloud, sometimes log management becomes expensive as, because of the dynamic nature of the cloud, instances can come and go at any time if placed under an autoscaling group. The other factor that we need to bear in mind is the storage cost as these instances produce large files, which will increase your storage cost.

This chapter will start by looking at how to set up the CloudWatch agent, a centralized place to store all the logs. As we are dealing with a large amount of data in the cloud environment, we need someplace where we can store it for a quicker search, and for that purpose, we will use Amazon Elasticsearch. Finally, we will need some visualization tools to view that data, and for this we will use Kibana.

In this chapter, we are going to cover the following main topics:

- Why do we need log management?
- Setting up the CloudWatch agent
- Setting up AWS Elasticsearch and Kibana

Technical requirements

To gain the most from this chapter, you should have a basic knowledge and awareness of any logging solution. You should be familiar with terms such as system and application logs.

Check out the following link to see the Code in Action video:

```
https://bit.ly/2WVOt8N
```

Why do we need log management?

The log is the first place to check on how your system is behaving. We generally enable logging in our application to debug issues related to application, performance, and even security issues. Now the challenge is that each log has its own format. For example, the format of `/var/log/messages` that store system messages is completely different from `/var/log/secure`, which stores all security-related information. Traditionally, we use tools such as `grep`, `sed`, and `awk` to parse information inside these files, but that is not fool proof or scalable solution. In the cloud, where we could be dealing with a terabyte or even petabyte of data, these tools will not work because of its inherent limitation of dealing with a limited set of data. To overcome these challenges and attain effective log management, AWS provides its own set of tools to push data and analyze it, which is the topic of this chapter. We will look at some of the solutions provided by AWS, such as the following:

- **CloudWatch agent**: Pushes data to centralized locations, such as CloudWatch Logs.

- **Elasticsearch**: A log analytic solution that provides a full-text search capability.

- **Kibana**: Provides a visualization dashboard for Elasticsearch.

Log management is an important topic as, at the time of writing, we need a single screen to check why the application is not working as expected. Rather than using the traditional approach (`grep`, `sed`, and `awk`), we can use cloud-native offerings (CloudWatch, Elasticsearch, and Kibana), which will help us debug our issues quickly. In the next section, we will start setting up the CloudWatch agent to push the logs to one centralized place.

Setting up the CloudWatch agent

In *Chapter 8, Monitoring AWS Services Using CloudWatch and SNS*, we learned how to set up the CloudWatch agent to push custom metrics—for example, memory and disk statistics—to CloudWatch. In this chapter, we will extend this concept further and use the CloudWatch agent to push system logs—for example /var/log/messages and /var/log/secure—to CloudWatch Logs.

Before setting up the CloudWatch agent, we need to understand what a CloudWatch log is. If you want all your logs at one centralized place, then you need to enable CloudWatch Logs. CloudWatch Logs enables you to store and access your log files from EC2, Route53, CloudTrail, and other sources at one centralized location. You can use them to search for a specific code, filter them based on specific fields, and archive them for future analysis. Before setting up the CloudWatch agent, we first need to set up CloudWatch Logs. These are the steps we need to follow:

1. Go to the CloudWatch console at https://console.aws.amazon.com/cloudwatch/.

2. Click on **Log groups** under **Logs**:

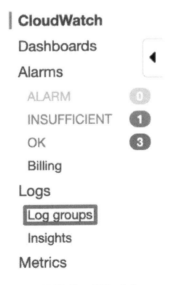

Figure 9.1 – AWS CloudWatch Logs groups

3.   Click on **Create log group** to create a new log group:

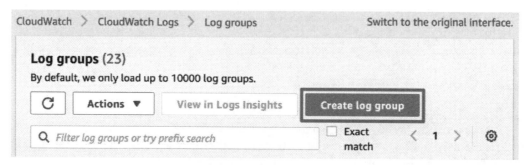

Figure 9.2 – Create log group

4.   Under **Log group details**, give your **Log group name**—for example, ProdCloudWatch. Click on **Create**:

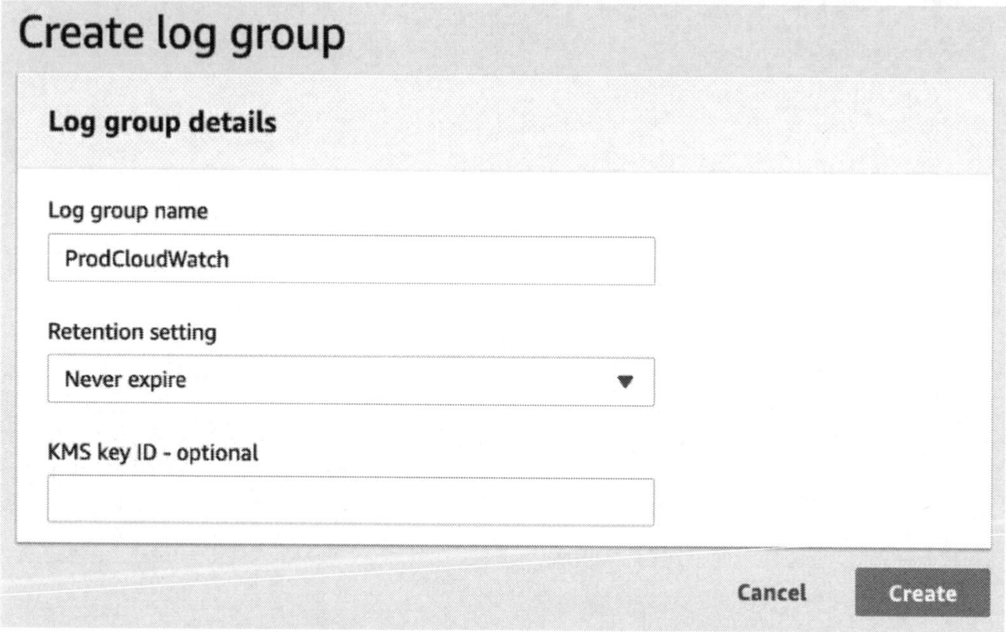

Create log group

Log group details

Log group name

ProdCloudWatch

Retention setting

Never expire

KMS key ID - optional

Cancel   Create

Figure 9.3 – Create log group screen with the name you selected

Now that we have CloudWatch Logs ready, there is one thing that we need to do in order to push system logs to CloudWatch Logs—namely, modify the IAM role. These are the steps we need to follow:

1. Go to the IAM console, click on **Roles**, and select **CloudWatchAgentServerRole**:

Figure 9.4 – Selecting the IAM policy

2. In the next screen, click on **Attach policies**:

Figure 9.5 – Attaching the CloudWatch Logs policy

3. In the search bar, search for `cloudwatchlogsfull`, select the policy, and click on **Attach policy**. This policy will give EC2 instance permission to push logs to CloudWatch Logs:

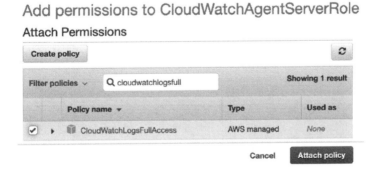

Figure 9.6 – Attaching the policy

With the IAM permission policy in place, we are going to follow the same steps that we did in *Chapter 8, Monitoring AWS Services Using CloudWatch and SNS*—that is, execute the `amazon-cloudwatch-agent-config-wizard`—but this time, with a slight modification. In the `Do you want to monitor any log files` step? Field, type `yes` and specify the name of the logfile—for example, `/var/log/messages` with the `LogGroup` set to `ProdCloudWatch`. We need to follow the same procedure for `/var/log/secure` with the `LogGroup` again set to `ProdCloudWatch`:

```
sudo /opt/aws/amazon-cloudwatch-agent/bin/amazon-cloudwatch-
agent-config-wizard
```

Once you run the preceding command, it will open a wizard and give you plenty of options to select. In most cases, the default option `[1]` will be sufficient, but you might need to select a different option in some cases. Let's try to break it down step by step:

1. First, it will ask you about the operating system on which you plan to run the agent. The available options are `linux` or `windows`—for this example, we will choose `linux`, which is the default option.

   It will then ask you whether you want to run this agent on `EC2` or `On-Premises` (as CloudWatch agent also supports installation to an on-premises data center)—for this example, you can choose `EC2`, which is the default option.

   Next, you need to choose the user under which you plan to run this agent. This is to define which user is used to run the agent once the agent is up and running. The available options are `root`, `cwagent` (CloudWatch agent), or others. For this example, you can choose `root`, which is the default option:

```
=============================================================
====
= Welcome to the AWS CloudWatch Agent Configuration
Manager =
=============================================================
====
On which OS are you planning to use the agent?
1. linux
2. windows
default choice: [1]:


Trying to fetch the default region based on ec2
metadata...
Are you using EC2 or On-Premises hosts?
```

```
1. EC2
2. On-Premises
default choice: [1]:


Which user are you planning to run the agent?
1. root
2. cwagent
3. others
default choice: [1]:
```

2. Next, you need to define additional stats which can enhance your monitoring experience. `StatsD` is a popular open source solution and is used to collect metrics from a wide variety of sources. In combination with the CloudWatch agent, you can use it to collect custom application metrics like the number of requests coming to your application or number of unique requests, and so on. You can turn on the `StatsD` daemon by specifying `yes/no` (the default is yes), in which port you want to run it (the default is `8125`), but you can always change it if it's a conflict with any existing service on that host (that is, any service running on same port, `8125`). You can also configure the frequency you want to collect data and to aggregate the data. For this example, you can choose the default option (`10s` and `60s`, respectively):

```
Do you want to turn on StatsD daemon?
1. yes
2. no
default choice: [1]:


Which port do you want StatsD daemon to listen to?
default choice: [8125]


What is the collect interval for StatsD daemon?
1. 10s
2. 30s
3. 60s
default choice: [1]:


What is the aggregation interval for metrics collected by
StatsD daemon?
```

```
1. Do not aggregate
2. 10s
3. 30s
4. 60s
default choice: [4]:
```

3. Like StatsD, you can turn on Collectd to collect more fine-grain control metrics, such as CPU and memory per core. Collectd is also a popular open source solution that is used to collect various system statistics from a wide variety of applications. Using Collectd, we can also collect additional EC2 dimensions such as ImageId, InstanceId, InstanceType, and AutoScalingGroupName. All these metrics are helpful if you are trying to debug any issue. It's highly recommended that you turn these on. To select this metric, use the default choice, 1. You can collect the metrics at intervals of 1s (second), 10s, 30s or 60s, but it all depend upon the type of application and your requirement:

```
Do you want to monitor metrics from CollectD?
1. yes
2. no
default choice: [1]:


Do you want to monitor any host metrics? e.g. CPU,
memory, etc.
1. yes
2. no
default choice: [1]:


Do you want to monitor cpu metrics per core? Additional
CloudWatch charges may apply.
1. yes
2. no
default choice: [1]:


Do you want to add ec2 dimensions (ImageId, InstanceId,
InstanceType, AutoScalingGroupName) into all of your
metrics if the info is available?
1. yes
2. no
```

```
default choice: [1]:
Would you like to collect your metrics at high resolution
(sub-minute resolution)? This enables sub-minute
resolution for all metrics, but you can customize for
specific metrics in the output JSON file:
1. 1s
2. 10s
3. 30s
4. 60s
default choice: [4]:
```

4. This is the most important part of the process, where you define the amount of metrics you want to collect via a CloudWatch agent. It all depends upon the configuration you select:

    - **Basic**: This will only provide you two additional metrics—the percentage of memory (mem_used_percent) and disk used (disk_used_percent).

    - **Standard**: This will provide you with some additional metrics, such as swap usage (swap_used_percent), disk inodes free (disk_inodes_free), CPU usage by user and system (cpu_usage_user and cpu_usage_system), and so on.

    - **Advanced**: This will provide you with a bunch of additional metrics—for this example, we will choose Advanced (option 3).

    As you can see, choosing Advanced gives us many additional metrics that are not present when you select the Basic or Standard option:

```
Which default metrics config do you want?
1. Basic
2. Standard
3. Advanced
4. None
default choice: [1]:
3
```

5. After this step, the wizard will give you a snippet of all the metrics you have selected so far. If you are satisfied with all the metrics, select yes (option 1, the default option), or 2 if you want to modify any of the configs:

```
Are you satisfied with the above config? Note: it can be
manually customized after the wizard completes to add
additional items.
```

```
1. yes
2. no
default choice: [1]:
1
```

6. In the next step, the wizard will ask whether you have a CloudWatch agent configuration file present on the host. If this is a fresh installation of the agent, then select no (option 2). If you have any configuration file present, then specify the path by choosing option 1:

```
Do you have any existing CloudWatch Agent (http://
docs.aws.amazon.com/AmazonCloudWatch/latest/logs/
AgentReference.html) configuration file to import for
migration?
1. yes
2. no
default choice: [2]:
```

7. This is the main step in defining the log files that we want to monitor via the CloudWatch agent. Select yes (option 1) and specify the log file path we want to monitor (/var/log/messages) and the CloudWatch log group that we created in *figure 9.3*. Repeat the same step for the /var/log/secure file:

```
Do you want to monitor any log files?
1. yes
2. no
default choice: [1]:
1
Log file path:
/var/log/messages
Log group name:
default choice: [messages]
ProdCloudWatch

Log stream name:
default choice: [{instance_id}]
Do you want to specify any additional log files to
monitor?
1. yes
```

```
2. no
default choice: [1]:
1
Log file path:
/var/log/secure
Log group name:
default choice: [secure]
ProdCloudWatch
Log stream name:
default choice: [{instance_id}]

Do you want to specify any additional log files to
monitor?
1. yes
2. no
default choice: [1]:
2
Saved config file to /opt/aws/amazon-cloudwatch-agent/
bin/config.json successfully.


Please check the above content of the config.
The config file is also located at /opt/aws/amazon-
cloudwatch-agent/bin/config.json.
Edit it manually if needed.
Do you want to store the config in the SSM parameter
store?
1. yes
2. no
default choice: [1]:
2
Program exits now.
```

8. Now, stop the CloudWatch agent and then start it by running the following commands:

```
$ sudo /opt/aws/amazon-cloudwatch-agent/bin/amazon-
cloudwatch-agent-ctl -m ec2 -a stop
```

```
amazon-cloudwatch-agent stop/waiting
```

```
$ sudo /opt/aws/amazon-cloudwatch-agent/bin/amazon-
cloudwatch-agent-ctl -m ec2 -a start
```
```
amazon-cloudwatch-agent start/running, process 13365
```

The cloud agent is up and running, which is streaming logs to the CloudWatch Log endpoint. In the next section, we will configure Elasticsearch, which will index the log data, and this index data we can visualize via Kibana.

Setting up AWS Elasticsearch and Kibana

Before setting up Elasticsearch, we need to understand what Elasticsearch is. It's a free and open source analytic engine based on the Apache Lucene library. It works by taking unstructured data from different sources, indexing it based on user-specified mapping, and making it searchable.

Companies such as Elastic (https://www.elastic.co/) provide the other alternative solutions, such as ELK, which stands for Elasticsearch, Logstash, and Kibana. Logstash, in this case, works similar to a CloudWatch agent, and is used to send data to Elasticsearch. Kibana lets you visualize your data using graphs and charts.

AWS provides its fully managed Elasticsearch solution known as Amazon Elasticsearch service. Using the Amazon Elasticsearch service has the following benefits:

- It's easier to deploy and manage, with Amazon taking care of heavy lifting activities, such as provisioning hardware, software installation, recovery, backup, and monitoring.

- It's highly scalable, and you can store up to 3 PB of data, which lets you run large log analytics.

- It's highly available and uses multi-AZ deployments, which allows you to replicate data in three availability zones in the same region.

- It's integrated with Kibana, which lets you explore and visualize your data.

Now you know about Elasticsearch, let's create the Elasticsearch cluster, also known as Amazon ES domain. The domain is a cluster where you can specify settings such as instance types, number of instances, and storage requirements. These are the steps you need to follow to create the Elasticsearch domain:

1. Go to the AWS console and under **Analytics**, click on **Elasticsearch Service**:

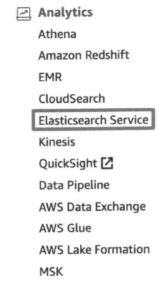

Figure 9.7 – Selecting Elasticsearch Service

2. Click on **Create a new domain**:

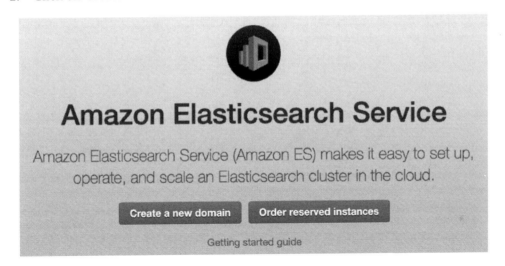

Figure 9.8 – Creating a new Elasticsearch domain

3.   On the **Create Elasticsearch domain** page, select the **Choose deployment type** as **Development and testing** (this domain uses a single availability zone) and the **Version** as the latest (for example, at the time of writing, version 7.7 is the latest). Click **Next**:

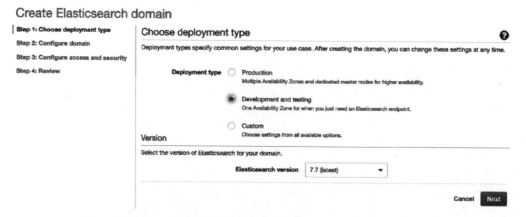

Create Elasticsearch domain

Figure 9.9 – Selecting the Development and testing environment

4.   Under **Configure domain** fill in the following details:

- **Elasticsearch domain name**: Here, you should give your domain a meaningful name—for example, myproddomain.

- **Instance type**: Choose an instance type for the data nodes—for example, **t3.medium.Elasticsearch**.

- **Number of nodes**: Choose the number of data nodes—for example, **1,** as shown in the following screenshot:

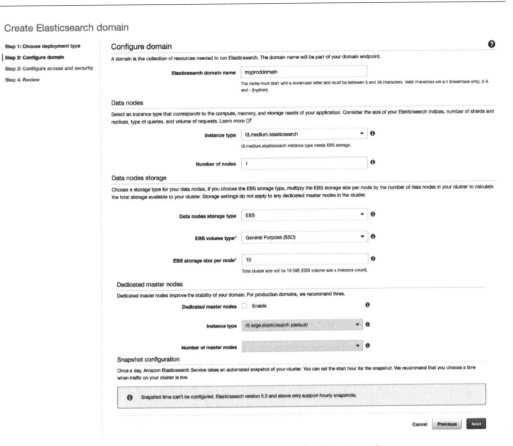

Figure 9.10 – Selecting instance type for Elasticsearch

- Under **Data nodes storage type** choose **EBS**, with the EBS volume type is **General Purpose (SSD)** and **EBS storage size per node** based on your data requirement—for example, 10 GB in this case.

- **Dedicated master nodes**: Optionally, you can enable **Dedicated master nodes**, which is useful in domains where your instance count is greater than 10 as it increases the stability of your cluster.

Click **Next**:

Create Elasticsearch domain

Step 1: Choose deployment type
Step 2: Configure domain
| Step 3: Configure access and security
Step 4: Review

Configure access and security

Amazon Elasticsearch Service offers numerous security features, including fine-grained access control, IAM, Cognito authentication for Kibana, encryption, and VPC access.
Learn more

Network configuration

Choose internet or VPC access. To enable VPC access, we use private IP addresses from your VPC, which provides an inherent layer of security. You control network access within your VPC using security groups. Optionally, you can add an additional layer of security by applying a restrictive access policy. Internet endpoints are publicly accessible. If you select public access, you should secure your domain with an access policy that only allows specific users or IP addresses to access the domain.

○ VPC access (Recommended)
● Public access

Fine-grained access control – powered by Open Distro for Elasticsearch

Fine-grained access control provides numerous features to help you keep your data secure. Features include document-level security, field-level security, read-only Kibana users, and Kibana tenants. Fine-grained access control requires a master user.

Set a master user to an IAM account using an ARN, or store a master user in the Elasticsearch internal database by creating a master username and password. After your domain is set up, you can use Kibana or the REST APIs to configure additional users and permissions. Learn more

☑ Enable fine-grained access control

○ Set IAM ARN as master user
By selecting an IAM ARN as the master user, your domain will only authenticate with IAM roles and users.

● Create master user
By creating a master user, your domain will have the internal user database enabled with HTTP basic authentication.

Master username | admin |
Master usernames must be between 1 and 16 characters.

Master password | •••••••• |
Master passwords must be at least 8 characters long and contain at least one uppercase letter, one lowercase letter, one number, and one special character.

Confirm master password | •••••••• |

Amazon Cognito authentication

Access policy

Access policies control whether a request is accepted or rejected when it reaches the Amazon Elasticsearch Service domain. If you specify an account, user, or role in this policy, you must sign your requests. Learn more

Custom policy builder allows at most 10 elements. Use a JSON-defined access policy to define a policy with more than 10 elements.

Domain access policy | Custom access policy ▼ |
Allow or deny access by AWS account ID, account ARN, IAM user ARN, IAM role ARN, IPv4 address, or CIDR block.

| IAM ARN ▼ | * | | Allow ▼ | Remove element |
Add element

ⓘ   IAM-based access policies can conflict with fine-grained access control. Learn more

Encryption

These features help protect your data. After creating the domain, you can't change most encryption settings.

Encryption   ☑ Require HTTPS for all traffic to the domain   ⓘ

☑ Node-to-node encryption   ⓘ

☑ Enable encryption of data at rest   ⓘ

KMS master key | (Default) aws/es ▼ | ⓘ

Description   Default master key that protects my Elasticsearch data when no other key is defined

Account   279503694119

Key ARN   arn:aws:kms:us-west-2:279503694119:key/afa5c8d8-5c52-4678-bbdb-dda8fbd9ec04

ⓘ   You enabled fine-grained access control, which requires HTTPS, node-to-node encryption, and encryption at rest.

▸ Optional Elasticsearch cluster settings

Cancel   Previous   Next

Figure 9.11 – Selecting node storage and dedicated master nodes

5. In the network configuration, we can choose a public access domain or VPC access. We created a VPC in *Chapter 3, Creating a Data Center in the Cloud Using VPC*. For the sake of simplicity, let's choose public access and also enable fine-grained access control to keep the data secure. To do this, you can create a **Master username** and **Master password**, and you can later use this to access Kibana or the Rest API. Keep all the other settings as default and click on **Next at the bottom of the screen**.

6. On the **Review** page, check all the configurations and click on **Confirm at the bottom of the screen**. Creating a domain usually takes 10–20 minutes but can take longer depending on the configuration.

7. Once you have an Elastic domain up and running, please make a note of the Kibana URL—for example, for me this is `https://search-myproddomain-pc67ikr3ryozvl4e53ey3k3rsq.us-west-2.es.amazonaws.com/_plugin/kibana/`, but it's going to be different in your case.

8. Now we have Kibana up and running; we can further explore the Kibana dashboard by looking at some sample data provided by Kibana. Go to the Kibana dashboard and click on **Add sample data**:

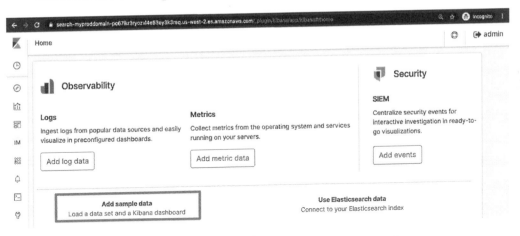

Figure 9.12 – Adding a sample data to Kibana dashboard

In the next screen, click on **Add data** to see the sample web logs:

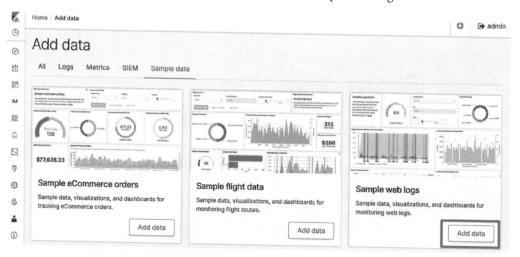

Figure 9.13 – Adding Sample web logs

9. You will see the dashboard as shown in the following screenshot. As you can see, Kibana is giving us a wealth of information—for example, OS-specific information (from which OS these requests are coming), country-wise stats, file-type information (gz or css), and so on and so forth:

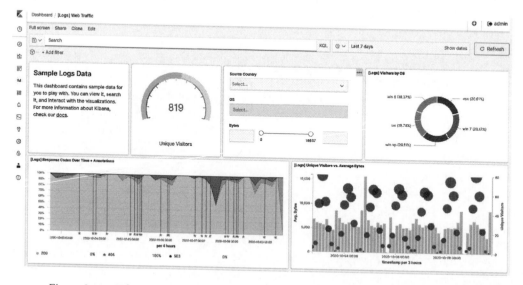

Figure 9.14 – Kibana dashboard showing various log statistics (OS and unique visitors)

In the following dashboard, Kibana is showing all fine-grained details, such as file type (gz and css) and unique visitors by country (for example, Canada (CN) and India (IN)):

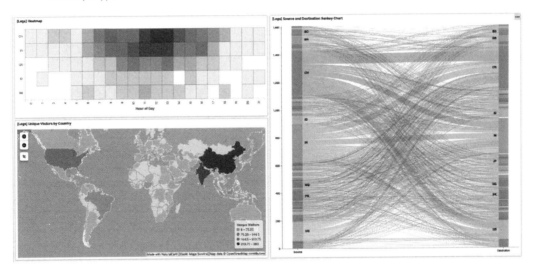

Figure 9.15 – Kibana dashboard showing various log statistics (type of files, unique visitors by country)

Now we have both Elasticsearch and Kibana up and running. We can utilize them for fast searching and visualizations to debug any system, security, or performance issue.

Summary

In this chapter, you have learned the importance of log analysis and how it helps us debug any issue. A log analysis tool is the backbone of any company. It helps your team debug issues at an earlier stage before the issue causes any severe damage to your environment (through security or performance issues).

You learned how to set up CloudWatch Logs to centralize all your logs in a single place. Then we set up Elasticsearch to stream these logs and then we set up Kibana, which gives us a dashboard to analyze them.

In the next chapter, we will focus on another critical component—backing up. We all understand the importance of backing up, especially in disaster recovery or accidental solution scenarios. In the next chapter, we will look at the various backup solutions offered by AWS. We will start setting up a script to store these backups in S3 and then, with the help of life cycle hooks, we will push that data in a glacier for long-term storage.

10
Centralizing Cloud Backup Solution

As system administrators or DevOps engineers, we all understand the importance of backing up. It's the first place we all check in the case of loss of data or disaster. Because of the cloud's dynamic nature (the instance can come and go at any time), it becomes challenging to decide which data to back up. We also need to decide how long we need to keep the backup, as the type of data and how much data we need to store will both incur a cost.

This chapter will start by looking at AWS's various backup solutions and which one you should choose under which condition. We will then move on to the **Data Lifecycle Manager** (**DLM**), which will help automate the process of snapshotting the EBS volume. Then we will look at the **Simple Storage Service** (**S3**), one of AWS's most reliable backup offerings, and how to automate backing up files in S3 using the command line. Finally, we will look at how we can transition our data to Glacier (a cost-effective way for long-term storage) using the Lifecycle Manager and how to automate the Lifecycle Manager using Terraform.

In this chapter, we are going to cover the following main topics:

- The various backup options offered by AWS
- Setting up the AWS DLM
- Backing up your data to S3 using the AWS CLI
- Transitioning S3 data to Glacier using a lifecycle policy

Technical requirements

There are no special technical requirements that you need to read through and understand this chapter; however, familiarity with the AWS command line and Terraform will help you better grasp the concepts that were discussed in *Chapter 1, Setting Up the AWS Environment*.

The GitHub link for the solution scripts for this chapter can be found at
`https://github.com/PacktPublishing/AWS-for-System-Administrators/tree/master/Chapter10`.

Check out the following link to see the Code in Action video:

`https://bit.ly/34WbLzR`

The v backup options offered by AWS

Before we start diving into AWS's various backup offerings, we first need to understand why we back up our data.

Why do we back up data?

One of the primary reasons we perform backups is to minimize data loss. Lost data will impact our business by impacting our brand, revenue, and trust in our customer relationships. So, the first thing we need to decide as an organization is how much data loss we can afford. Data loss can be defined in terms of a **rcovery point objective** (**RPO**). The RPO will dictate the backup frequency, which is the solution that we use to perform the backup, as it's the measurement of the maximum tolerable limit of our data loss. The other factor we need to consider is the **recovery time objective** (**RTO**), the amount of time it will take to recover, which is directly correlated to how much your business can afford to operate with that particular application offline or down.

Now the question is, why don't we back up all of our data? The reason for this is its cost. Applications have different requirements and levels of importance to your organization—some are critical and some are not. If we start backing up all individual applications, then our backing-up cost will go high. Now the next question is, what are the options that we have to back up? The answer to that question is that we need to find a balance between cost versus risk and start with our requirements. We can start with the following requirements:

- Identify critical applications in your organization which are required to be protected

- Define clear RTO and RPO requirements

- Examine the impact on the business if the application is down

- Examine any compliance considerations—for example, data only needs to be backed up from a specific location or country

Now, with all these considerations in place, let's look at some of the backup options provided by AWS:

- **Amazon S3 and Glacier**: This is the first place that most customers look backing up their data. Both S3 and Glacier provide 11 9s of durability, which means that if you have 10 million objects (files) stored in S3 with over 10,000 years, then you will lose one object. If your compliance requirement allows (for example, EU countries don't allow their data to be copied to any other country), then S3 also supports cross-region replication, which means that we can copy S3 data from one region to another. This will help if the data in one AWS region goes down, as we will have a backup copy available in other regions.

> **Information box**
>
> For more information on the 11 9s of durability, refer to `https://aws.amazon.com/s3/storage-classes/`.

- **File gateway**: The file gateway backs up on-premise data to the cloud. You can deploy a file gateway as a virtual machine, an appliance in your datacenter, or **Amazon Machine Image** (**AMI**). It works by enabling you to connect your on-premise application to the file gateway using the **Network File System** (**NFS**) / **Server Message Block** (**SMB**) protocol; when you write data to the file gateway, it will convert it into object storage. Then, the data gets saved durably to your S3 bucket. The other advantage of using the file gateway is that it provides a local cache of up to 32 TB, with data in cache, which means that you have low latency access to your data.

- **Tape gateway**: The tape gateway is used to replace an on-premise tape library. It works similarly to the file gateway, where you have a virtual appliance sitting between the on-premise facilities and S3 bucket, but this time, it's a virtually emulated tape gateway, which means that no physical tape device is involved. You can access this appliance using a standard protocol, such as NFS or SMB, and the data will be stored durably in S3.

- **Volume gateway**: The volume gateway provides the block storage where on-premises data is backed up in cloud storage. The workflow is the same as the file and tape gateways, but this time, to access the volume gateway, you need to use the **internet Small Computer Systems Interface (iSCSI)** protocol, which provides block-level access to storage devices by using SCSI commands. The data will eventually be stored in an EBS snapshot.

- **EBS snapshot**: Using snapshots, we can take the backup of our EBS volumes to S3. These snapshots are point-in-time and incremental, which means that after the first snapshot, the next snapshot only has the blocks that have been changed. This will help to reduce the storage cost and duplication of data.

Out of the backup solutions that AWS offers, which one you should choose is entirely dependent on your requirement and where you are running your workload. If your workload runs on AWS, then the snapshot option will be an ideal solution for you, but if your workload is running on-premise, you can choose the gateway solution (file, tape, or volume). If you are looking for a hybrid option, then S3 is an optimal solution. In the next section, we will see how to set up the EBS volume snapshot creation using DLM.

Setting up the AWS DLM

AWS **Data LifeCycle Manager** (**DLM**) is used to automate the creation, deletion, and retention of snapshots, which we use to back up our EBS volumes. AWS DLM comes with no additional cost and provides a complete backup solution for your EBS volumes. Some of the advantages of using it are as follows:

- Regular backup schedule

- Retains the backup, which is required for internal compliance and auditing

- Deleting the old backup will reduce your storage cost

To use the Amazon DLM to manage the backup of your EBS volumes via the AWS management console, we need to go through the following series of steps:

1. Go to the EC2 console at `https://console.aws.amazon.com/ec2/`, and in the navigation pane, click **Lifecycle Manager** under **Elastic Block Store**:

▼ **Elastic Block Store**

Volumes

Snapshots

Lifecycle Manager

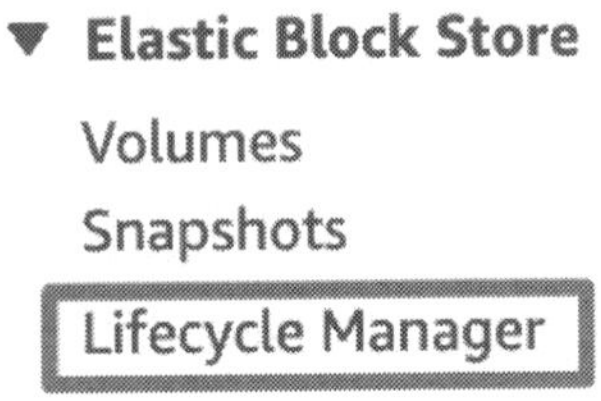

Figure 10.1 – Lifecycle Manager under Elastic Block Store

2. In the next screen, click on **Create Snapshot Lifecycle Policy**:

Welcome to Data Lifecycle Manager

Schedule and manage the creation and deletion of EBS snapshots

Create Snapshot Lifecycle Policy

Figure 10.2 – Welcome to Data Lifecycle Manager

3. You need to provide the following information for your policy:

    - **Description**: Give a meaningful name to your policy—for example, `my-prod-server-snapshot`.

    - **Select resource type**: This is the type of resource you want to backup. **Volume** refers to creating a snapshot of an individual volume. **Instance** refers to a multi-volume snapshot, which means that it will take a snapshot of all the EC2 volumes attached to that instance. In this case, we will choose **Instance**, as we want to take a snapshot of all the volumes attached to this instance.

- **Target with these tags**: These are the resource tags that are used to identify the volumes or the instance to back up—for example, the tag **Name : prod-server**.

- **Lifecycle Policy Tags**: These are tags for the lifecycle policy. For this example, we will not be adding any tags.

The following screenshot shows the form filled in with the preceding details:

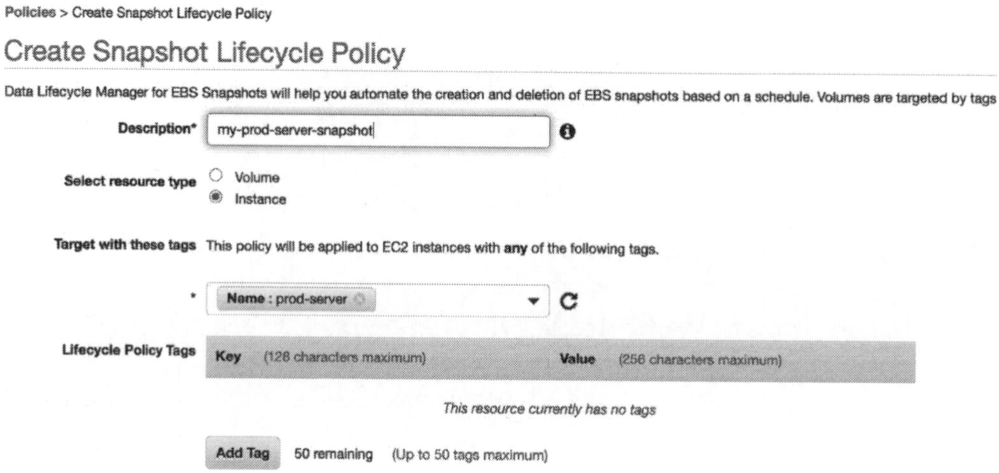

Policies > Create Snapshot Lifecycle Policy

Create Snapshot Lifecycle Policy

Data Lifecycle Manager for EBS Snapshots will help you automate the creation and deletion of EBS snapshots based on a schedule. Volumes are targeted by tags

Description* [my-prod-server-snapshot] 🛈

Select resource type ○ Volume
                      ● Instance

Target with these tags This policy will be applied to EC2 instances with **any** of the following tags.

* [Name : prod-server ⊗   ▼] C

Lifecycle Policy Tags **Key** (128 characters maximum)   **Value** (256 characters maximum)

This resource currently has no tags

[Add Tag] 50 remaining (Up to 50 tags maximum)

Figure 10.3 – Create Snapshot Lifecycle Policy after filling in all the details

4. For the IAM role, we need to choose the IAM role that has the permission to describe volumes and to create, describe, and delete snapshots. By default, AWS provides the `AWSDataLifecycleManagerDefaultRole` default role, but you can create your own IAM role. For this example, let's choose the default role:

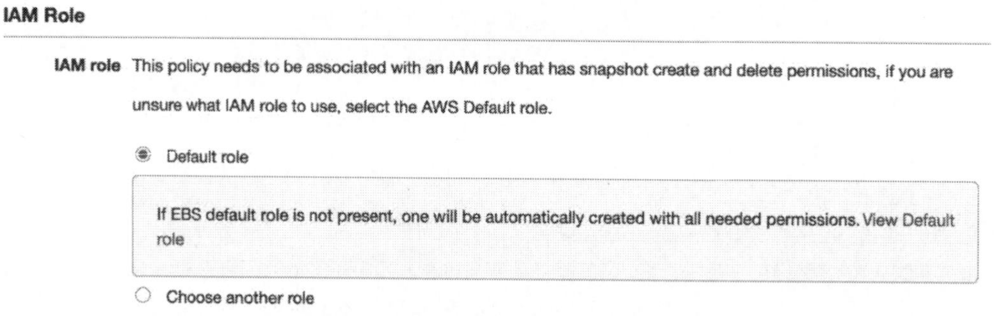

IAM Role

IAM role This policy needs to be associated with an IAM role that has snapshot create and delete permissions, if you are unsure what IAM role to use, select the AWS Default role.

  ● Default role

  If EBS default role is not present, one will be automatically created with all needed permissions. View Default role

  ○ Choose another role

Figure 10.4 – Choosing the default IAM role

5. In this step, we need to add the policy schedule. For each policy schedule, we need to specify the following information:

- **Schedule name**: Give a meaningful name to your schedule—for example, `prod-server-snapshot-schedule`.

- **Frequency**: The interval between the different policy runs. You can select either **Daily**, **Weekly**, **Monthly**, or **Yearly** from the dropdown or you can specify your own **Custom** cron expression. For this example, let's choose **Daily**.

- **Every**: How often you want to run. It all depends upon your RTO and RPO. You can choose to run it every **1**, **2**, **3**, **4**, **6**, **8**, or **12** hours. In our case, you can choose **1** hour, which means that this policy is going to make a backup of your volumes every hour.

- **Starting at**: This is the time when the policy run is scheduled to start. Please note that the timing is in the UTC time zone, so please adjust it according to your server time zone. For example, in this case you can see that our backup will start at 9.00 am UTC.

- **Retention type**: You can retain the snapshot based on a total count of the snapshot or the age of the snapshot. For example, in our case you can retain the last 2 snapshots. After the retention period expires, the snapshot will be deleted:

▼ **Policy Schedule 1**

Schedules define how often snapshots are to be created by the policy, as well as the configuration for those snapshots. You must configure the default schedule for this policy. You can optionally configure up to three additional schedules for the policy.

Schedule name*	prod-server-snapshot-schedule
Frequency	Daily
Every	1 Hours
Starting at	09 : 00 UTC
Retention type*	Count
Retain*	2

Figure 10.5 – Creating the DLM Policy Schedule

6. Keep the rest of the parameters, such as the tags, Policy Schedule, and others, as their default and click on **Create Policy**.

7.   You will see something like this after you click **Create Policy**:

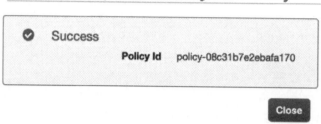

Figure 10.6 – Create Snapshot Lifecycle Policy

Once the policy creation is complete, it will create a snapshot of the `prod-server` instance every hour starting from 9.00 am UTC and it's going to manage a maximum of two snapshots.

Before DLM, we need to write the manual script to take the EBS volume snapshot. With DLM, AWS provides a managed service, which does all the heavy lifting in the background and automates the EBS volume snapshot creation. In the next section, we will see how to back up your data in S3 using the AWS CLI.

Backing up your data to S3 using the AWS CLI

AWS S3 is an ideal place to back up your data as it is infinitely scalable and can store and retrieve any amount of data. This section will show you how to use the AWS **Command Line interface** (**CLI**) (which we set up in *Chapter 1, Setting up the AWS Environment*) to access S3. We will build our script for backing up our files and easily retrieving them as needed. We will then add this script in cron to schedule tasks at regular intervals—for example, 5 minutes, which means that our script will make a backup of our files every 5 minutes. These are the steps we need to follow:

1.   The first step is to create the bucket. This is an optional step; if you already have a bucket created you can use it. To create a new bucket named `my-backup-bucket-master-aws-system-administration`, we need to pass the `mb` (make bucket) option to the `s3` command:

```
$ aws s3 mb s3://my-backup-bucket-master-aws-system-
administration

make_bucket: my-backup-bucket-master-aws-system-
administration
```

> **Note**
> Bucket names must be globally unique, which means that two different AWS users can't have the same S3 bucket name.

2. To verify it whether bucket has been created successfully, you need to pass `ls` (list bucket) to the AWS S3 command line:

```
$ aws s3 ls
2020-10-09 15:03:28 my-backup-bucket-master-aws-system-
administration
```

3. To upload the file/directory located in your local directory to the S3 bucket, you need to use the `cp` (copy) command. For example, in this case we are passing `cp` to the AWS CLI to copy `mybackupdir` to the `my-backup-bucket-master-aws-system-administration` S3 bucket. As this is a directory, we need to use the `--recursive` option; if it was a file, then we could simply omit that option:

```
$ aws s3 cp mybackupdir s3://my-backup-bucket-master-aws-
system-administration --recursive
upload: mybackupdir/3 to s3://my-backup-bucket-master-
aws-system-administration/3
upload: mybackupdir/1 to s3://my-backup-bucket-master-
aws-system-administration/1
upload: mybackupdir/2 to s3://my-backup-bucket-master-
aws-system-administration/2
upload: mybackupdir/4 to s3://my-backup-bucket-master-
aws-system-administration/4
upload: mybackupdir/6 to s3://my-backup-bucket-master-
aws-system-administration/6
upload: mybackupdir/5 to s3://my-backup-bucket-master-
aws-system-administration/5
```

4. In order to download the file from S3 to your local directory, we simply need to reverse the command:

```
$ aws s3 cp s3://my-backup-bucket-master-aws-system-
administration . --recursive
download: s3://my-backup-bucket-master-aws-system-
administration/1 to ./1
download: s3://my-backup-bucket-master-aws-system-
administration/3 to ./3
```

```
download: s3://my-backup-bucket-master-aws-system-
administration/4 to ./4
```

```
download: s3://my-backup-bucket-master-aws-system-
administration/2 to ./2
```

```
download: s3://my-backup-bucket-master-aws-system-
administration/6 to ./6
```

```
download: s3://my-backup-bucket-master-aws-system-
administration/5 to ./5
```

5. Let's come back to our use case, where we want to create a backup of our local files/ directory to S3. In most cases, only a certain percentage of files will change on a daily basis, not all of the files. Our aim will be to only copy those files that change to S3 rather than the entire directory, and to achieve this, we need to use the `sync` parameter with S3. The `sync` parameter is used to synchronize the content of a bucket and directory. For example, inside the `mybackupdir` directory, you will only create one file, `7`, and you will want to copy this file only to S3. This is where the `sync` option will come in handy:

```
$ cd mybackupdir/
```

```
$ touch 7
```

```
$ aws s3 sync mybackupdir s3://my-backup-bucket-master-
aws-system-administration
```

```
upload: mybackupdir/7 to s3://my-backup-bucket-master-
aws-system-administration/7
```

6. In the next step, we will need to put the `sync` command in `crontab` so that we can take the backup on a regular basis. Run the `crontab -e` command to open the `crontab` console and then type `*/5 * * * *` followed by the command. What this will do is sync the file from your local directory to the `my-backup-bucket-master-aws-system-administration` bucket every 5 minutes:

```
crontab -e
```

```
*/5 * * * * aws s3 sync mybackupdir s3://my-backup-
bucket-master-aws-system-administration
```

The AWS CLI is a quick way to automate your daily tasks. In this section, by using a few code lines, we saw how we can sync data between our local folder and S3. In the next section, we will focus on saving costs by using the lifecycle policy and transitioning our data from the S3 bucket to Glacier for long-term storage.

Transitioning S3 data to Glacier using a lifecycle policy

You can define a lifecycle policy where you can define the action that S3 takes during an object's lifetime. Some examples of these actions are deleting an object after a specified time, archiving objects, and transitioning to another storage class. A lifecycle policy can be applied to all objects or a subset of objects in a bucket. In this section, we will see how to transition S3 objects to Glacier using the lifecycle policy. The Glacier is the data-archiving and long-term secure and durable solution offered by AWS at an extremely low cost. Using Glacier, you can store your data cost-effectively for months, years, or even decades. To achieve this, you need to go through the following series of steps:

1. Log in to AWS S3 console at `https://console.aws.amazon.com/s3/` and in the bucket list, select the bucket in which you want to create the lifecycle policy. For example, in this case, we can choose the `my-backup-bucket-master-aws-system-administrator` bucket:

Figure 10.7 – Choosing an S3 bucket

2. Choose the **Management** tab and click on **Add lifecycle rule**:

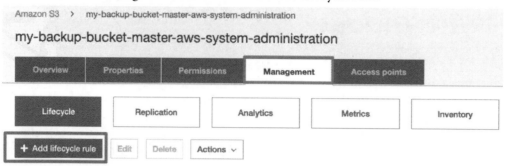

Figure 10.8 – Add lifecycle rule

3. In the **Lifecycle rule** dialog box, enter the following details:

    - **Enter a rule name**: Give a meaningful name to your rule. The name must be unique within the bucket.

    - **Choose a rule scope**: You can apply this rule to a specific prefix—for example, to all files ending with .txt—or you can apply it to all the objects in the bucket. For this example, you can choose **Apply to all objects in the bucket** and click **Next**:

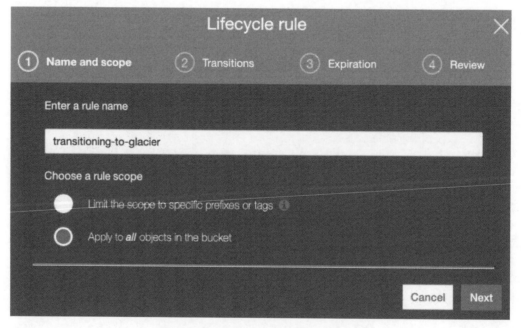

Figure 10.9 – Naming your lifecycle rule

4. In the **Storage class transition** screen, you can choose the current version (meaning that the rule will be applied to all new objects uploaded to this bucket) or you can also apply it to the previous objects. Under **Object creation**, you can choose which storage class you want your object to be transitioned to. Under S3, you have multiple options—for example **Transition to Standard-IA**, **Transition to Intelligent-Tiering**, **Transition to One Zone-IA**, and **Transition to Glacier after**. In order to keep the cost down, for this example, you should choose **Transition to Glacier** and click **Next**:

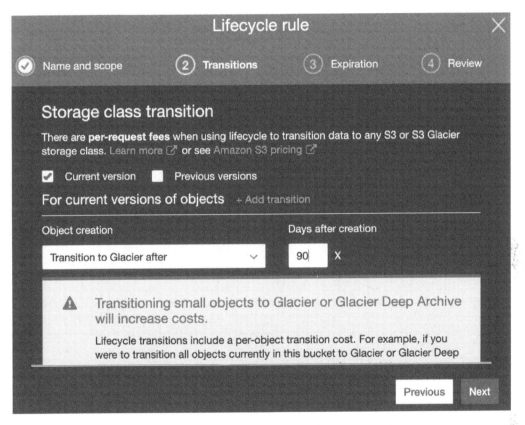

Figure 10.10 – Choosing Transition to Glacier after 90 days

5. Under **Configure expiration**, choose the current and previous versions and set **Expire current version of object** to 455 and **Permanently delete previous versions** to 365. What we are trying to do here is to delete the object after 365 days to save costs. Click **Next**:

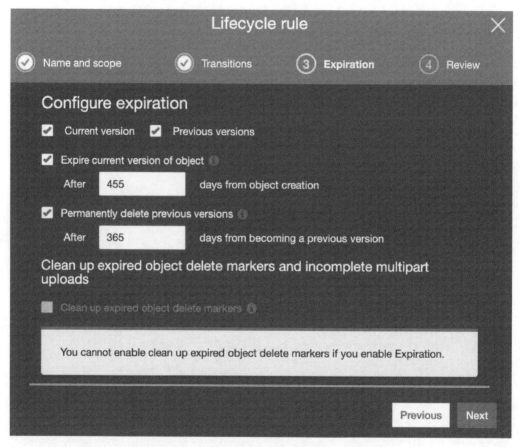

Figure 10.11 – Choosing expiration after 365 days

6. Review all the settings for your rule, acknowledge it, and click **Save**:

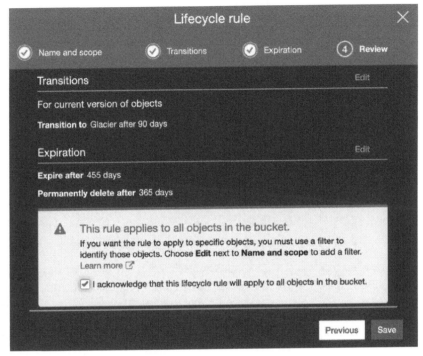

Figure 10.12 – Review your lifecycle rule

7. If the rule doesn't contain any errors, you will see something like the following on the **Lifecycle** page:

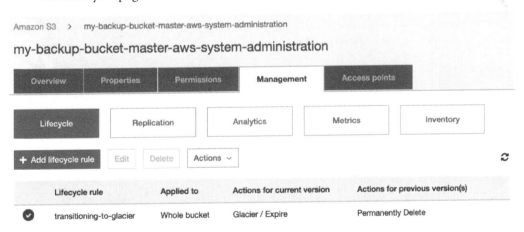

Figure 10.13 – Your newly created lifecycle rule

Transitioning data to Glacier will have huge cost benefits. As our AWS infrastructure grows, keeping all the data in S3 will incur a huge cost. By storing the data in Glacier and then using the lifecycle policy, we can define when we delete data depending upon our compliance requirement. In the next section, we will see how to automate the lifecycle rule using Terraform.

Automating transitioning S3 data to Glacier using Terraform

In the last section, we learned how to transition S3 data to Glacier using the AWS console. This section will further solidify the concept by performing the same task, but this time using Terraform. These are the steps we need to follow:

1. The first step is to specify the provider block. The provider is a plugin that is used by Terraform to interact with the remote system. Terraform supports multiple providers, such as AWS, Google Cloud, Azure, and others. In our use case, we need to use AWS, as we are building our infrastructure in AWS. Next, we need to define the region in which we are creating our infrastructure—in this case, us-west-2 (Oregon):

```
provider "aws" {
   region = "us-west-2"
}
```

2. In this step, we are going to use a Terraform random_id resource. As the S3 bucket needs to be globally unique, we are going to use this so that our bucket will not conflict with any other bucket. The byte_length defines the number of random bytes to produce. In this case, it will produce eight random bits, which means it will add eight extra bits at the end of bucket:

```
resource "random_id" "my-random-id" {
   byte_length = 8
}
```

3. As the last step, we are going to create the S3 bucket and define the lifecycle rule. To create an S3 bucket, we are going to use the `aws_s3_bucket` resource. Then we will use the `random_id` resource we defined earlier to add randomness to our bucket name. Then we will define the lifecycle rule, which is exactly what we defined via the AWS console—that is, after 90 days, transition the S3 object to Glacier and, after 365 days, expire it:

```
resource "aws_s3_bucket" "my-bucket" {
   bucket = "my-bucket-${random_id.my-random-id.dec}"
   acl     = "private"
   lifecycle_rule {
     enabled = true
      transition {
        days           = 90
        storage_class = "GLACIER"
      }

      expiration {
        days = 365
      }
   }
}
```

Now we have our Terraform code ready, the next step is to execute the code and create our resource.

4. The `terraform init` command will initialize the Terraform working directory or it will download plugins for a provider (for example, `aws`):

```
$ terraform init

Initializing the backend...

Initializing provider plugins...
- Checking for available provider plugins...
- Downloading plugin for provider "random" (hashicorp/
random) 3.0.0...

The following providers do not have any version
```

```
constraints in configuration,
so the latest version was installed.


To prevent automatic upgrades to new major versions that
may contain breaking
changes, it is recommended to add version = "..."
constraints to the
corresponding provider blocks in configuration, with the
constraint strings
suggested below.


* provider.aws: version = "~> 3.10"
* provider.random: version = "~> 3.0"


Terraform has been successfully initialized!
```

5. The `terraform plan` command will generate and show the execution plan before making the actual changes:

```
$ terraform plan


Refreshing Terraform state in-memory prior to plan...
The refreshed state will be used to calculate this plan,
but will not be
persisted to local or remote state storage.


---------------------------------------------------------
---------------


An execution plan has been generated and is shown below.
Resource actions are indicated with the following
symbols:
  + create


Terraform will perform the following actions:


  # aws_s3_bucket.my-bucket will be created
  + resource "aws_s3_bucket" "my-bucket" {
```

```
      + acceleration_status           = (known after apply)
      + acl                           = "private"
      + arn                           = (known after apply)
      + bucket                        = (known after apply)



Plan: 2 to add, 0 to change, 0 to destroy.


-----------------------------------------------------------
--------------
23: To create the S3 with lifecycle policy, you need to
run the terraform apply command.
```

6. After this, as mentioned in the last line of the preceding output, we will run the
    terraform apply command:

```
$ terraform apply
provider.aws.region
   The region where AWS operations will take place.
Examples
   are us-east-1, us-west-2, etc.


   Enter a value: us-west-2



An execution plan has been generated and is shown below.
Resource actions are indicated with the following
symbols:
   + create


Terraform will perform the following actions:


   # aws_s3_bucket.my-bucket will be created
   + resource "aws_s3_bucket" "my-bucket" {
      + acceleration_status           = (known after apply)
      + acl                           = "private"
      + arn                           = (known after apply)
      + bucket                        = (known after apply)
```

```
        + bucket_domain_name              = (known after apply)
        + bucket_regional_domain_name = (known after apply)
        + force_destroy                   = false
        + hosted_zone_id                  = (known after apply)
        + id                              = (known after apply)
        + region                          = (known after apply)
        + request_payer                   = (known after apply)
        + website_domain                  = (known after apply)
        + website_endpoint                = (known after apply)


Plan: 2 to add, 0 to change, 0 to destroy.


Do you want to perform these actions?
  Terraform will perform the actions described above.
  Only 'yes' will be accepted to approve.


  Enter a value: yes


random_id.my-random-id: Creating...
random_id.my-random-id: Creation complete after 0s
[id=571zAM3yNhU]
aws_s3_bucket.my-bucket: Creating...
aws_s3_bucket.my-bucket: Creation complete after 2s
[id=my-bucket-16698629440652064277]
```

As you can see in the output, the `random_id` resource added a random ID after the bucket name.

Automating S3 bucket creation with a lifecycle policy using Terraform is a great time saver when you need to repeat this task in different AWS accounts and regions.

Summary

We can't emphasize the importance of backup enough. But the critical balance we all need to achieve is to configure our process so that it isn't too little to impact our RTO and RPO and isn't so much that it shoots down our AWS budget.

In this chapter, we learned about the various backup solutions offered by AWS and how they help us make backups. We also learned which solution to use under which conditions. We looked in more detail at DLM, and now, rather than writing our own custom snapshot solution, we can use DLM to automate the snapshot of our EBS instances. We also looked in more detail at S3, which provides us the 11 9s of durability, and with a few lines of code, we learned how to push our backup to S3. In the end, we looked at Glacier as a long-term archival solution, and at the same cost-effectiveness.

Glacier is one of the most cost-effective backup solutions available in the cloud, from just $0.00099 per GB-month (less than one-tenth of one cent, or about $1 per TB-month). As you can see, AWS makes it easy to make a backup in the cloud, but the solution you will choose entirely depends upon your requirement. If your workload runs in a hybrid model (on-premise and cloud), you can leverage solutions such as S3 and Glacier. If the workload is fully migrated to the cloud, then you can use a solution like S3.

In the next chapter, we will look at various **disaster recovery** (**DR**) solutions offered by AWS. Choosing a DR solution is again dependent upon the RTO, RPO, and cost. We will look in more detail at a real-world example, where we deploy a static website in S3 and see how it works as a failover solution if our primary website goes down.

11
AWS Disaster Recovery Solutions

In the previous chapter, we learned about the backup solutions offered by AWS. This chapter extends that concept further, and will show us how to use backup during **disaster recovery (DR)**.

DR refers to planning that aims to protect an organization from any unfortunate events that can disrupt its services. These events can be power outages, natural disasters, equipment failure, or cyberattacks. A DR plan will ensure that critical business functions will continue to operate or recover quickly despite severe disasters. DR enables the continuation of infrastructure and systems following a disaster. DR is a hot topic for several reasons. There are some applications that we never thought to put under DR because of their noncriticality or because they were too expensive to put in an on-premises environment. The cloud provides an effective, economical solution—for example, storing 1 GB of data in Amazon Glacier will cost you $0.004 per month.

In this chapter, we will start by looking at the various DR solutions offered by AWS. Then we will look at a real-time example of how to fail to an S3 static website in case our primary website goes down. These static pages will let our customers know that we are working on the issue.

In this chapter, we're going to cover the following main topics:

- Discussing the various DR solutions offered by AWS

- Configuring a website to failover to an S3 bucket

Technical requirements

There are no special technical requirements that you need to read through and understand this chapter; however, familiarity with the S3 and **Domain Name Server (DNS)** will help you better grasp the concepts.

The GitHub link for solution scripts can be found at the following link: `https://github.com/PacktPublishing/Mastering-AWS-System-Administration/tree/master/Chapter11`

Check out the following link to see the Code in Action video:

`https://bit.ly/34TqueO`

Discussing the various DR solutions offered by AWS

Before we discuss the various DR solutions offered by AWS, we first need to define the business impact analysis, **recovery time objective (RTO)**, and **recovery point objective (RPO)** for an application and fit a DR solution to that objective. We already discussed the RTO and RPO in *Chapter 10, Centralizing Cloud Backup Solution*.

AWS offers four levels of DR support:

- Backup and restore

- Pilot light

- Warm standby in AWS

- Hot standby (with multi-site)

We will cover all these in detail in the following sections.

Backup and restore

This solution suits less critical applications where RTO/RPO is measured in hours. This is one of the most common solutions implemented by many AWS customers, where they store their application backup to S3 for short-term storage, and for long-term storage, to Glacier. Now compare this solution to a traditional on-premise environment where data is backed up to tape and sent off-site regularly. The recovery time is the longest in this type of scenario. AWS S3 is an ideal solution for backup. It provides 11 9s of durability (99.999999999%). Data is transferred via a network; it will be accessible from any location.

If you need to transfer a very large dataset to S3, you can use AWS Import/Export service. If you are dealing with petabytes of data, AWS offers the Snowball service, which is a petabyte-scale data transport solution.

If your infrastructure is running on AWS, then you can copy the file directly into S3. You can snapshot your EBS volumes or backup AWS **Relational Database Service** (**RDS**), which, under the hood, eventually stores snapshot/RDS data in S3.

Backing up your data only solves half of the problem. The other half of the problem is to recover your data quickly and reliably in case of disaster. Here are some of the key points that we should remember for backup and disaster:

- Select the appropriate tool based on the criticality of your application and RTO/RPO.

- Test your backup and recovery process regularly.

- Make sure you have a proper retention policy based on your compliance requirement.

Backup and restore is the least expensive solution and is ideal for the noncritical application. Next, we will look at the pilot light, which is a costly solution compared to backup and restore, but the recovery time is much faster.

Pilot light

The main idea behind the pilot light comes from a gas heater analogy. A gas heater has a small idle flame called the pilot light, which is always on and can quickly ignite the entire furnace to heat up the house as needed. The same principle is applied to the DR scenario, where all the system's critical core elements are always configured and running. We can rapidly provision a full-scale production environment around this critical core during the time of the disaster.

The typical infrastructure element included as a part of the pilot light scenario is the database that is continuously in sync with the master. Depending upon the application, we might need to replicate application data too.

To restore the business-critical services by provisioning the remaining infrastructure, we should typically have a preconfigured AMI that boots up our instances as soon as possible. From a network point of view, you can use Elastic IP (a reserve static IP associated with your AWS account), which is generally preallocated during the DR preparation phase, and associate that with our instance. The other alternative is to use **Elastic Load Balancing (ELB)**, which is used to distribute traffic to multiple instances. We then need to update the Route53 record to point to a new EC2 instance, or, if we are using ELB, we can use **canonical name (CNAME)**. After the creation of a new ELB, we will get a new CNAME, and that's why it's crucial to update the Route53 record with this new CNAME record.

The pilot light method will give you a quick recovery as the core piece of infrastructure is always running and is continually kept up to date. To scale up your infrastructure, AWS provides a solution in the form of CloudFormation, which will automate infrastructure resources, provisioning, and configuration.

Here are some of the key points we should remember when following a pilot light method:

- Always replicate or mirror EC2 instance data.
- Maintain the AMI for the critical application that will speed up the recovery process.
- Automate the provisioning of AWS resources.
- Regularly test pilot light servers.

As you learned in the pilot light scenario, your infrastructure's bare-minimum, critical servers are always running, so it's an expensive solution compared to backup and restore. Still, your application will always be available to your customer. In the next section, we are going to explore the warm standby option.

Warm standby in AWS

We can think of warm standby approach as an extension to the pilot light methodology. It will reduce the downtime as some of the services are already running. You first need to identify all of your business-critical systems, then fully duplicate them on AWS and get them running. These servers can be running the minimum possible instance size but should still be fully functional. You can use these systems for nonproduction workloads, such as testing, **quality analysis (QA)**, and so on. In the case of disaster, you should scale up infrastructure quickly to handle production load. Scaling can be done horizontally by adding more servers behind the load balancer or vertically by bumping up the instance family. As a best practice, horizontal scaling is always preferred over vertical scaling because with vertical scaling, there is a possibility that you will hit a limit, such as the maximum CPU or RAM available for a given EC2 instance family, which is not the case with horizontal scaling, where you are adding additional servers.

Here are some of the key points we should remember for warm standby:

- Replicate/mirror EC2 data.
- Create and maintain the AMI of your application.
- Run a minimal version of your infrastructure.
- Regularly patch and update software and configuration files.

Warm standby is an extension to pilot light, but in this case, we have our critical business infrastructure running all the time with the minimal possible instance size. In the next section, we will look at the hot standby solution.

Hot standby (with multi-site)

This is the most expensive solution of all the available options to maintain an exact copy of your production in an active/active configuration. In this case, a weighted DNS service, such as Route53, is used to route production traffic to different sites. With weighted routing, a specific portion of traffic is routed to an on-premise facility; for example, 60% could be routed to an on-premise facility and the remaining 40% could be routed to AWS.

In the case of disaster, you only need to adjust the DNS weighting and send all traffic to the AWS servers. The capacity of your AWS infrastructure can be rapidly increased by using solutions such as auto-scaling (as covered in *Chapter 6, Increasing Application Performance using AWS Auto Scaling*). At the database end, we must add the logic at the application level to detect the failure and cut over to the AWS database.

Here are some of the key points we should remember for hot standby:

- Set up your environment similar to the production.
- DNS weighting or similar technology should distribute traffic to both sites.

Out of all the available DR solutions provided by AWS, which one you should choose depends on the application's criticality and cost. Backup and restore is the cheapest of all the solutions, but your RTO/RPO time will be high, which means your application will be inaccessible to the customer for a long time. If you choose hot standby (with multi-site), then your RTO/RPO will be less as your instance is always running and you can easily switch the DNS endpoint within seconds, but it will increase your infrastructure cost.

Configuring a website to fail over to an S3 bucket

In a real-time scenario, we will configure an S3 static website, which we will use as a failover if there's an issue with our primary website. To do the failover, we are going to use the Route53 health check.

Our primary website is hosted on EC2 behind an application load balancer:

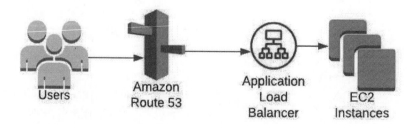

Figure 11.1 – Primary website using ALB and EC2 instances

If the primary EC2 instances go down, Route53 will route traffic to an S3 bucket using a failover policy that is hosting our static website:

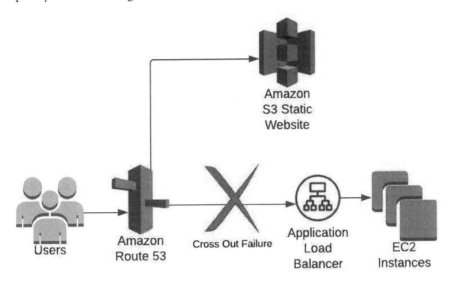

Figure 11.2 – Route53 failover to S3 in case of EC2 failure

This chapter assumes that you already have a Route53 public hosted zone that is hosting your website. A public hosted zone holds information such as how to route traffic on the internet for a specific domain, for example, `amazon.com`. For more information about public hosted zones, check out the following link: `https://docs.aws.amazon.com/Route53/latest/DeveloperGuide/AboutHZWorkingWith.html`

To register/purchase a domain from AWS, check out the following documentation. To configure a website, we need a public hosted zone. The following guide is the step-by-step process of registering a new domain using Route53: `https://docs.aws.amazon.com/Route53/latest/DeveloperGuide/domain-register.html`.

Once you have purchased a new domain, let's check out the steps involved in registering a new domain:

1. To verify the domain, which you have already purchased via Route53, go to the URL at `https://console.aws.amazon.com/route53/`. If you've already purchased the domain via AWS or transferred any domain from any other provider to AWS, you will see it under the Route53 console. For the purpose of this example, I am using `plakhera.com`, which is a public hosted zone. The main difference between public and private hosted zones is that public hosted zones route traffic to the internet. A private hosted zone is used to route traffic within AWS VPC:

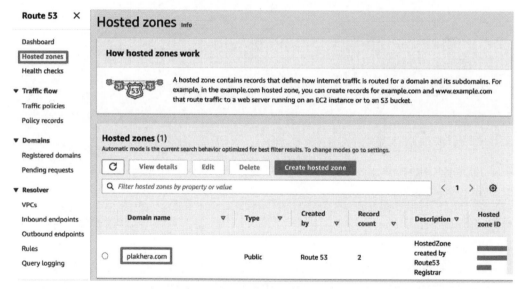

Figure 11.3 – Route53 hosted zones

2. In the next step, you need to create an alias record that maps our domain to the application load balancer, which we have already configured in *Chapter 5, Increasing an Application's Fault Tolerance with Elastic Load Balancing*. An alias record is specific to AWS, and it adds a Route53 extension to your DNS functionality. It's used to route traffic to selected AWS resources, such as an S3 bucket, load balancer, and so on.

3. As shown in the preceding screenshot, click on the **plakhera.com** domain. You should see the following screen. Click on **Create record**:

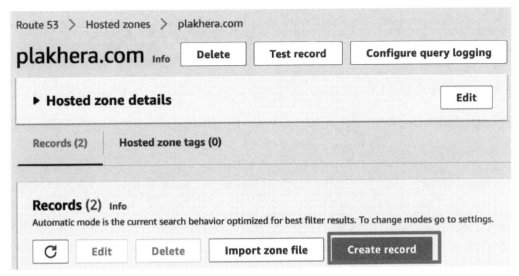

Figure 11.4 – Create record

4. On the next screen, select the **Simple routing** policy under **Routing policy** and click **Next**:

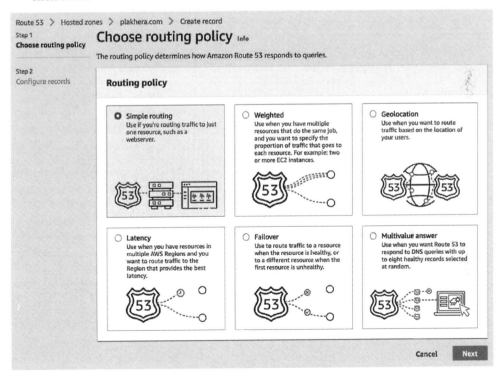

Figure 11.5 – Route53 choosing the Simple routing policy

5.   On the next screen, click on **Define simple record**:

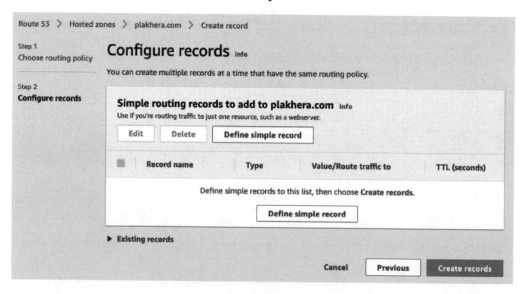

Figure 11.6 – Define simple record

6.   On the **Define simple record** screen, fill in the following details:

- **Record name**: Leave it blank (as we want to route all the traffic to the main domain (`plakhera.com`)).

- **Value/Route traffic to**: From the dropdown, select **Alias to Application and Classic Load Balancer**, **us-west-2** as the region, and then enter the name of the application load balancer (this is the same application load balancer that we created in *Chapter 5, Increasing an Application's Fault Tolerance with Elastic Load Balancing*). Under **Record type**, select **A – Routes traffic to an IPv4 address and some AWS resources**.

Click on **Define simple record** to proceed, as shown in the following screenshot:

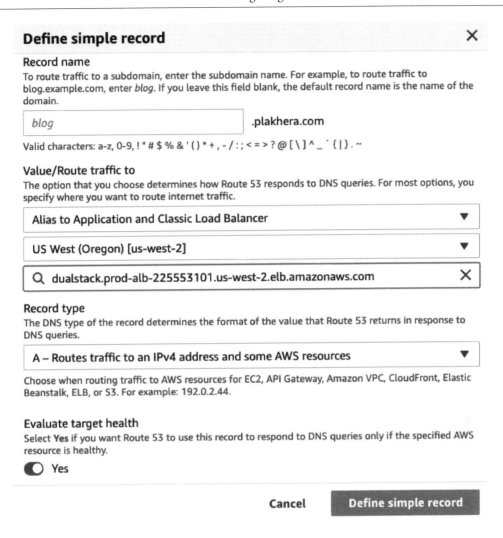

Figure 11.7 – Define simple record with values

7. At the bottom of the page, click on **Create records**.

8. Try to browse your domain (`plakhera.com` in this example) on any browser and you will see the default page that you created in *Chapter 5, Increasing an Application's Fault Tolerance with Elastic Load Balancing*:

This is coming from default apache page

Figure 11.8 – Browse your website

In the next step, we are going to create a static website that we will use as a failover if there is any outage in our primary website:

1. To create a static website using S3, go to the S3 console at `https://s3.console.aws.amazon.com/s3/home` and click on **Create bucket**:

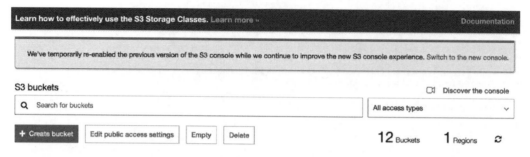

Figure 11.9 – AWS S3 console

2. Give your **Bucket name** as `plakhera.com` (it needs to be the same as our hosted zone) and under **Region**, from the dropdown, select **US West (Oregon)** and click on **Create**:

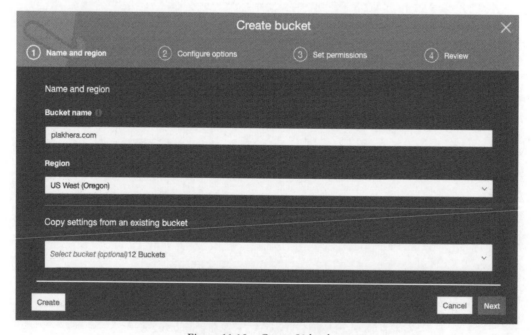

Figure 11.10 – Create S3 bucket

3. Click on the bucket we have created:

Figure 11.11 – Select the S3 bucket

4. Click on **Properties** and then **Static website hosting**:

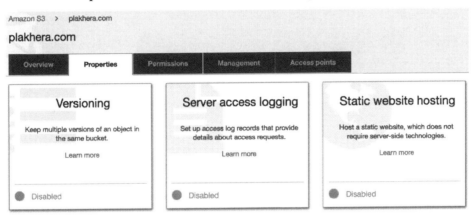

Figure 11.12 – Static website hosting

5. In the next window, select **Use this bucket to host a website** and under **Index document**, type index.html (you can choose any name, but index.html is the standard name; S3 returns this index document when requests are made to the root domain). Click on **Save**:

Figure 11.13 – Defining values for static website hosting

6. Go back to the S3 console at `https://s3.console.aws.amazon.com/s3` and click on the **Overview** tab and then click on **Upload**. Upload the file provided via the GitHub link at `https://github.com/PacktPublishing/Mastering-AWS-System-Administration/blob/master/Chapter11/index.html`, which is going to display `This is my S3 backup website`:

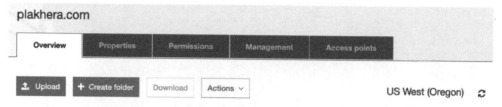

Figure 11.14 – Uploading file to S3

7. On the next screen, click on **Add files** and add `index.html`:

Figure 11.15 – Add the file to your bucket

8. Once the file is added, click on **Upload**:

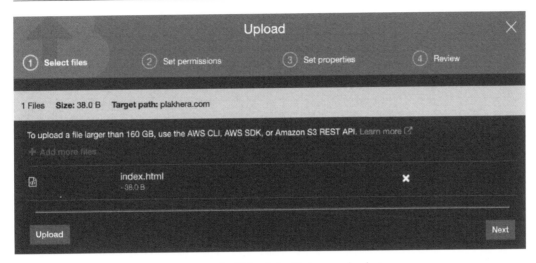

Figure 11.16 – Upload the file to your bucket

9. Now what we need to do is grant the public access to this S3 bucket so that we can browse its content. To do this, go back to your S3 bucket and click on **Edit public access settings**:

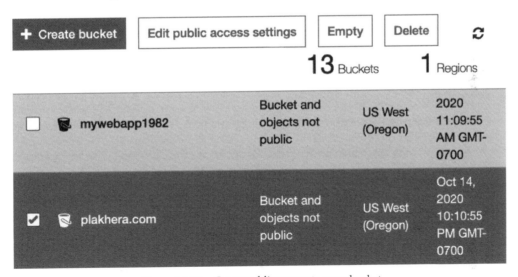

Figure 11.17 – Grant public access to your bucket

10. Uncheck the **Block all public access** and click on **Save**:

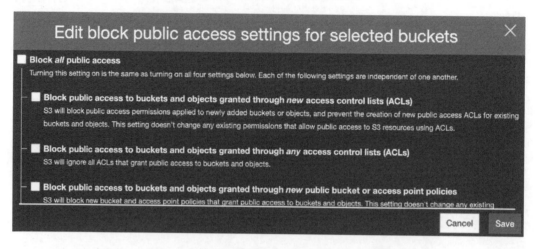

Figure 11.18 – Edit block public access settings for selected buckets

11. As of this stage, we make our bucket public, but in order to grant all the objects inside the bucket read-only permission, we need to add an S3 bucket policy. To do this, again inside the bucket, navigate to **Permissions | Bucket Policy** and copy the following policy. This policy allows all the action `s3:GetObject`, which means that it grants read-only permission to all the `plakhera.com` bucket objects:

```
{
    "Version": "2012-10-17",
    "Statement": [
        {
            "Effect": "Allow",
            "Principal": "*",
            "Action": "s3:GetObject",
            "Resource": "arn:aws:s3:::plakhera.com/*"
        }
    ]
}
```

Copy the preceding policy and click on **Save**:

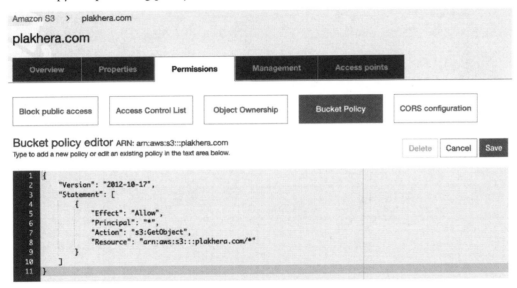

Figure 11.19 – S3 Bucket Policy

12. You will now see the change under **Bucket Policy**. Under **Bucket Policy**, it will now show the word **Public**:

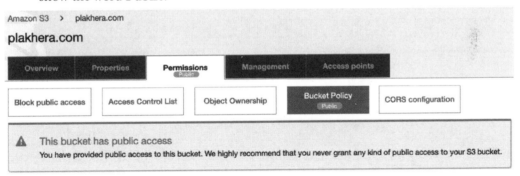

Figure 11.20 – S3 bucket with public access

13. Go to the **Properties** tab and click on **Static website hosting**. You will see your website endpoint:

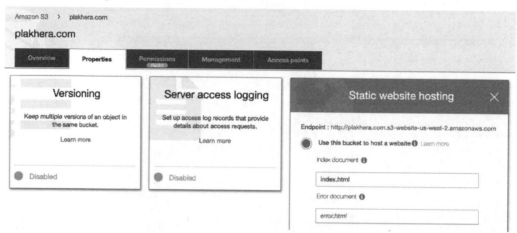

Figure 11.21 – S3 bucket URL

14. When browsing to the endpoint; you will see the pages that we uploaded in step 8 to this S3 bucket:

Figure 11.22 – S3 bucket endpoint

At this stage, we have our primary site and backup site running. Now we need to modify our Route53 and set up the routing policy for a failover. Failover routing acts like an active/passive setup, in that it will route all the traffic to the primary site if the resource is healthy and then to different resource when the first resource is unhealthy. We configure it using the following steps:

1. In order to configure it, go back to the Route53 record that we created earlier, select it, and this time click on **Edit**:

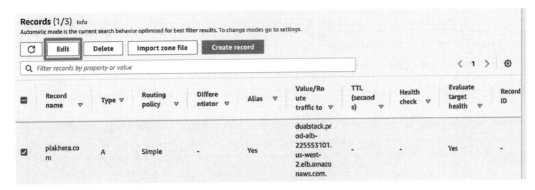

Figure 11.23 – Editing your Route53 record

2. This time, under the **Routing policy**, you need to select a different policy
    (**Failover**). Select **Failover** as the **Routing policy**:

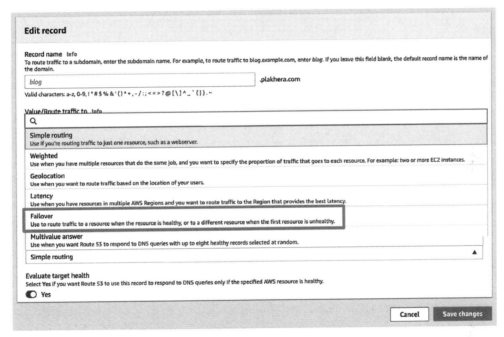

Figure 11.24 – Select Failover as the routing policy

3. With the routing policy set to a failover routing policy, you need to add a few more
    details:

    - **Failover record type**: From the dropdown, select **Primary**. **Primary** is where
    the traffic is routed by default unless it becomes unhealthy, in which case it will be
    routed to **Secondary**.

- **Record ID**: This gives a description of your record. Choose any meaningful name here—for example, `Route53-Primary`.

Click on **Save changes**, as shown in the following screenshot:

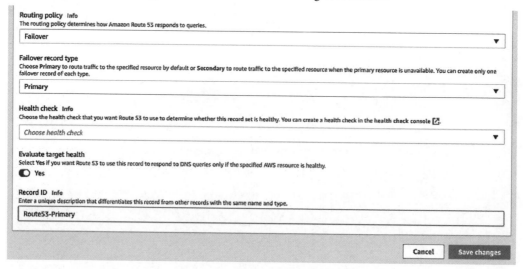

Figure 11.25 – Add values to your policy and save the changes

4. With the **Primary** record in place, next we need to create a secondary record. To do this, go back to the Route53 **Records** and click on **Create record**:

Figure 11.26 – Create a secondary record

5. Under **Routing policy**, choose **Failover**:

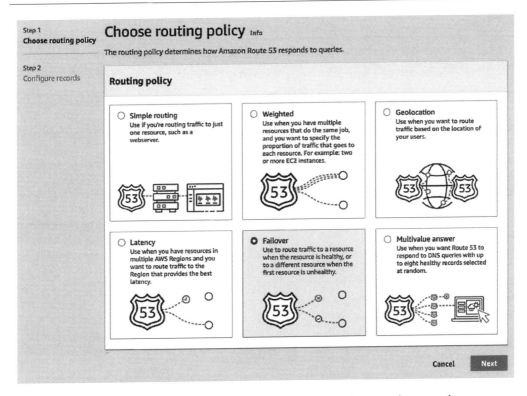

Figure 11.27 – Select Failover as the routing policy for the secondary record

6.   On the next screen, scroll down to the bottom and click on **Define failover record**:

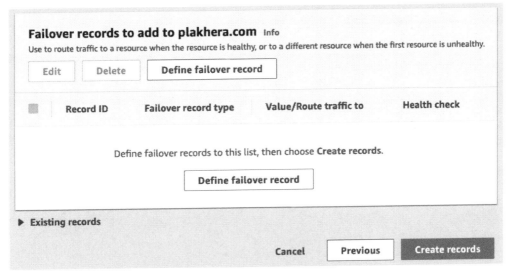

Figure 11.28 – Define failover record

7. Under **Define failover record**, we need to define our secondary failover record. This is used if the primary goes down:

    - **Values/Route traffic to**: From the dropdown, choose **Alias to S3 website endpoint**, **US West (Oregon) [us-west-2]** for the region, and then select the static S3 website that we created earlier.

    - **Failover record type**: As we are creating the secondary record, choose **Secondary**.

    - **Record ID**: This is to give a description of your record. Choose any meaningful name here—for example, Route53-Secondary (you will see this when you scroll down to the bottom).

    Keep the rest of the settings as their defaults and click on **Define failover record**:

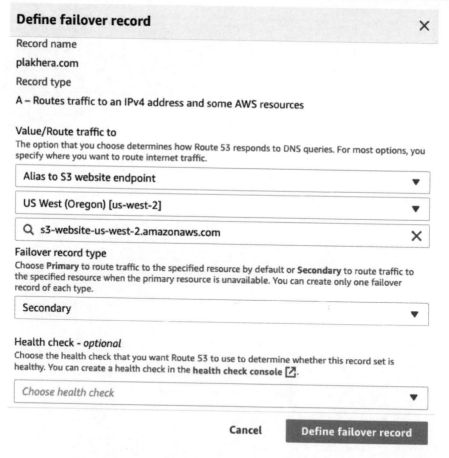

Figure 11.29 – Define failover record with values

8. Scroll down to the bottom and click on **Create records**:

Record name Info
To route traffic to a subdomain, enter the subdomain name. For example, to route traffic to blog.example.com, enter *blog*. If you leave this field blank, the default record name is the name of the domain.

| blog | .plakhera.com |

Valid characters: a-z, 0-9, ! " # $ % & ' ( ) * + , - / : ; < = > ? @ [\ ] ^ _ ` { | } . ~

Record type Info
The DNS type of the record determines the format of the value that Route 53 returns in response to DNS queries.

| A – Routes traffic to an IPv4 address and some AWS resources ▼ |

Choose when routing traffic to AWS resources for EC2, API Gateway, Amazon VPC, CloudFront, Elastic Beanstalk, ELB, or S3. For example: 192.0.2.44.

TTL (seconds) Info
The amount of time, in seconds, that DNS resolvers and web browsers cache the settings in this record. ("TTL" means "time to live.")

| 300 | | 1m | 1h | 1d |

Recommended values: 60 to 172800 (two days)

Failover records to add to plakhera.com Info
Use to route traffic to a resource when the resource is healthy, or to a different resource when the first resource is unhealthy.

| Edit | Delete | **Define failover record** |

	Record ID	Failover record type	Value/Route traffic to	Health check
☐	Route53-Secondary	Secondary	s3-website-us-west-2.amazonaws.com	-

▶ **Existing records**

| | | Cancel | Previous | Create records |

Figure 11.30 – Create records

9. Under your Route53 console, you will see a record like that shown in the following screenshot, with **Primary** pointing to a load balancer and **Secondary** pointing to an S3 static website:

Records (4) Info
Automatic mode is the current search behavior optimized for best filter results. To change modes go to settings.

| C | Edit | Delete | Import zone file | **Create record** |

Q *Filter records by property or value*

	Record name ▽	Type ▽	Routing policy ▽	Differe ntiator ▽	Alias ▽	Value/Ro ute traffic to ▽	TTL (second s) ▽
☐	plakhera.co m	A	Failover	Primary	Yes	dualstack.pr od-alb-225553101. us-west-2.elb.amazo naws.com.	-
☐	plakhera.co m	A	Failover	Secondary	Yes	s3-website-us-west-2.amazonaw s.com.	-

Figure 11.31 –Primary and secondary failover record

10. In order to replicate the scenario, go back to the EC2 console at `https://us-west-2.console.aws.amazon.com/ec2` and shut down both of the instances behind the load balancer:

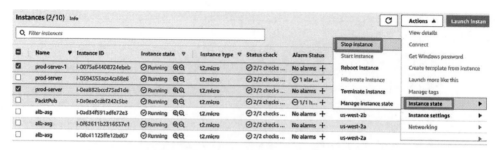

Figure 11.32 – Stopping the EC2 instances

11. Stopping these instances and failing over to the secondary (S3 in this case) will take some time. After a few seconds, if you try to browse to your website, you will see that it's coming from S3:

This is my S3 backup website

Figure 11.33 – Primary website is now redirected to failover

Failing over to a static S3 website is useful in a real-time scenario. In most cases, companies create pages displaying We are working on the issue or We will get back to you or Contact our customer care page so that their customer will be aware that someone is already looking into the issue. These things will help to build customer trust and experience.

Summary

Some of the keys to having a successful DR solution are testing, monitoring and alerting, backups, and automation. You can introduce a solution such as a Game Day (where you can simulate the failure and failover to a replica) to exercise a failover in the DR environment. You can also introduce a modern discipline such as chaos engineering, where you can experiment on a software system in production to build confidence that your system can withstand any unexpected conditions. A good monitoring system will enable you to get a notification as soon as your system is down. If you go one step up, then your monitoring system, such as CloudWatch, will be tightly integrated with an automation solution, such as Lambda, which will spin up your new instance. Automation is the key, as it will reduce your downtime. Last but not least, you should take your backup regularly and restore it on a regular basis.

In this chapter, we have learned about the various DR solutions offered by AWS and which one to use under which condition. We then looked at real-time use cases of failing over to a static S3 website if our primary website goes down.

In the last chapter of this book, we will look at some more real-time cases. These are the problems that you face in your daily work, and with a real-time example, you will learn how to solve it. The chapter covers different cases from compute to networking, and even how to reduce your AWS bill.

12
AWS Tips and Tricks

In the final chapter of this book, we will look at 10 tips and tricks to get the most out of **Amazon Web Services** (**AWS**). We will start with the networking side of the infrastructure and learn about some common **virtual private cloud** (**VPC**) limitations and which subnet to choose while building a VPC. We will then move on to one common issue: the difference between a dedicated instance and a dedicated host, and which one to select under which conditions. Then, we will look at a fairly new feature in the **Identity and Access Management** (**IAM**) permission boundary and how it restricts access.

Then, we will move to the monitoring side and look at the custom CloudWatch metrics and how they are useful. We will also look at the importance of tagging. We will then look at safety measures and how to prevent the accidental deletion of your **Elastic Compute Cloud** (**EC2**) and **Elastic Block Store** (**EBS**) volumes. We will also look at a critical question in our daily system admin/DevOps, which is how to reduce/save money on our AWS bill. We then move on to how to create a random **Simple Storage Service** (**S3**) bucket name, and we will finally wrap up with how to automate **Amazon Machine Image** (**AMI**) creation. These tips will help you improve your AWS skills and will also assist you in your daily job.

In this chapter, we're going to cover the following main topics:

- Some common pitfalls—VPC limitations
- Which VPC subnets to choose while building a VPC
- Dedicated instance versus dedicated host—which should you choose?
- The power of the IAM permission boundary

- Custom CloudWatch metrics

- Tagging, tagging, and tagging—why is tagging important?

- Protecting your EC2 instances and EBS volumes using termination protection

- How to reduce your AWS bill

- Choosing an AWS bucket name and how to create a random bucket name

- Automating AMI creation

Technical requirements

The GitHub link for solution scripts can be found at the following link: `https://github.com/PacktPublishing/AWS-for-System-Administrators/tree/master/Chapter12`

Check out the following link to see the Code in Action video: `https://bit.ly/38Fj7bS`

Some common pitfalls – VPC limitations

The VPC is one of the most critical components as this is the place where we start our AWS journey, and it is where we begin setting up our network before deploying other resources such as EC2. Before we start using it, there are some limits for VPC resources, but most of them are soft limits (unless indicated), and you should always contact AWS customer support to increase these resource limits. Some of these limits that you should be aware of are presented here:

- You can only have five VPCs per region. This is generally an AWS newbie error, initially in the **Proof of Concept** (**POC**) phase, when trying to create multiple VPCs in a region. The good news is this is a soft limit, and you can always contact AWS Support to increase this value.

- By default, you can have 200 subnets per VPC, but again this is a soft limit.

- By default, you can have five internet gateways and **Network Address Translation** (**NAT**) gateways per region, but this is a soft limit.

- By default, you can have 200 network **Access Control Lists** (**ACLs**) per VPC and 20 rules per **Network Access Control List** (**NACL**). You can have 20 ingress and 20 egress rules. The maximum you can have is 40 rules per ACL, as a hard limit, which means you can't increase it. One of the primary reasons for there being a hard limit is that it would impact network performance to process these additional rules.

- The default route table limit is 200, and you can have 50 routes per route table. This quota for routes per table can increase to a maximum of 1,000 (hard limit), but you will start seeing network performance issues after 125 routes.

- The default security group limit per region is 2,500 (soft limit), and the maximum it can be increased to is 5,000 (hard limit). The quota for security group rules is 60 inbound and 60 outbound, with a hard limit of 1,000. As we have seen with other resources, you will start seeing network performance issues as the number of security group rules increases.

Always keep these limits in mind, especially the hard limits, before designing your VPC solution. As networking is a critical part of any infrastructure, these limits may severely impact your infrastructure performance.

Which VPC subnets to choose while building a VPC

AWS gives us a lot of flexibility while designing the VPC network. AWS supports the following subnet blocks: /16 to /28. If you choose a /16 netmask, it will give you 65,536 **Internet Protocol** (**IP**) addresses, and if you decide on a /28 IP address, it will provide you with 16 addresses. Now, which subnet block to choose depends entirely upon your network requirements. Typically, companies choose a bigger subnet as this helps them if their infrastructure expands.

AWS now supports the addition of IPv4 **classless inter-domain routing** (**CIDR**) to your VPC. The default quota is 5, and the soft limit can be increased to 50 for IPv4. For IPv6, the default limit is 1, which can't be increased (hard limit). In order to add additional CIDR blocks to your VPC, we perform the following steps:

1. Go to the VPC console at https://us-west-2.console.aws.amazon.com/vpc/home. Select the VPC to **prod-vpc**, as in this example, and click on **Actions**. From the dropdown, select **Edit CIDRs**, as illustrated in the following screenshot:

Figure 12.1 – AWS VPC Edit CIDRs

2. In the next screen, you can add additional CIDRs to your VPC using **Add new IPv4 CIDR**, as illustrated in the following screenshot:

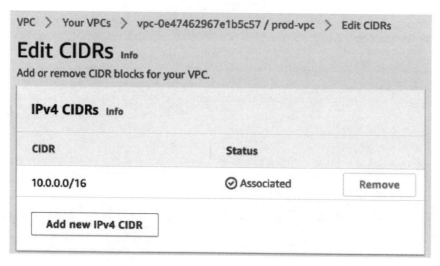

Figure 12.2 – Adding a new VPC CIDR

> **Note**
> The CIDR you choose must not overlap with the existing VPC CIDR.

Choosing the right subnet is the first thing to get right when designing the network infrastructure. Make sure that you always keep company growth in mind, and select the optimal subnet.

Dedicated instance versus dedicated host – which should you choose?

This is always a confusing topic, but let's first learn about dedicated instances with reference to an on-demand context, which most of us know about. On-demand is the preferred choice for most of us as it's cost-effective. When you spin up your EC2 instance, if you don't choose any option, by default it picks on-demand, which means your instance can be launched in any hypervisor running in AWS.

This might be an issue for some customers who want a hypervisor (a hypervisor is a piece of software that creates and runs **virtual machines (VMs)**) dedicated to their AWS account. There can be many reasons for that, but one common concern is security. You want the hypervisor you are using to only run the AWS instances of your company. This is where a dedicated instance comes into the picture. When you pick the dedicated instance option, hardware will be dedicated to your account. AWS now provides you with isolation at the hardware level in that if you launch any instance, it will always be launched in the same dedicated instance reserved by your AWS account.

A dedicated host goes one level deeper. In the case of a dedicated instance, multiple instances can be launched on the same hypervisor. But in cases where you have strict license requirements that your license be bound to a specific host, you can choose the dedicated host option. Both of these options come with an additional cost, such as $2 per hour for AWS, to keep this host reserved for you.

Before you choose a dedicated instance or a dedicated host, please be aware of some of their limitations. Not all instance types support a dedicated instance, such as the t2 instance family. For more information, check out the following web page: `https://aws.amazon.com/ec2/pricing/dedicated-instances/`.

For a dedicated host, if you plan to run **Red Hat Enterprise Linux (RHEL)** or SUSE Linux, you need to bring your own AMI. The AWS AMI available in the Marketplace can't be used for dedicated hosts, and an AWS **Relational Database Service (RDS)** instance is not supported. There is no AWS free usage tier for dedicated hosts.

Choosing between dedicated instances and dedicated hosts will all depend upon your requirements. If you plan to use software with a license bound to a specific host, then a dedicated host is the default choice, but this comes with an additional cost. If you don't want your instance to be shared with other companies but for your company instance to boot on the same host, you should choose a dedicated instance.

The power of the IAM permission boundary

The main idea behind a permission boundary is to provide a safety net. It's a set of access rights that an entity such as user, group, or organization can never exceed. A permission boundary on its own doesn't grant any permissions. The primary purpose of it is to restrict access. To understand permission boundaries, let's take a simple example, as follows:

1. Create an IAM user using an `aws iam create-user` command. We need to pass `--user-name` at the end of the command and then give the username—in this case, `mypermuser`. This will create an IAM user, as follows:

```
$ aws iam create-user --user-name mypermuser
```

2. In the next step, we will assign full permissions to the user by attaching an `AdministratorAccess` policy. To attach this policy, we need to use an `aws iam attach-user-policy` command and then pass the username, `mypermuser`, which is the same user we created in the previous step. The code for this can be seen in the following snippet:

```
$ aws iam put-user-permissions-boundary --permissions-
boundary arn:aws:iam::aws:policy/AmazonS3FullAccess
--user-name mypermuser
```

3. Now, we will attach the permission boundary to the `mypermuser` user. The primary purpose of the permission boundary is to restrict access, as in the previous step we attached an `AdministratorAccess` policy to the user, which means this user has full admin access, but now we are attaching a permission boundary as a safety net and assigning only S3 access to the user. The net effect of this is that the user only has S3 full access. To perform this action, we need to use an `aws iam put-user-permission-boundary` command and pass the `permissions-boundary` S3 access and username, which is `mypermuser`. The code for this can be seen in the following snippet:

```
$ aws iam put-user-permissions-boundary --permissions-
boundary arn:aws:iam::aws:policy/AmazonS3FullAccess
--user-name mypermuser
```

4. With the permission boundary in place, if we try to access any other AWS resource except the S3 bucket, it will fail. Let's try to access an EC2 instance—as you can see in the following code snippet, it's failing:

```
$ aws ec2 describe-instances
An error occurred (UnauthorizedOperation) when calling
the DescribeInstances operation: You are not authorized
to perform this operation.
```

5. Let's try to access an S3 bucket, which is the only allowed permission. As you can see in the following code snippet, it's working:

```
$ aws s3 ls
2020-10-01 22:31:47 aws-cloudtrail-logs-xyz12345
```

As you can see, the IAM permission boundary is a powerful concept, and it helps restrict access to the IAM entity.

Custom CloudWatch metrics

If you look at the CloudWatch dashboard, there are four default metrics, as follows:

- CPU
- Disk I/O
- Network
- Instance/system status check

These default metrics (CPU, status check, and network) can be seen in the following screenshot:

Figure 12.3 – CloudWatch default metrics

But why are some of the standard metrics such as memory utilization or disk space not default metrics? The reason behind that is that an EC2 instance is a VM that emulates computer hardware such as CPU, **random-access memory** (**RAM**), and disk. Your AWS service can't look inside your instance because its operating system controls how many resources need to be allocated, such as how much memory is required. This is the main reason why it's not possible to determine memory utilization by looking at the virtual hardware. We need to install solutions such as CloudWatch agents to get these metrics and push them to CloudWatch. In *Chapter 8, Monitoring AWS Services Using CloudWatch and SNS*, we have already seen how to install these CloudWatch agents and push these metrics to CloudWatch.

With these custom metrics now available in CloudWatch, you can now enable a **Simple Notification Service** (**SNS**) notification to alert you if any of these metrics cross the threshold, or create a dashboard to view these metrics in a single pane.

Tagging, tagging, and tagging – why is tagging important?

Tagging is a way to manage your AWS resources by assigning metadata or a label to each resource in the form of tags. It helps you to categorize your AWS resources in different ways, such as by environment, owner, and so on—for example, we can set a tag as equivalent to a production or a development environment. This way, you can quickly identify a specific resource based on the tag you have as this belongs to a production or a development environment.

Tagging is a simple but powerful concept in AWS, helping you to categorize your resources as well as keep track of your resources.

Protecting your EC2 instances and EBS volumes using termination protection

You can always delete an EC2 instance that is no longer needed, and the process is called terminating your instance. Simultaneously, you need to be very careful not to accidentally delete any instance in use, as this will cause downtime. This is where enabling instance termination protection comes in handy.

By default, you can delete any instance using the following:

- EC2 console
- AWS **command-line interface (CLI)**
- **Application Programming Interface (API)**

We can use the `DisableApiTermination` attribute to control whether we can terminate the instance using the console, the AWS CLI, or an API. This attribute can be set at the following times:

- During instance launch
- When the instance is running (for EBS-backed instance)
- While the instance is in a shutdown state

To enable termination protection of a running instance, proceed as follows:

1. Go to the EC2 console at `https://console.aws.amazon.com/ec2/`. Select the instance, click on **Actions** then on **Instance settings**, and click on **Change termination protection**, as illustrated in the following screenshot:

Figure 12.4 – Changing EC2 termination protection

2. In the next screen, check the **Enable** box and click on **Save**, as illustrated in the following screenshot:

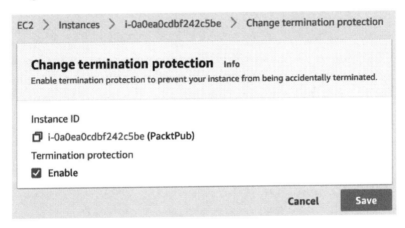

Figure 12.5 – Enabling EC2 termination protection

3. In order to enable termination protection via the AWS CLI, you need to use a `modify-instance-attribute` command, and your command will look like this (replace `instance-id` with the EC2 instance ID of your instance):

```
aws ec2 modify-instance-attribute --disable-api-
termination --instance-id <instance id>
```

These small checks will help safeguard your resources and prevent your infrastructure from any accidental termination or deletion of resources.

How to reduce your AWS bill

One of the common problems to which we are all looking for a solution is how to reduce your AWS bill. There are a variety of ways you can achieve this, as follows:

*   In *Chapter 4, Scalable Compute Capacity in the Cloud via EC2*, we already discussed activating an AWS billing alarm when a certain threshold was reached.

- Use AWS Trusted Advisor, which gives you real-time guidance to help you provision your resources following AWS best practice, helping you to identify resources not running at their full capacity. You can decide later whether you want to keep the resource or delete it. For more information about Trusted Advisor, please refer to the following web page: `https://aws.amazon.com/premiumsupport/technology/trusted-advisor/`.

- If your load is stateless and fault-tolerant and you want to reduce the operating cost, you can use Amazon EC2 Spot Instances. EC2 Spot Instances lets you take advantage of AWS unused capacity, and a 90% discount compared to on-demand prices is available. For more information about Spot Instances, please refer to `https://aws.amazon.com/aws-cost-management/aws-cost-optimization/spot-instances/`.

- As we discussed in *Chapter 4, Scalable Compute Capacity in the Cloud via EC2*, other methods you can adopt are shutting down instances in the dev environment on a scheduled basis, cleaning up any unused AMI, or detaching any unused EBS volumes.

From finance to infrastructure, everyone wants to reduce their AWS bill. Taking these small measures will significantly help to reduce your bill.

Choosing an AWS bucket name and how to create a random bucket name

An Amazon S3 bucket name must be globally unique, as the S3 namespace is shared with all AWS accounts. This means no two buckets should have the same name.

By using Terraform, you can achieve this using the `random_id` resource. `byte_length` defines the number of random bytes to produce, and in this case, there are 8 bits of random bytes, which means it will add 8 extra bits at the end of bucket, as illustrated in the following code snippet:

```
resource "random_id" "my-random-id" {
byte_length = 8
}
```

Then, you can pass `random_id` to the `aws_s3_bucket` resource to add randomness to the bucket, as illustrated in the following code snippet:

```
resource "aws_s3_bucket" "my-bucket" {
bucket = "my-bucket-${random_id.my-random-id.dec}"
}
```

By choosing the `random_id` resource, you can simplify and automate your S3 bucket random bucket name creation.

Automating AMI creation

AMI contains information that is required to launch an instance. It consists of information such as the operating system image, the different software installed in it, and configuration information. It's important to regularly update the AMI to contain information such as operating system patches, updated software, and the latest config changes. To create an AMI, we can follow any of these three procedures:

- Creating an AMI using the AWS console

- Creating an AMI using the AWS CLI

- Automating AMI creation using Packer

Let's discuss these procedures in detail in the following sections.

Creating an AMI using the AWS console

The steps to create an AMI using the AWS console are listed as follows:

1. Go to the EC2 console at `https://us-west-2.console.aws.amazon.com/ec2/v2/home`. Select the instance (in this case, **prod-server**), and under **Actions**, click on **Image and templates** and then click on **Create image**, as illustrated in the following screenshot:

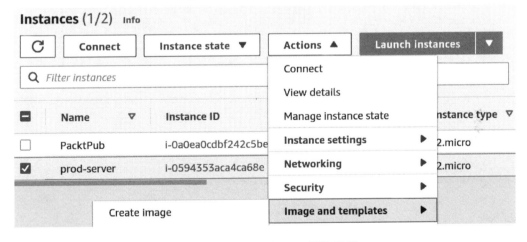

Figure 12.6 – Creating an AWS AMI

2. In the next screen, give your image some name—for example, `my-test-image`—under **Image name** and click on **Create image**, as illustrated in the following screenshot:

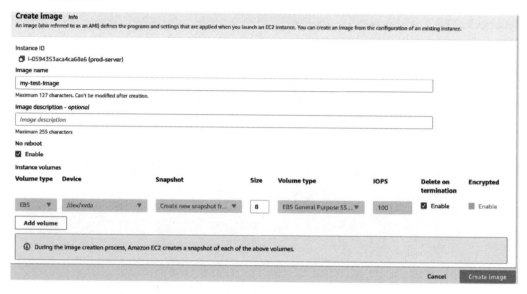

Figure 12.7 – Assigning a name to your AMI

3. If you now click on **AMIs** under **Images**, you will see the newly created image, as illustrated in the following screenshot:

Figure 12.8 – Newly created AMI

At this stage, you know how to create an AMI using the AWS console. In the next section, we will see how to create an AMI using the AWS CLI.

Creating an AMI using the AWS CLI

A second way to create an image is by using the AWS CLI. To do so, we perform the following steps:

1. We need to pass the `create-image` parameter along with the EC2 instance ID (instance ID of an EC2 instance for which we want to create an image) to the AWS EC2 command line, as follows:

```
$ aws ec2 create-image --instance-id i-0594353aca4ca68e6
--name "my-test-server-ami"
{
    "ImageId": "ami-098f764eb24c00288"
}
```

2. To get the status of this newly created image, use a `describe-images` command and pass the image IDs of the newly created image to the AWS EC2 command, as follows:

```
$ aws ec2 describe-images --image-ids
ami-098f764eb24c00288 --query Images[].State
[
    "available"
]
```

Using the AWS CLI, we can automate the process of AMI creation. In the next section, we will look at one more tool—Packer—that uses the AWS CLI internally to automate this process.

Automating AMI creation using Packer

Packer is an automation tool that is useful in creating any type of machine image. It uses a **JavaScript Object Notation (JSON)** template and lets you define your infrastructure. In order to automate the AMI Packer must be installed, and these are the steps we need to follow to do this:

1. Add the official Packer repository for Ubuntu and the **GNU Privacy Guard (GPG)** key, as follows:

```
curl -fsSL https://apt.releases.hashicorp.com/gpg | sudo
apt-key add -
sudo apt-add-repository "deb [arch=amd64] https://apt.
releases.hashicorp.com $(lsb_release -cs) main"
```

2. Update and install Packer by running the following command:

```
sudo apt-get update && sudo apt-get install packer
```

3. Create a basic Packer template with the following details:

- `type`: This is a mandatory field in the Packer template, and each builder needs to define it. As we build this image in AWS, we use an `amazon-ebs` type, which means EBS backs this image.

- `region`: The region in which we want to build an image, as image ID differs per region.

- `source_ami`: This is the AMI on which our image is based. In this example, I am using an Amazon Linux image, but you can use any image for this.

- `instance_type`: This is the instance type Packer uses while building this image. For this example, you can use `t2.micro` as this comes under the free tier.

- `ssh_username`: This is to tell Packer which username to use. This is the username you can use when launching an instance using this AMI. As we are using an Amazon Linux image, we can use `ec2-user`.

- `ami_name`: The name of the AMI that Packer creates.

The following code shows the preceding details filled in:

```
{
    "builders": [{
      "type": "amazon-ebs",
      "region": "us-west-2",
      "source_ami": "ami-067f5c3d5a99edc80",
      "instance_type": "t2.micro",
      "ssh_username": "ec2-user",
      "ami_name": "my-test-packer-example-1.0"
    }]
}
```

4. Before running your Packer script, you need to export a few environment variables. To export the environment, you can run the command shown in the code block that follows. Packer uses these environment variables to interface with the AWS API. We already discussed about environment variables in *Chapter 1, Setting Up the AWS Environment*. The code can be seen here:

```
export AWS_ACCESS_KEY_ID=
export AWS_SECRET_ACCESS_KEY=
```

5. Build your first image using Packer, like this:

```
$ packer build firsttemplate.packer
amazon-ebs: output will be in this color.


==> amazon-ebs: Prevalidating any provided VPC
information
==> amazon-ebs: Prevalidating AMI Name: my-test-packer-
example-1.0


==> Wait completed after 2 minutes 17 seconds


==> Builds finished. The artifacts of successful builds
are:
--> amazon-ebs: AMIs were created:
us-west-2: ami-08cf87c123456sff
```

Automating AMI creation is handy in a disaster recovery scenario, when you want to create your infrastructure quickly. If this process is automated, you will always have the latest copy of your AMI ready, with all the configuration and changes embedded in it.

Summary

In this chapter, you have learned some of the tips and tricks that you can utilize in your daily job to automate and manage your infrastructure. These tips can help troubleshoot any issue and enhance your productivity. You can use these tips during the initial stage while designing your infrastructure, and some tips will help you reduce your AWS bill.

As the internet is filled with infinite resources, I am sincerely thankful to you for spending time reading this book. I hope you learned something new. In this book, you have learned some of the ways to automate an infrastructure. As the cloud world changes almost every day and there is always scope for improvement, you can use these examples as building blocks and build something on top of them. As you continue to learn new technologies and grow in your career, always improve and share your knowledge with the rest of the world. As you are now empowered with this new knowledge, please use it in your daily job or enhance your existing infrastructure.

Other Books You May Enjoy

If you enjoyed this book, you may be interested in these other books by Packt:

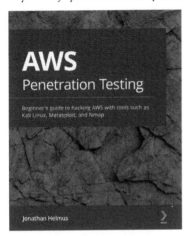

AWS Penetration Testing

Jonathan Helmus

ISBN: 978-1-83921-692-3

- Set up your AWS account and get well-versed in various pentesting services
- Delve into a variety of cloud pentesting tools and methodologies
- Discover how to exploit vulnerabilities in both AWS and applications
- Understand the legality of pentesting and learn how to stay in scope
- Explore cloud pentesting best practices, tips, and tricks
- Become competent at using tools such as Kali Linux, Metasploit, and Nmap
- Get to grips with post-exploitation procedures and find out how to write pentesting reports

AWS Security Cookbook

Heartin Kanikathottu

ISBN: 978-1-83882-625-3

- Create and manage users, groups, roles, and policies across accounts
- Use AWS Managed Services for logging, monitoring, and auditing
- Check compliance with AWS Managed Services that use machine learning
- Provide security and availability for EC2 instances and applications
- Secure data using symmetric and asymmetric encryption
- Manage user pools and identity pools with federated login

Leave a review - let other readers know what you think

Please share your thoughts on this book with others by leaving a review on the site that you bought it from. If you purchased the book from Amazon, please leave us an honest review on this book's Amazon page. This is vital so that other potential readers can see and use your unbiased opinion to make purchasing decisions, we can understand what our customers think about our products, and our authors can see your feedback on the title that they have worked with Packt to create. It will only take a few minutes of your time, but is valuable to other potential customers, our authors, and Packt. Thank you!

Index

Made in United States
Orlando, FL
15 February 2023

30057705R00213